ASSISI AND UMBRIA
REVISITED

ASSISI. Duomo, San Rufino.

ASSISI AND UMBRIA REVISITED

BY
EDWARD HUTTON

Intra Tupino e l'acqua che discende
Del colle eletto dal beato Ubaldo,
Fertile costa d'alto monte pende,
Onde Perugia sente freddo e caldo
Da Porta Sole, e dirietro le piange,
Per grave giogo Nocera con Gualdo.
Di questa costa là, dov' ella frange
Più sua rattezza, nacque al Mondo un Sole,
Come fa questo, tal volta, di Gange.
Però chi d'esso loco fa parole
Non dica Ascesi, che direbbe corto,
Ma Oriente, se proprio dir vuole.

DAVID McKAY COMPANY, INC.
NEW YORK

First published 1953

MADE AND PRINTED IN GREAT BRITAIN
BY JARROLD AND SONS LTD, NORWICH

TO
KATHIE

"And sweeter woman ne'er drew breath
Than my son's wife . . ."

CONTENTS

vii

LIST OF ILLUSTRATIONS

ix

*Acknowledgments for permission to reproduce these
photographs are made to: J. M. Marcel for
Nos. I, II, V, VI, XIII–XV; Anderson for
Nos. III, IV, VII, X, XI, XVI, XVII, XIX–
XXII; Alinari for Nos. VIII, IX, XII, XXIII
and XXIV.*

PREFACE

WHEN I was a young man I wrote a book, *Cities of Umbria,* which went into eight or more editions and finally fell out of print in the war of 1939–45. I have not thought to reprint it. Since it was written I have wandered about Umbria many times and most recently spent some months of spring, summer and autumn in that country where one cannot go a mile but one finds oneself in the footsteps of Saint Francis. And now that my life has nearly completed its circle, the pages which follow recount these fortunate wanderings and recall those, happier still, of earlier days.

I must thank my old friend F. Mason Perkins and my son Peter Hutton for many suggestions and for reading the proofs.

E. H.

CHAPTER I

ASSISI

THE CITY OF SAINT FRANCIS

Assisi is the city of S. Francis. It is impossible to think of anything but his simple and lovely life within the walls of what is now a great shrunken village, ruddy with the pale coloured stone of Subasio from whose side it has as it were been hewn, lean and emaciated with the years.

One of the oldest cities of Italy, it still retains more than a memory of Rome. It was, or was said to be, the birthplace of Propertius in 46 B.C. and of the Italian poet Metastasio in 1698 —but who recalls these facts today? We are indeed nonplussed and astonished when we learn that Goethe climbed the long hill from the high road up to the city, not for the sake of S. Francis, but to see and adore the façade of the modest Roman Temple of Minerva which still stands in the ancient Forum, the Piazza Grande of Assisi.

"I left on my left the vast mass of churches piled Babel-wise one over another (in one of which rest the remains of the holy S. Francis of Assisi) with aversion, and at last I reached the old town and, behold, before my eyes stood the noble edifice, the first complete memorial of antiquity I had ever seen."

Perhaps Roman antiquity is more accessible to us than it was to Goethe, though the portico of the Temple of Minerva in Assisi is still the first "complete memorial of antiquity", in the way of a temple a traveller from the north will meet on his way to Rome. However it may be, no one today would turn away "with aversion" from the medieval Franciscan city with its marvellous Romanesque and Gothic churches, its frescoes by Cimabue, Giotto, Simone Martini and Pietro Lorenzetti for the sake of any Roman antiquities whatsoever. We should doubtless revere them both, and it is surely a grave limitation in the culture of Goethe that he found himself unable to do the same.

Today there is nothing, can be nothing, in Assisi but the memory of him who took Lady Poverty to wife. Yet the city we see but little resembles what it was in Francis's day. What we see is not what he saw, but is, in fact, his creation. The city S. Francis knew had no San Francesco, no Sacro Convento, no Santa Chiara and no Rocca towering over all.[1] The western hill on which the triple church of San Francesco stands, the *Collis Infernus* or *Collis Inferni*, was divided from the city, quite outside which it stood, by a deep ravine which was only finally filled up and the upper and lower piazzas of San Francesco constructed in the sixteenth century. Before that the church was reached by a bridge over the ravine. Perhaps from very far off, from Perugia, for instance, we may have an impression of the city as S. Francis knew it, crouched on the skirts of Subasio. But there are, of course, many buildings within the city which he knew well: the Roman Temple, the great façade of the Duomo, and the churches, Santa Maria Maggiore, San Pietro, San Giacomo within the wall, San Damiano and the Carceri without. And he seems to have loved this, his birthplace, so well that, great traveller though he was, he never wanted to leave it, to go far away from it. The places he loved best were Monte Subasio, Rivotorto, the Portiuncula, San Damiano, the island in Lago Trasimeno, and Assisi itself, which he turned to bless with words of love as they bore him to the Portiuncula to die. Hardly one of these places, however, at all resembles what it was in his day, least of all his best-loved Rivotorto and Santa Maria degli Angeli. It is only the wide landscape that is the same and there is surely a divine harmony between the soul of S. Francis and this landscape of the valley of Spoleto which his early biographers seem instinctively to have understood.

And yet one finds oneself on his account wandering up and down the steep and climbing ways, through street and piazza where he played as a child, where he went gaily as a young man, which presently saw him begging his bread, and echoed alike with the scorn of his fellows and the irresistible words of his preaching. Here is the house, here is the stable, in which he was born; here the font in which he was baptised. Just beyond the walls is San Damiano where the Crucifix spoke to him. Here before Santa Maria Maggiore he stripped himself and repudiated

---

[1] The Rocca where Frederic II spent some time in his youth was overthrown by the Assisans in 1198 when S. Francis was about sixteen years old. It was rebuilt by Cardinal Albornoz in 1367 and is now again and long since a ruin.

his earthly father, Pietro Bernardone. There is the house of his first companion, Bernard of Quintavalle. And there in the Vescovado he lay till they bore him out of Porta Moiano on his last journey when he turned and blessed the city he loved, but could no longer see, on the way to S. Mary of the Angels, where he was to die. And finally, here in the great triple church dedicated in his honour, on the Collis Inferni, now the Collis Paradisi, we may venerate his dust.

THE CHURCH OF SAN FRANCESCO

It is to this great triple church one comes first, by Porta San Francesco and the cloistered Piazza Inferiore, into the cool darkness of the lower church of San Francesco. It seems more like a fortress than a church as you climb the hill, built as it is on arches of stone against the hill-side; and this impression is greater yet if you approach Assisi by the old road from Bastiola. But as you enter the church you seem to have wandered back into the north with its twilight churches, where the sun never shines and they worship God in semi-darkness. And, indeed, it is not till evening that the level light of the setting sun throws a glory over a splendour that in the morning is rather felt than seen.

San Francesco is the grandiose tomb of the little poor man, who should have been buried in the lee of some wood where birds sing and the earth is carpeted with primroses. Begun by Frate Elias in 1228 for the Holy See, immediately after the death of the saint, San Francesco consists of two churches, superimposed one on another, to which a large crypt is now added. The lower church has a cavernous nave, lined with chapels, with an apse, and eastern and western transepts. Beneath this is the crypt, now enlarged, in the midst of which towers the rock to which the tomb of the saint, hidden for seven hundred years, is chained. Above the lower church is the radiant upper church, consisting of nave, apse and wide transept. San Francesco was completed in 1253.

At the end of the Piazza Inferiore is the gate of the Sacro Convento, and beside it stands the Renaissance Cappella di S. Bernardino.

One enters by the beautiful portal of the fourteenth century into the eastern transept. The church under the embowed, dark-blue roof is full of twilight through which here and there the frescoes shine and the windows gleam and glow with their fourteenth-century glass.

Originally the lower church, it would appear, was nothing more than a nave and small choir and western transepts— indeed, very like the upper church as we see it today, but without, of course, its height and sunshine; but gradually during the thirteenth and fourteenth centuries the chapels and eastern entrance transept were added, and in recent years the crypt much enlarged. The great convent beside the church was built then, too, and is, as it always has been, in the hands of the Conventuals of the Franciscan Order and not, as is Santa Maria degli Angeli, in the possession of the Friars Minor.

In the recently much enlarged crypt, exactly under the high altar of the lower church is the tomb of S. Francis, a great sarcophagus chained to the rock of the Collis Inferni which, because of it, is now the Hill of Paradise. S. Francis was canonised by Gregory IX, his friend, the sometime cardinal protector of the Order, on July 16, 1228, less than two years after his death. By 1230 the great church was sufficiently in being to receive his corpse. On May 25 of that year, as his most venerable body was borne from San Giorgio, Elias by a *coup* seized it and secretly buried it. No one knew where the body of the saint exactly lay, till in 1818 the sarcophagus and its sacred treasure were discovered. Elias may have acted as he did to prevent the Perugians or others from stealing the body.

It is here, in the upper and lower churches, perhaps, better than anywhere else in Italy, that the beginnings of Italian art can be studied.

The lower church, one of the most impressive buildings in the world, is precious with the paintings and the glass of the masters of the fourteenth century. It is the irony of fate that the darkness which fills the church should make a sight of all the splendour so difficult.

To the left of the entrance is a fresco of the Madonna and Child with S. Francis and S. Antony Abbot and some bishop

ASSISI. San Francesco.

ASSISI. San Francesco,
Lower Church:
Cimabue, Madonna and

by Ottaviano Nelli of Gubbio, a charming picture, if less delightful than his better-known work in Santa Maria Nuova in his birthplace.

At the end of the vestibule, opposite the entrance doors, is the Albornoz chapel. Cardinal Gil Alvarez Carillo di Albornoz was related to the royal houses of Leon and Aragon: he was born at Cuenca. While still a young man he was made Archbishop of Toledo by Alfonso XI of Castile, whose life he is said to have saved at Tarifa in battle with the Moors in 1340. Pedro el Cruel hated him because he rebuked him for his licentious life, and on this account he fled to the Pope at Avignon; Clement VI it was, a learned man, who made him cardinal. In 1355 the Pope sent him to Italy as his general, to prepare for the return of the Holy See. Here, in Assisi, he rebuilt the Rocca Maggiore. Albornoz, certainly one of the most terrible captains Italy has ever seen, little by little swept the Patrimony and Romagna clean of those *signorotti* and bandits who, in the absence of the Papacy, had fallen on the country like a pestilence. He succeeded in re-establishing Pope Urban V in Rome. Like all the world, he seems to have loved S. Francis. He founded this chapel not long after he was made cardinal, and, dying in 1367, at Viterbo, was buried here in that year.[1] The frescoes, which Vasari tells us are by Buffalmacco, but which certain later critics have given to Andrea da Bologna, are not in the Giottesque tradition, and, indeed, in many ways are but third-rate works: they represent the story of S. Catherine of Alexandria; while under the arch we may see the consecration of Albornoz, and opposite S. Louis between two bishops. Third-rate though they be, in the Marriage of S. Catherine, where at the supreme moment she seems to faint with awe and love, much force and beauty have found exquisite expression.

As one passes into the nave of the great church the darkness is deeper. The walls are decorated with much destroyed frescoes by the Maestro di S. Francesco. The first chapel on the left, of San Martino, is painted in fresco by Simone Martini with scenes from the life of S. Martin. Simone Martini, born probably in Siena in 1283 was the pupil of Duccio, and not, so far as his

[1] Four years later his body was exhumed and carried to Toledo and entombed with almost royal honours, in the Capilla de S. Ildefonso in the cathedral.

2

work tells us, much influenced by Giotto. He has been called "the most lovable of all the Italian artists before the Renaissance", and, indeed, looking on the strange beauty of his work here, who can doubt it? He is more aristocratic and refined than Giotto; has, indeed, a sense of beauty subtler, though, perhaps less profound, than his. Is there anything in all pre-Renaissance art more lovely than these frescoes where S. Martin divides his cloak with a beggar, and later, as he lies asleep, has a vision of Christ wearing that very cloak? And best of all, perhaps, is that in which one sees the young S. Martin girded with the sword and all the accoutrements of knighthood, his hands clasped in prayer. The gaiety of all that—the beauty of the young men who look on, the splendour and magnificence of the emperor, the charm of the thought, the perfection of the craft! A great master, you might say, and then you think of the life-enhancing work of Giotto, and all it meant to Italy, and means to us. And yet Simone Martini is a great painter, though scarcely an original painter, as Giotto is. He was content to carry out more exquisitely the ideas of his master, Duccio, by whom he seems always to have been overshadowed. There is nothing of the immense vitality of the Florentine. When his young men stretch out their arms, as in this fresco, you do not feel as though they might embrace you, as you do with Giotto over and over again. Yet in his equestrian portrait of Guidoriccio da Fogliano, in Siena, he has created a captain who moves as surely and irresistibly towards his enemy as the Colleoni of Verrocchio or the Gattamelata of Donatello. It might be said that he was the most beautiful illustrator of the book of life in all the pre-Renaissance, the whole vitality and reality of life being in the text. One looks on these frescoes always with new joy, but never with the sense of life with which one gazes at Giotto's work at Padua. S. Martin, in the upper line of the frescoes, is ordained and retires to Albenga; he preaches in some city, possibly Tours; he restores a child to life, and at last dies. In all this work, too detailed to describe, one finds the same grace and entrancing beauty. The jambs of the windows are frescoed with fine busts and the entrance arch has beautiful full-length figures of saints. Even the glass in the windows here was also probably designed by Simone.

Passing down the nave, one comes on the left to the Cosmatesque pulpit, certainly one of the loveliest things in the church. Beneath it Madonna Iacoba de' Frangipani was buried in 1239; you may still read the epitaph: *Hic iacet Iacoba sancta nobilisque romana.* This noble Roman lady was with S. Francis when he died. It was in her house he had stayed when in Rome, and she was one of his most eager disciples. Above the pulpit is a lovely fresco, attributed to Giottino, of the Coronation of the Blessed Virgin.

Opposite the chapel of San Martino is the chapel of S. Louis, with a fine window; and next to it the chapel of S. Anthony of Padua, which contains nothing to keep the traveller. The chapel next to it, however, that of S. Mary Magdalen, is of the highest interest. Here are frescoes by a very close pupil of Giotto's, representing the legends of S. Mary Magdalen and S. Mary of Egypt. The roof is painted with figures of Christ, Lazarus, the Magdalen and Mary of Egypt. Below we see the Raising of Lazarus, and Christ in the house of Simon, where the Magdalen anoints His feet, the Noli Me Tangere and S. Mary miraculously coming to Marseilles, where, according to the legend, she and Lazarus and Martha founded a church. In the lunettes are the communion of the Magdalen and the Magdalen carried to heaven. The finest of the series, and the nearest to Giotto's own work, are the Noli Me Tangere and the Raising of Lazarus.

As one passes on out of this chapel into the transept, on the right wall one sees some marvellously lovely half-figures of saints by Simone Martini—five Franciscan saints—among them S. Clare, an especially beautiful portrait of the aristocratic girl who ran away from home to join S. Francis and was the first Abbess of the Second Order of S. Francis, called "Poor Clares", after her, and another of S. Louis of Toulouse.

One comes now to the huge Cosmatesque high altar, over which are the famous Allegories by Giotto's assistants. These frescoes of the Poverello's triumph are very difficult to see because of the darkness; the light—such as it is—is, I think, best in the afternoon, when the sun streams through the windows of the choir and transept. There we see S. Francis in glory vested as a deacon, in the dalmatic, enthroned and surrounded by angels. Opposite this is the Mystical Marriage of S. Francis with Lady Poverty. Christ Himself marries them, while Poverty, in tatters, stands among the flowers and thorns. On her left is Charity, who gives her a burning heart; on her right, Faith hands her a ring. Of the crowd which watches this most strange wedding, part is scornful, yet part is full of understanding. At the feet of Poverty a dog barks, a boy pelts her with stones, and even a child thrusts at her with a stick. A kind of fear seems to possess the crowd, and it is for this cause they hate her. Among the crowd itself, many kind or malicious, simple or worldly actions may be found; the whole picture is, as it were, an action. Above, angels are witnesses of this mystical marriage. Beside this fresco is that of Chastity praying in a strong tower; some knight is receiving baptism before putting on his armour; while Penance drives away a demon, S. Francis receives certain novices. A winged figure dressed as a friar drives away a woman who seems to symbolise Desire, for she is blindfolded, and her feet are talons; she is girt with human hearts, and her head is crowned with roses. Behind all comes Death. On the other side you see Obedience betwixt Prudence and Humility. Behind is a vision of Christ on the Cross, while before, a friar kneels, holding a yoke upon which Obedience lays her hand, and with a gesture commands silence.

In the right-hand transept is the grandly impressive work of Cimabue, a great fresco of the Madonna enthroned with angels and with S. Francis himself standing there. Though not painted in the saint's lifetime, it is, one might think, a fine portrait and well preserved, whereas the figures of the Virgin and Child have suffered much from restoration. Beneath is a fresco with half-figures of four Franciscan friars, his companions, by Pietro Lorenzetti.

The other frescoes in this right transept are the work of the assistants of Giotto and are for the most part concerned with the life of Our Lord. They are of great beauty; the frescoes of the Birth of Christ, and of the Flight into Egypt, are among the sweetest and loveliest things in the Lower Church. They cover both the eastern and the western walls and vaults. Above, on one side, we see the Birth of Christ, the Visitation, the Adoration of the Magi, the Presentation in the Temple, and the

Crucifixion; on the other, the Flight into Egypt, the Massacre of the Innocents, Christ in the Temple, Christ led home by His parents, a miracle of the resurrection of a child of the Sperelli family, S. Francis by the side of a skeleton representing Death, and, over a door, a half-figure of the Saviour. As one looks at these frescoes, one realises, perhaps more easily than in the works in the vaults over the high altar, to what splendour Italian art was being called. And yet, if we compare them with that early picture of the Madonna and Child, by Cimabue, we are aware that, after all, something has been lost. How lovely that fresco of the Madonna and Child is, how sacred and noble, and how surely it marks for us the change that is coming from the Byzantine manner, to the manner of Giotto.

The chapel of San Niccolò at the end of this transept, decorated with frescoes of the legend of S. Nicholas, contains the Cosmatesque tomb of Giovanni Orsini who died in 1292. It closes this transept, as that of San Giovanni Battista closes the opposite transept, and together they are the two earliest chapels built in San Francesco. Vasari tells us that the architect was Agnolo of Siena, who about 1310 built these chapels for the two members of the Orsini house, Giovanni and Napoleone. The frescoes in the chapel of S. Niccolò are attributed to Giottino. Fine as they are, full of life and action, they seem to me less splendid than the frescoes on the outside of the entrance arch. These represent the death of a child, and his resurrection by S. Francis, one of the finest compositions in the church; while above is a fresco of the Annunciation, which some have given to Puccio Capanna. Whoever may have painted these frescoes, and it matters little enough, they are among the most remarkable things in the Lower Church.

Giovanni Orsini's brother, Napoleone, lies in the chapel at the head of the opposite transept. This left transept is entirely decorated with Sienese frescoes, the work of Pietro Lorenzetti and his assistants. They are indeed, as a whole, Lorenzetti's most considerable creation. By far the most beautiful thing here is a work apart. It is a fresco, also by Pietro Lorenzetti, in the form of an altarpiece and stands behind the altar on the left. It represents the Madonna and Child with S. John the Evangelist and S. Francis; and the Madonna, who is looking intently into the eyes of her little Son, is pointing with her thumb and drawing His attention to S. Francis. Below is a Crucifix with the donors. Whenever I look on this most beloved painting I think there is nothing more powerful and more lovely in Sienese art.

The other frescoes which cover the roof and walls of this transept are concerned with the Passion of Christ; and those more certainly by Pietro Lorenzetti himself are the most moving: the Descent from the Cross and the Entombment and the large Crucifixion on the left wall, so unfortunately damaged by the breach in the wall. Nothing more harmonious is to be found anywhere. The rest of these Passion frescoes might seem to be the work of assistants under Pietro Lorenzetti's supervision, though the fresco of S. Francis receiving the stigmata on the wall near the apse is probably by Pietro himself.

The fresco in the form of an altarpiece over the altar at the end of this transept, under which Napoleone Orsini lies buried, is also by Pietro Lorenzetti. In the midst are the Madonna and Child and on one side the Baptist, on the other S. Francis.

It is out of this transept one climbs up to the Upper Church past the sacristies, which are full of wonders, the most important treasure there being the autograph Blessing written on parchment for Brother Leo by S. Francis on Monte La Verna, on the back of which are his *Laudes Creatoris*.

The Upper Church, in contrast with the Lower Church, is a temple of colour and light. It is as though the one symbolised the humble life of S. Francis on earth, the other his glory in heaven. Of the same form as the Lower Church, save that it has no chapels and no eastern transept, it gives us an idea of space and light and beauty such as we never receive in the Lower Church, where the low roof and the twilight mask the frescoes, the chapels, the colour on wall and ceiling, and even the very church itself, in the sombre, mysterious night of the catacombs. But in the Upper Church all is changed; it seems to glow like some perfect jewel, and almost to illumine itself rather than to receive light from the sun shining over the world outside. And it is here are preserved some of the most precious early frescoes in Italy.

The nave, choir and both transepts were painted by Cimabue, according to Mr. Berenson, between 1277 and 1280, and at any rate by 1296, the date we find inscribed in the apse. These frescoes, ruined though they be, are Cimabue's most important work and the most important series of medieval wall-paintings in Italy. The finest of these is the great Crucifixion on the left wall of the left transept, most tragic in its majesty, and the arch-angels and angels above. Scenes from the Apocalypse and again and again angels cover the walls of this transept.

In the apse are scenes from the life of the Blessed Virgin and portraits of Popes Gregory IX and Innocent IV, while above are medallions of angels and saints and on the roof the four Evangelists.

In the right transept on the right is another tremendous Crucifixion. On the left are scenes from the Acts of SS. Peter and Paul, above which are six medallions of angels, and above again, Christ surrounded by symbols of the four Evangelists. On the window wall the Acts of SS. Peter and Paul are continued and above two half-figures of saints, one in armour.

Unknown painters of the Roman school have painted the roof with a perfect understanding of the decorative value of colour and design. Pre-eminent among these painters is the "Isaac Master", the most classical and accomplished artist of the school, as one sees in his painting here of Abraham in the Sacrifice of Isaac. Their work here in the Upper Church had an immense influence on Italian art. Over the choir, the four Evangelists, with their symbols, and the Angel who should bring all things to their remembrance, speak to the four quarters of the world. Then in the nave we find Christ in benediction, the Blessed Virgin, S. John Baptist and S. Francis. And in the vault at the west end, the four Doctors of the Church— S. Gregory with the Dove, S. Ambrose, S. Jerome and S. Augustine. In the upper parts of the walls are painted scenes from the history of the world and the life of Christ. Terribly ruined, in a state of almost complete destruction, they are yet enough to prove to us the power of that Roman school which died so early and which has been forgotten. Even yet, we may see the strong influence of antiquity in those genii lurking so delightfully among the fruit and flowers. Are they not the ancient world itself almost, in its lightness, its gaiety, its natural and yet fanciful beauty? In the fresco of the four Doctors of the Church, in the last vault towards the end of the nave, we find this painter of the Roman school at his strongest. It is very obviously the work of a man who was thinking in mosaic rather than in fresco—the immense dignity of the figures, and even the furniture, being really the inspiration of an artist in the more durable material. But after all, for us at least, it is in the decorative value of these frescoes that we shall find our delight. They are perfect, at least as decoration, and the colour has grown magical with age. The same painter is supposed to have painted the walls in their upper parts, of which, however, almost nothing remains but a lovely and ruined suggestion of precious colours on the damp *intonaco* through which we discern those archangels of whom Milton sang.

Greater, and certainly more dramatic, are the two Cruci-fixions by Cimabue in the transept, before whose tragic majesty we can only stand in awe and bow the head.

Giotto or others, working on the long spaces below these marvellous works, could not have escaped their authority. Day by day as they worked on the frescoes of the life of S. Francis, which it may well be are not from Giotto's own hand, those frescoes of the earlier masters, in all their noble beauty, no doubt told many a secret. There are twenty-eight frescoes.[1] Those on the long wall are grouped in threes by the architecture of the church. The subjects, all taken from the Legends of S. Bonaventura, are as follows:

1. S. Francis honoured by the Simpleton. 2. S. Francis gives his cloak to a poor knight. 3. The Vision of the Palace. 4. The Crucifix speaks to S. Francis at San Damiano. 5. S. Francis renounces his father. 6. The Vision of Pope Innocent III. 7. The Pope approves the first Rule. 8. S. Francis in the fiery chariot. 9. The Vision of the Thrones. 10. The Devils driven from Arezzo. 11. S. Francis before the Soldan. 12. S. Francis in ecstasy. 13. The Prespio. 14. The Miracle of the spring. 15. S. Francis preaches to the birds. 16. The death of the knight of Celano. 17. S. Francis obtains the Portiuncula Indulgence

[1] See Appendix, pp. 235 *et seq.*

from Honorius III. 18. S. Francis appears to S. Anthony.
19. S. Francis receives the Stigmata. 20. Death of S. Francis.
21. Vision of Augustine and the Bishop of Assisi with regard to
the Stigmata. 22. Hieronymus convinced of the Stigmatisation
of S. Francis. 23. S. Francis's body borne to San Damiano—
the last meeting of S. Francis and S. Clare. 24. The Canonisa-
of S. Francis. 25. Pope Gregory IX convinced of the Stigmatisation of S. Francis. The last three frescoes are of miracles worked
by S. Francis. 26. Heals the gentlemen of Ilerda of a wound.
27. Raises a woman from the dead. 28. Frees Pietro d'Assisi
accused of heresy from prison. I shall not describe these frescoes
of the Poverello. They are among the best-known works of art
in the world and have been written about again and again.
Though there might seem to be little if anything of the work
of Giotto himself in these frescoes how magnificent is the gesture
of Pietro Bernardone in the fresco where S. Francis has been
taken before the bishop only to renounce his father for ever;
how naturally, in another fresco—that of the death of the
Lord of Celano—the saint rises in haste from the table where he
is sitting; how lovely are those angels who bear him to heaven,
clothed in light, in the ruined picture of his death. Designed or
not by the young Giotto, these frescoes are, in their simplicity
and naturalness, the centre of the movement that was soon to
excite all Italy to enthusiasm. They are earlier than the work
attributed to him in the Lower Church, and they remain among
the most precious things in Italy, strewn though she is with the
triumphs of art.

Before leaving San Francesco, it is delightful to pass out of the
dark nave of the Lower Church, through the Cappella di Sant'
Antonio, to spend an hour in the little cloistered Campo Santo,
where the tall cypresses, like flameless tapers, tower over the
dead. It is a place divided from the world, as certain days are
from the rest of life, by an inviolable and sacred silence. Slowly
in the soft air the cypresses stir under the sky, and in that little
sequestered place, noiseless with the footsteps of the dead, all
that is really precious in the world seems to come to one graciously, silently obliterating everything else. Scarcely anything
of sorrow is there in that quiet graveyard, and the brutal

sentimentality of such a place of death, often so vulgar and common with indifference, is not to be found there, and those who once went up and down with so much dignity and simple goodness, forgotten though they be, do not resent an intrusion made for love, meditation or refreshment.

Nor should a visit to the great convent, the Sacro Convento, be omitted. So little like S. Francis, it is the work of Frate Elias and the Popes, who built it no doubt as a Papal treasury and stronghold; the great and splendid Papal apartment, overlooking the winding Tescio, with wonderful views to Perugia and beyond even to Mont' Amiata, attests it. The museum formed here contains many precious things, a unique collection of vestments from the fourteenth century onwards, silversmiths' work, too, and among other paintings two Crucifixes of great interest and beauty, characteristic works by the Maestro di San Francesco.

UP AND DOWN ASSISI

It is really after many nights and days spent in its desolate piazzas, its tawny palaces, and its silent, cool churches, that Assisi becomes for one something real, something more actual than the life of its saint. How many beauties it has! That little chapel, for instance, Cappella dei Pellegrini in Via San Francesco, all that is now left of the Ospedale founded in 1431;[1] some of its frescoes have been carried away to the Museo Civico, but those in the chapel still remain, as does the chapel itself, a little shadowy place in the wide deserted street. Over the doorway under the eaves is a much damaged work of Matteo da Gualdo, the Eternal Father among the Cherubim. Within, over the altar, the same master has painted his masterpiece, the Annunciation above, and below the Madonna enthroned with her little Son between S. Antonio and S. Giacomo, to whom the chapel is dedicated. The walls were painted by Pier Antonio da Foligno, called il Mezzastris, about 1482; on the right is the story of S. James of Compostella, and on the left that of S. Antony Abbot. Above in the vault are the four Doctors of the Church, or, as some think, S. Leo III, S. Isidore of Seville,

[1] The Hospital of the Pilgrims was demolished in 1885.

S. Augustine and S. Bonaventura, by the same master, who was obviously a pupil of Beneozzo Gozzoli.

Then there is the Tempio di Minerva, close to the Palazzo Municipio, the fabric of a vision as once seen from the plain before the houses which now close the piazza on the south were built.

Thence one passes up the steep ways to the Duomo of San Rufino, whose façade is the most majestic piece of architecture in the city, a work of the twelfth century. Unfortunately the interior of the church was entirely remade in the eighteenth century. At the font here S. Francis and the Emperor Frederic II were baptised. There, too, in the sacristy is a beautiful early triptych by Niccolò da Foligno, painted in 1460, where the Madonna and Child are enthroned between S. John the Evangelist, S. Rufino, S. Civellino and S. Pietro Damiano, with their legends in the predella, one panel of which is missing. In the beautiful frame is the Annunciation with angels.

From San Rufino one descends to that strange church built in honour of S. Clare in place of the old church of San Giorgio, where the enormous buttresses seem to await transformation into chapels, as at San Francesco. Within, under the high altar, is the still incorrupt body of S. Clare; while in the convent is the Crucifix which spoke to S. Francis at San Damiano. In the church itself is a great panel of the end of the thirteenth century with a full-length figure of S. Chiara surrounded with scenes from her legend; and high in the apse hangs another colossal Crucifix traditionally but surely wrongly attributed to Cimabue and everywhere are fourteenth-century frescoes, though far less splendid certainly than those in San Francesco. It was here, in the church of San Giorgio over which the church of Santa Chiara has been built, that S. Francis went to school, and it was hither his body was borne from the Portiuncula, and here it lay till the great basilica was ready to receive it.

Those churches, too, which now bear witness to various events in S. Francis's life—the Chiesa Nuova built over the house in which according to tradition he was born and which still preserves some vestiges of antiquity; Santa Maria Maggiore, the old cathedral of the eleventh century, beside the Vescovado, where he stripped himself of his clothes and repudiated his

earthly father, Pietro Bernardone—bear witness to the life of
him who not only changed the spirit of Assisi but the spirit of
the Church, and restored that first commandment of Christ,
"that ye love one another as I have loved you". Indeed, the
very stones of these narrow, climbing, difficult ways are trodden
today because of him who, as tradition will have it, was, like his
Master, born in a stable between an ox and an ass and whose
greeting was *Pax*. Something of this *Pax*, of the Peace which
passeth all understanding, seems still to linger in this little
broken city because of him, to hover over the ineffable landscape, wonderful, spellbound, in which it lies.

Other churches, too, there are, the finest of which is San
Pietro just within the gate which bears its name; a Benedictine
church of the twelfth century. And then there is that little
church in the wall near Porta San Giacomo, San Giacomo di
Murorupto of the twelfth century: but these, and others like
them, I leave for the discovery of those who linger here.

SAN DAMIANO AND THE CARCERI

It is on the way past Santa Chiara, leaving the town by the
Porta Nuova and the Borgo Aretino, with its memory of an old
war, that you go down through the olives to the little church of
San Damiano, which owes its very being to S. Francis and which
alone preserves itself more or less as it was in his day. In the
court of the convent, many pleasant hours of a spring evening
slip by almost unheeded—so quietly, so sweetly do they pass
among the flowers and the thoughts that come to you from long
ago, fragrant with the innocence of S. Clare and her company.
For it was here that S. Francis established his Sister Clare and
the nuns of his Second Order. The church and convent are
now in the hands of the Friars Minor, for the Poor Clares left
here after the death of S. Clare, when the new church which
bears her name was built in her honour. The frescoes here are
sometimes by some country disciple of Giotto, sometimes by
Tiberio d'Assisi, or another. Almost as plentiful as the flowers,
we pass them by with the same silent acceptance, as just the
delightful gifts of nature, which indeed they are, painted for
love in a land of sunshine.

The story is well known how after his conversion S. Francis, praying here, before an ancient Crucifix, in the little church then ruinous, heard Christ speak from that cross, saying, "Francis, go and repair My house which, as thou seest, is wholly falling into ruin." And he, supposing this command to refer to ruined San Damiano, began to bring stones to rebuild it, and to that end took some bales of cloth from his father's warehouse and sold them in Foligno together with his horse, and, returning, brought the money to the priest here at San Damiano. This was the immediate cause of the quarrel with his father which ended in the scene before Santa Maria Maggiore, the subject of one of the frescoes in the upper church of San Francesco.

In course of time San Damiano was restored by his efforts and came into the use of his Order and there he established S. Clare with her nuns. There, too, later he came, sick and half blind, towards the end of his life, and in a little hut of straw and wattles, after a sleepless night of misery, he composed the Hymn of the Sun, one of the earliest poems to be written in the vernacular and assuredly the most beautiful of them all. San Damiano only saw him again when on the morning after his death at the Portiuncula on October 3, 1226, his body was borne here by his friars and a vast company of the citizens of Assisi, in order that, as he had promised her, S. Clare should see him once more. Thence they bore him into the city.

Here, too, S. Clare was to die later, and one may still see the place where she lay, for the little church and convent now used by the Friars Minor is scarcely changed from those long past days. One may still see the tiny refectory where the Pope bade S. Clare bless the bread set out for the nuns, when each little loaf was instantly marked with a cross. One may still see the *dormitorio*, the room in which she died, and the place called S. Clare's garden, whence she could see the Portiuncula. Every corner seems to be filled with a peace no longer to be found elsewhere in the world. The frescoes of Tiberio d'Assisi, that characteristic Umbrian master, breathe just this sense of ideal tranquillity, as though here and here alone Christianity had known how to possess itself of that Elysian air of which Virgil speaks:

Largior hic campos aether et lumine vestit

but in more sacred wise.

And then there is the Eremo delle Carceri.

The way to the hermitage of the Carceri is rough and long, but I am not sure that a sight of this lonely refuge from the world is not the best way for the traveller to realise the life of the friars of the thirteenth century. A little more than one hour's walk from Assisi, the rude convent on the slopes of Subasio, hidden in a wooded groin of the bare mountain, seems to be surrounded by silence as by a rampart. Save to the pilgrim, however, the relics preserved there are of little interest; the pillow and the hair-shirt, pitiful enough today, move one less than the place itself. The tiny chapels in their simplicity, founded as they are in the bare rock, bring back to one perhaps, as nothing else can, the humility of the great saint. Even to pass through the doors it is necessary to stoop, and one is but divided from nature by the greater silence. Just outside is the forest, a wooded cleft in the hill-side, cool and dark, and full of mystery.

One comes back to Assisi after a day on that mighty hill-side as to a new world. Its warmth, its colour, its fantastic beauty seem more friendly, more homely than before. San Francesco is less dark, and all the people of the city have friendly faces.

UP AT THE ROCCA MAGGIORE

There is one other visit, easier but quite as rewarding, to be paid at Assisi. I mean the climb up to the Rocca Maggiore, high above the Cathedral and the old ramshackle windy convent of San Lorenzo. Wandering about those ruined walls and turrets or lying in their shade you have before you, but in its fullness, the great view with which the loggias, balconies and windows of the Hotel Subasio have already delighted you on your first evening, only from here what is perhaps the loveliest and certainly the most serenely spacious of landscapes is more widespread under a greater breadth of sky. From here, before you lies the whole wide valley from Perugia to Spoleto —*Umbria verde*—they say, *Umbria Santa* rather, for your

impression, in early morning or at sunset, is one of ineffable
benediction. Under the great flank of Subasio and on the other
side of the wide valley stand the little cities: on this side under
the cypresses Spello and pyramided Trevi, with the castle of
Spoleto under the ilex-woods of Monteluco beyond; Foligno
in the plain scarce visible, Montefalco clear above Foligno's
roof-tops and the Topino-misted Bevagna with Cannara beside
it and Bettona above on its long ridge of mountain, behind
the dome of S. Mary of the Angels, where the Tescio stream
winds away to Bastia, and the Topino and Chiascio meet and
Torgiano stands with its towers, and at evening maybe one may
catch a glimpse of amethystine Amiata on the verge of the
Senese. Nothing more lovely, nothing more serene and full of
a Franciscan peace could well be imagined.

No, but now look northwards: the great bare mountains
rise in a formidable rampart, seemingly impassable save
where cut and gashed by precipitous gorges and ravines.
It is a landscape of a nightmare, as tragic and bitter as that on
the south is peaceful and serene. It was through those ravines
that his companions, under the guard sent from Assisi, bore
the dying saint by night in the glare of torches on his way
home by that circuitous route from Siena, for fear of the
Perugians. One has not really possessed oneself of Assisi and
what it stands for till one has seen and considered both these
views, not only the view over the valley of Spoleto, but this,
too, over the gaunt mountains to the north. For in the life
of S. Francis there was not only the serenity and peace of
Rivotorto and the Portiuncula, there was also the despair and
bitterness of Poggio Bustone and Fonte Colombo. Those
landscapes seem to sum up, as it were, the life of the little poor
man, who, at so great a cost, saved the Church and civilisation
in the thirteenth century, and who remains in our minds, as
Renan has said, as "after Jesus the only perfect Christian".

And, indeed, men as different as Dante, Mussolini and Pius
XI seem to have been of similar opinion. In *The Divine Comedy*
Dante finds S. Francis in the Empyrean in the snow-white Rose
of Paradise enthroned beside the Baptist and before S. Benedict
and S. Augustine. In fact it is next to the Precursor of Christ
that Dante places His most perfect imitator in whose body were

renewed the sacred stigmata of His Passion. Already in the
Heaven of the Sun Dante had summoned the most learned and
the most profound and, as he thought, the wisest of Christian
intellects—he had summoned S. Thomas Aquinas to praise
S. Francis in Paradise. Why? Perhaps because the innermost
essence of wisdom is love. As for Mussolini, he called S. Francis
"*il più santo dei Santi*". While Pope Pius XI declares in
his Encyclical, on the occasion of the seventh centenary of
S. Francis's death in 1926, "It seems necessary for Us to affirm
that there has never been anyone in whom the image of
Jesus Christ and the evangelical manner of life shone forth more
lifelike and strikingly than in S. Francis. He who called himself
the Herald of the Great King was also rightly spoken of as
'another Jesus Christ' appearing to his contemporaries and to
future generations almost as though he were the Risen Christ.
He has always lived as such in the eyes of men and so will
continue to live for all future time."[1]

UNDER THE OLIVES

One afternoon I had been to visit my friends at Santa Maria
degli Angeli, and Padre Bernardino had wished, in spite of all I
could say, for he is a very old man, to walk back with me through
the vineyards up to Assisi, chiefly, I think, because he wished to
talk to me concerning that great virtue, humility, upon which
he conjectured, no doubt with reason, that I required some
elementary instruction.

It was the Saturday before Palm Sunday, and all those
country paths through the *poderi* were strewn with olive branches
fallen by the way, cut for the ceremony of the morrow. Whenever I looked up as we climbed, there above me, over the olives,
was the little brown city of S. Francis, on the skirts of Monte
Subasio. To the left, on its bastioned rock, rose the great triple
church of San Francesco, gaunt as a fortress. To the right
soared up the slim and graceful campanile of Santa Chiara, and
between them lay the little holy city, too small now for its

---

[1] *Encyclical of His Holiness Pope Pius XI on the Seventh Centenary of the death of
S. Francis of Assisi*, translated by Most Rev. J. H. Ryan, Bishop of Omaha (Washing-
ton, 1926).

ASSISI. San Francesco, Upper Church: ? Giotto, S. Francis honoured.

ASSISI. Santa Chiara.

broken rosy walls, against which the olives tossed in silver, crowned by its vast castle ruined against the sky.

We lingered by the way, in the lovely spring afternoon.

"*Ebbene, caro figlio mio*, touching this virtue so dear to our holy father, S. Francis."

"Yes, Father?"

"It is not, *caro mio*, a grace often vouchsafed to your country-men, and we might say even less often to the *Americani*. To tell the truth, they seem scarcely to understand it at all. Listen, then, *caro figlio*.

"Not long since there used to come every day and all day to the Portiuncula a certain man, unkempt, in rags, dirty, forlorn, unspeakable. It was thought he was a Russian, for he wore a long beard half-way down to his waist and his hair fell on his shoulders. A rough customer, one might say. Yet his devotion seemed to be quite extraordinary. All day long, as soon as the church was open, before the first Mass was said; all day long till the church was closed at nightfall, he haunted the Portiuncula, passing in and out, to and fro, as one is accustomed to do, praying—obviously intent on our great Plenary Indulgence, that *Perdono* once confined to one day in the year, but now to be gained, as you know, every day, *toties quoties*, for the living and the dead, each time you pass in and out of that holy place.

"One day, some of your countrymen and women, *caro figlio*, no doubt from the great hotel at Perugia, seeing this dirty and forbidding figure incessantly performing his devotions in the Portiuncula, before the altar of S. Mary of the Angels—and, no doubt, loathing the sight of so much dirt, and, as they thought, superstition—when they returned to the rich hotel at Perugia, like true *Protestanti* they protested and complained that they had been alarmed at this disgusting spectacle and in-commoded in their sight-seeing by this poor wretched one, who, as we shall see, was, though most displeasing to them, quite otherwise than displeasing to God. Perhaps they threw him a soldo, perhaps they didn't. I know not. At any rate, they complained.

"Now, *caro mio*, in these days, as you may have observed, we are very sensitive about the good opinion of foreigners. And this sensitiveness, quite an official thing I assure you, compelled

the authorities in Perugia to complain to the authorities of
Assisi, so that they sent for the poor one and, believing him, as I
said, to be a Russian, wanted to turn him not only out of Assisi
but out of Italy. However, it soon appeared that he was no
Russian at all, but a Calabrese. Nevertheless, they would have
kicked him out, but that the bishop heard about it and inter-
vened, so that he was only forbidden to haunt the Portiuncula.

"Ah, *caro mio*, the grief of that poor man was terrible to see,
for the *frati* said to him as he wept at the door, 'Go!' Nevertheless, he was there every day just the same, though the Padre
Guardiano would not let him in, because he feared a scandal.
Till at last, taking compassion on him, he said, 'Listen, now.
You must obey the bishop, who has forbidden you to incommode
foreigners in our church. We cannot therefore admit you while
the church is open. Nevertheless, if you care to come when we
close it at nightfall, we will let you in and you can make your
prayers in the Portiuncula till we open the church in the
morning. Then you must go. But tell me what you would be
doing, and why you haunt this place the whole day long. No
doubt, it is the Indulgence."

"And he answered, 'I am trying to empty Purgatory.'"

"Father," said I, "let us sit down here under this cypress
and you shall tell me something more about humility, this
Franciscan virtue, which we English lack so sadly."

Just then three urchins spied us and came dancing and running to Padre Bernardino, demanding holy pictures, which he
produced at once from some pocket or other, and presently the
mother came also from the little farm hard by and asked his
blessing.

When they had left us, Padre Bernardino turned to me and
said, "Ah, *caro figlio*, it is not only the English who lack humility.
I remember when, fifty years ago, I was in England, I would
wear the habit everywhere. It was not the custom then."

"No, Father, nor now."

"Well, I arrived at the station called Victoria, and as I went
through the streets it was the hour when the children come out
of school, and they all ran after me and surrounded me,
shouting and jeering. Then I made an act of contrition for my

pride of the habit, and I prayed S. Mary of the Angels to deliver me from those children, for I was afraid. And, *caro figlio*—pouf! in a moment I was alone in the street, for they had all run away."

Evening was coming. The setting sun filled the wide valley of Spoleto with benediction. Looking back across the olives down the hill-side, my eyes rested on the great dome of Santa Maria degli Angeli, where S. Francis gave the habit to his friars to wear.

"All the same," said Padre Bernardino suddenly, "one should love the habit, which is a mark of humility, and one should wear it, and in time all will love it again, and especially the children. How can they learn to love it if they never see it?"

"How is the habit a sign of humility, Father?" I asked absent-mindedly, while, at Ave Maria, Santa Chiara called to San Francesco over the city.

"If I do not wear the habit how can one know that I am only a friar? Why, I might, in a short jacket, be taken—nay, I might presently take myself—for something great, a parish priest, or even a Jesuit father!"

"O, dear Father, no one would ever take you for a Jesuit."

"Ah, I suppose not," he said ruefully.

"You may have heard," he went on. "Have you heard of that little friar who had only one relation in the world, and he a Jesuit father? Too much honour, no doubt, and so indeed it proved. For this learned father was so disgusted with his only relation—and he a young man—for becoming a friar of S. Francis that he not only refused to see him or even to answer his letters, but to have anything whatever to do with him at all.

"Ah, *caro mio*, how miserable, how unhappy was that little friar. His only relation in the world would have nothing to do with him. He went to the Padre Guardiano and begged him to help and advise him. 'What can I do?' said he, 'he is my only relation, and he will have nothing to do with me.'

"*Caro*, it was no use. What could the Padre Guardiano do? Nothing at all, save tell him to pray to our Blessed Lady of the Angels and our Holy Father S. Francis. And this, with tears, he did.

"*Caro figlio*, never is a prayer unanswered, if it come from the heart. One night, as that learned father of the Society was going to bed, appeared to him his Angel Guardian, who said, '*Reverendo Padre mio*, tonight as you sleep the Padre Eterno sees fit to vouchsafe to you a vision, a vision indeed of Paradise. Look you to it.'

"And, *figlio mio*, it befell just as the Angel Guardian said. For as he slept that father saw in a vision the very streets of Paradise, all of gold and chrysoprase and jasper, and walking there, San Benedetto, San Bernardo, San Domenico, Sant' Agostino, Sant' Ambrogio, all the *pezzi grossi*, and there, too, Sant' Ignazio Loyola with them.

"Oh, *figlio mio*, how was his heart uplifted when he saw this sight and Sant' Ignazio in such magnificent company. Tears filled his eyes; he experienced not mere thankfulness, gratitude, benediction; *caro mio*, as he lay in his bed he felt at least two inches taller. And they passed down the ways of gold.

"And then, *caro figlio*, came one so beautifiul, so wonderful, so marvellously tender and full of grace and love that that learned father turned to his Angel Guardian and whispered, '*Quello lì è il Gesù Cristo, non è vero?* This is Jesus Christ Himself, is it not?' But the Angel Guardian only smiled and said, '*Che! che!* that is San Francesco.' "

It was quite dusk when we came at last to the gate of Assisi.

CHAPTER II

SAINT MARY OF THE ANGELS

THE PORTIUNCULA

SANTA Maria degli Angeli, the Portiuncula, was, S. Bonaventura tells us, the spot on earth most beloved by S. Francis. Today the half-industrialised village which bears this name, in the plain about two miles below Assisi, close to the railway station, will, it may be, disappoint the traveller. In the midst of rather squalid surroundings he sees an enormous basilica, originally of the sixteenth century, under a dome which is said to have been designed by Vignola and which covers like a casket the little sacred chapel, the Portiuncula. But in the time of S. Francis the valley hereabouts was wooded and the little chapel of the Portiuncula was lonely among the trees, and until some wattle huts were built about it by his companions, nothing encroached upon its solitude.

The chapel was indeed very ancient and was known originally as Santa Maria di Josaphat. It was said to date from the fourth century, when it had been built by four pilgrims returning from Jerusalem, and presently it got the name of Santa Maria degli Angeli because it was believed angels were used to descend there at night and sing divine praises. The place came then into the possession of the Benedictines of the abbey on Monte Subasio and was known in that Order as the Portiuncula or "little portion", for it was the smallest of their possessions, and when S. Francis came upon it it was in ruins.

Now S. Francis had, according to the legend, been bidden by the Crucifix which spoke to him in San Damiano: "Francis, seest thou not that My house is falling into ruin? Go therefore and repair Me it." Trembling and astonished, he answered, "Gladly will I do it, O Lord," for he understood the saying to be of that very church of San Damiano, which through age seemed likely to fall, not discerning that it was of the Church Universal the Crucifix spoke. Having repaired San Damiano, he later "betook him to another place which is called Portiuncula, where in ancient days a church of the Blessed Virgin had been built, but now it was forsaken and cared for by none, and when he saw it thus brought to ruin, being moved with pity he began to dwell there and was diligent in repairing it."[1]

He resolved to live there, and presently (c. 1210) begged the place of the Benedictines, who granted it to him, and the Portiuncula thus became the cradle of the Franciscan epic and was established by S. Francis himself as the chief house and head of the Order.

There it was on October 18, 1208, on the feast of S. Luke, as the priest read the passage in the Gospel in which Jesus established the rule for His Apostles,[2] "heal the sick, carry neither purse nor scrip, nor shoes...," that S. Francis made this the rule for himself and his company. There it was he received S. Clare when she fled away from her father's house to become the bride of Christ; there it was he ate with her when all the place seemed on fire; there it was the great Chapter of Mats (1219) assembled, attended by more than five thousand friars; there it was he established the Perdono and there it was he came to die on October 3, 1226.

The fame of the Portiuncula became so great, it was so thronged and so sacred, that other buildings were built about it[3] already in the thirteenth century, but they were found too small for the crowds of pilgrims who came there, and Pope Pius V, in 1569, in view of the multitude which flocked thither in August for the Perdono, the Indulgence granted by Honorius III in 1216, threw them down and erected in their place the vast basilica we see. The architect is said to have been Vignola, but, certainly after his death, Galeazzo Alessi and Giulio Danti of Perugia modified his design. The church was more than a hundred years in building, and then in 1831 and 1832 earthquakes for the most part overthrew it, though the cupola remained, miraculously as it seemed, over the sacred little chapel, which S. Francis had rebuilt with his own hands.

[1] I Celano, cap. 9. For the origins of the Portiuncula, see P. E. d'Alençon: *Des Origines de la Portiuncula* (Louvain, 1909).

[2] Luke x. According to some authorities this happened on S. Matthias's day and in Assisi in the church of S. Nicola. As to these two dates, see *Analecta franciscana*, III, p. 2.

[3] Cf. P. E. M. Giusto, O.F.M., *La topografia dell'antica chiesa della Portiuncola* in *L'Oriente*, 1916–17.

In 1836 Gregory XVI rebuilt the basilica, the architect being Pelotti, who was by no means faithful to Vignola's design. Moreover, the façade with its enormous portico is even more modern and the immense bronze statue of the Madonna which crowns it is of yesterday.

Within, the basilica is ample and full of light, well suited to the needs of a multitude of pilgrims, which in very recent times have increased again owing to the supposed movements of the great bronze statue of the Madonna which crowns the façade. Thousands have flocked from all parts of Italy to witness this presumed marvel.

The only works of art in the great church are two terra-cottas by Andrea della Robbia. One of these is in the left transept. This is an altarpiece of much beauty, a Coronation of Our Lady, with side panels of S. Francis receiving the Stigmata and S. Jerome in the wilderness, and three predella panels of the Annunciation, Adoration of the Child and the Magi, by the school.

But the basilica is only a casket which holds the very precious and sacred relic of the Portiuncula. This stands directly under the dome and is of the highest interest, for it was actually rebuilt by S. Francis himself and has been generally little tampered with.[1] It measures seven by four metres and is roughly built of the stone of Monte Subasio. A modern Gothic tabernacle has been erected on the façade. There is a fresco by Overbeck (1830) of little merit. On the right side is a fresco of the fifteenth century of the Madonna and Child enthroned with S. Francis and S. Bernardino; on the back of the chapel is a cut-down fresco of the Crucifixion. Within, over the altar, is a large picture by Ilario da Viterbo (1393) of the Annunciation with, at the sides, S. Francis tempted by demons, two angels accompanying S. Francis to the Portiuncula, the Confirmation of the Rule and S. Francis proclaiming the Indulgence. In the predella are five scenes of the miracles of S. Francis. The central Annunciation seems to be a free copy of Simone Martini's Annunciation, now in the Uffizi.

There is always someone praying, in this tiny chapel glimmering with lamps, for it is here that the great Indulgence,

---

[1] Little tampered with in comparison with the cell of S. Francis in which he died, which is also within the basilica.

the famous Perdono, may be won—now every day in the
year as often as you pass through the chapel. No conditions
are attached to this Indulgence, which is applicable to the souls
in purgatory, save, of course, that of being in a state of grace.

Brother Peter Catanii, one of the earliest companions of
S. Francis, was buried in the Portiuncula in 1221, as an inscription tells us. From the day of his death he worked so many
miracles that the people began to crowd to his tomb with
offerings, to the great inconvenience of the friars. Learning
this, Francis went to the tomb of the miracle worker, "Brother
Peter," said he, "thou didst ever obey me in life; obey me still,
now that we are infested with all these people of the world. I
enjoin thee by Obedience to make an end of thy miracles and
allow us to recover peace." And from that moment Peter did
no more prodigies.

A friar speaking English (it used to be Frate Bernardino, then
in his eighties) leads one round the church and, with the
simpleness and kindness common in Italy, tries to make everything plain. To him it is a work of infinite pleasure, he
assures you, yet one cannot but think it must often be tedious.
Almost all the world he has to show, and with such eager
courtesy, must be fairyland to so many of his guests. "They do
not understand, they do not understand," is his excuse for them.
Yet it seems difficult to misunderstand so expressive a place.

Having shown you the Portiuncula, the little friar leads you
to the Cappella del Transito—the cell where S. Francis died,
which is under the dome on the Epistle side of the great church.
This tiny cell, now a chapel, is scarcely large enough for more
than two or three to assist at Mass. It has been a good deal
spoiled, at least outside, where unfortunately the walls have
been plastered up and decorated with a poor modern fresco
(1886) of the saint's passing. Within there are frescoes representing the first Franciscan saints, possibly originally by
Lo Spagna, but much repainted in the eighteenth century. The
cell is moving in its simplicity; it is still authentic, with its broken
door guarded from those eager for relics: but the only beautiful
thing here is the white enamelled terra-cotta statue of S. Francis
by Andrea della Robbia, who has here produced a most
sympathetic masterpiece, an exquisite interpretation of the

ascetic spirit at its most gentle. It is a thoughtful work of great beauty, delicate and yet strong; the sensitive face and hands are typical of Andrea.

As to S. Francis's death: he had for long lain sick in the bishop's palace within the walls of Assisi, but presently he asked to be borne to S. Mary of the Little Portion that he might yield up the breath of life in the place he had so much loved and in which he had received the breath of grace. When he had been borne thither he lay on the ground, here in what is now the Transito Chapel, his habit laid aside, naked in honour of Lady Poverty, while his companions wept, and one of them, divining his wish, took a habit with the cord and brought it, saying, "These I lend thee as unto a beggar and do thou receive them under holy obedience." And at this he rejoiced, for in his zeal for poverty he was minded to possess not even a habit unless it were lent him by another. As at the outset of his conversion he had stood naked before the bishop, so in the ending of his life he was minded to quit the world naked. He recommended to his brethren the beloved Portiuncula. "This place is holy," he told them; "hold it ever in veneration and never abandon it. If you are driven out by one door, return by another, for it is here the Lord has multiplied us and has shown us His light and poured out His love in our hearts."

He did not forget Sister Clare and sent her a message forbidding her to give way to sadness and promising that she and her daughters should see him again, which came to pass when his body was borne to Assisi by way of San Damiano. He remembered, too, the noble Roman Lady "Frate Jacoba", as he called her. She too would be sad to learn he had left the world without warning her, and he was already dictating a letter to her when the noise of a cavalcade was heard and the Lady Jacoba was herself come from Rome with her two sons. "The Lord be praised," he said; "let the door be opened for the Rule is not for Brother Jacoba." She had come furnished with all that was necessary for the burial of the Poverello, a veil for his face, a cushion for his head, a sheet of haircloth for his body and wax for the funeral ceremonies. She had brought, too, some of the sweetmeat made of almonds which he loved.[1] He could

[1] She was a Frangipani and the sweetmeat bears her name to this day.

but taste it; it was Bernard of Quintavalle, his first companion, who ate it.

Then, turning to those about him, he told them to lay him on the ground and after he was dead to let him lie there for the space in which one may gently walk a mile. At his desire the Canticle of the Sun was constantly heard in the hut with the verse in praise of our Sister the Death of the body which he had so recently made. He asked for bread, and having blessed it, distributed it to the brethren in imitation of Christ at the Last Supper.

The next day, his last, the Passion according to S. John was read to him, and at dusk of October 3, 1226, she to whom no one willingly opens the door entered. He saw her, received her courteously. "Be welcome, my Sister Death." They placed him on the ground, ashes on his head, ashes and dust. Then with failing voice he intoned a Psalm[1] with those about him: *Voce mea ad Dominum clamavi*: "Bring my soul out of prison that I may give thanks unto Thy Name. . . ."

Evening had stolen into the hut. There was a great silence. He seemed to be sleeping.

And immediately a multitude of crested larks rose wheeling about the roof of the hut and for long with their chirping bewailed the loss of their friend. And at the same hour a brother saw a shining star borne on a white cloud mounting towards heaven.

> . . . *l'anima preclara*
> *Mover si volle, tornando al suo regno* . . .

Through the long night the forest resounded with the psalmody of the friars mingled with the rumour of an immense and gathering multitude.

On Sunday, October 4, they bore his body to Assisi, with haste within the walls, lest the Perugians by a *coup de main* might possess themselves of it. But they went by way of San Damiano where S. Clare looked on him for the last time.

The friendly little friar presently leads you out of the church into the great sacristy which is furnished, as is the choir of the

---

[1] Psalm 141 (A.V. 142).

church, with fine intarsia furniture work of the seventeenth century, and thence past the small chapel of San Carlo Borromeo into the famous rose garden, which is perhaps something of a disappointment. Perhaps one expected too much, but it is railed in so securely and is so small that S. Francis must have had much ado to roll in it at all.

"Well," said the friar, "this is S. Francis's rose garden. One night he was tempted, oh, tempted of the devil in the grotto close by, which you will see in a moment, and so he ran into this little garden which was then full of briars; then he rolled among the thorns, but they suddenly burst into flower, and always they grow without thorns now. If we take them away, either they die," he said, "or they grow with thorns. Either they die or they grow with thorns," he repeated sorrowfully. And in answer to a question, "Yes, they blossom still in June and are red. It was in January that this miracle happened," he continued softly, "and his angel led him to the altar of the Portiuncula and he saw the Madonna and the angels and Christ on His throne in heaven. The leaves," he added, "are still sometimes marked as though spotted with blood."

But it is the chapel which takes its name from these roses, the Cappella delle Rose, which S. Bonaventura built over a poor hut where S. Francis would spend much time in prayer, that is of considerable interest. It consists of three parts, the grotto or hut of S. Francis, the oratory above it of S. Bonaventura, and a vestibule or atrium which S. Bernardino added in the fifteenth century. The walls of this last are covered with frescoes by Tiberio d'Assisi (c. 1470–1524), a pleasing local artist, and strongly influenced by Perugino and Pintoricchio. They consist of the story of the Indulgence, and in one we see S. Francis offering the thornless roses to Our Lady. In the oratory of S. Bonaventura are frescoes by the same painter of various Franciscan saints: S. Francis in the midst of his companions, over the altar; on the left, S. Bonaventura, S. Bernardino, S. Louis of Toulouse and S. Anthony of Padua; on the right, S. Clare and S. Elisabeth; above in the vault, God the Father in benediction. These frescoes are dated 1516. Beneath the oratory in the grotto or hut in which S. Francis was used to pray is a kneeling effigy of the saint. It is hard to leave this moving little chapel with its brightly coloured frescoes as in a child's picture book, its serenity and air of happiness.

The vast convent has not much of interest for the traveller, but the museum should not be missed.

The major treasures here, apart from the notable collection of vestments, are a Crucifix by Giunta Pisano and the panel with a full-length figure of S. Francis with half-figures of two angels, painted by the master who takes his name from this picture—the Maestro di S. Francesco. The beautiful and rather small Crucifix by Giunta Pisano used to stand over the altar of a chapel, demolished when the big basilica was built, near the chapel where S. Francis died and which took one of its names from this Crucifix. Its other name was Cappella dello Spirito Santo, and it was so called in memory of the celestial fire that appeared to consume all this place of Santa Maria degli Angeli when S. Francis and S. Clare sat at meat together and spoke so marvellously of God that all those present were rapt in ecstasy, as is narrated in the *Fioretti*, Chapter XV. The Crucifix is well preserved and finer in quality and execution than the other extant Crucifix from his hand in the church of SS. Ranieri e Leonardo in Pisa. The mutilated signature should read: *Iuncta Pisanus Capitini me fecit*. Giunta was active between 1229 and 1255, and seems to have come under Franciscan influence to judge by his Crucifixes, the characteristic of which is the tragic aspect of suffering which he gives to the figure of Our Lord, whose features have been distorted by pain, and he seems to express thus the compassion which S. Francis and his followers felt and expressed for the sufferings of the Saviour.

Giunta's great follower, the Maestro di S. Francesco, is seen here in the panel portrait of S. Francis. The very long figure of the saint is largely repainted, and was, I have sometimes thought, once not so long as we see it. The inscription below I have never been able to decipher, but that above reads HIC LECTUS MIHI VIVENTI FUIT ET MORIENTI. The picture is thus said to have been painted on the bed of the saint, that is to say, on the plank on which he slept and died. Two half-figures of angels fill the top corners of the panel about the small head of the saint, whose hair looks like a close-fitting cap. Similar angels are found in the large Crucifix by the master in the Perugia Gallery. A lovely patterned border surrounds three sides of the panel within the frame. Here too is preserved a portrait figure of S. Francis very close to Cimabue.

RIVOTORTO

Some mile and three-quarters to the south of Santa Maria degli Angeli, left of the high road to Foligno, beyond the chapel of Santa Maria Maddalena with its arched belfry, stands Santa Maria di Rivotorto, a modern church in Gothic style built after the earthquake of 1853 had destroyed an earlier building, which commemorated the tiny hut, which, even before the Portiuncula, was the first home of S. Francis and his companions.

A good deal of controversy has arisen as to the authenticity of this site, though for centuries it has been venerated as that of S. Francis's earliest sojourn where Brother Fly was turned out of the Order and where the peasant thrust in his ass and finally drove away the whole company. The difficulty has arisen on a question of its distance from the Portiuncula as stated by Bartholi in his *Tractatus* on the Indulgence of the Portiuncula,[1] but accuracy in a matter of distance is not characteristic of medieval treatises and may perhaps be disregarded. Here, at any rate, is the traditional site of the famous hut which was so small that the little company could scarce sit down or rest in it, so that S. Francis wrote the name of each of his companions over the narrow place he must occupy. Within the modern church is a replica of this hut.

It was at Rivotorto that S. Francis and his company were wont to assemble before the first journey to Rome and the official recognition there of the Rule and the Order by Innocent III; and on their return it was here they lived for a considerable time, perhaps even for as long as twenty months, and thus it was the first Franciscan convent. And it was when they were so characteristically turned out by the obstinate peasant and his ass[2] that S. Francis obtained from the Abbot of San Benedetto on Monte Subasio the possession of the chapel of

---

[1] F. Bartholi, *Tractatus de Indulgentia S. Mariae de Portiuncula* (Paris, 1900), p. 4.
[2] *Tres Socii*, 55.

the Portiuncula, which then became the *caput et mater* of his Order.

At Rivotorto S. Francis had twelve disciples, that is to say, the eleven who went with him to Rome and Frate Silvestro, the first priest to join the Order, which he had done after the return from Rome.[1] In the *Speculum Perfectionis* we read that in the first days of the Order when the brethren were living at Rivotorto, among them was a certain brother that did hardly pray at all and never did any work. "He would not go forth for alms, but did eat bravely; and, perceiving these things, the Blessed Francis knew by the Holy Spirit that he was a carnal man, and he said unto him, 'Go thy ways, Brother Fly, forasmuch as thou art minded to devour the labour of thy brethren and to be slothful in the work of God. . . .' And so he went his way."[2] This "carnal" brother is supposed to be Fra Giovanni di Capella, the sixth companion of S. Francis.

Rivotorto was the scene of the brief and marvellous springtime of the fraternity in which the most characteristic of the Franciscan virtues blossomed, whose excellence the troubadour of God greeted in salutation, "Hail, O holy Lady Poverty and thy sister holy Humility: hail, Lady Charity and thy sisters Lady Obedience and holy Simplicity." These virtues were eagerly practised at Rivotorto.

Not far from the hut, the first convent of the Order, were the leper houses about the two chapels of Santa Maria Maddalena and San Rufino d'Arce or San Rufinella, which one passes on the way to Rivotorto, and it was certainly in the service of the afflicted persons there that S. Francis had established himself at Rivotorto. And if Lady Charity led him and his companions to the service of the lepers, Lady Poverty, too, brought rude trials to Rivotorto. It sometimes happened that for lack of bread they had to eat the roots abandoned in the fields. And then one night, "in a time when the Blessed Francis began to have brethren and was sojourning with them at Rivotorto, it so fell out while all the brethren were asleep about the middle of the night that one of the brethren cried out saying, 'I am dying! I am dying!' Whereupon all the brethren awoke from

---

[1] Bonaventura: *Legenda Major*, cap. IV, 5.
[2] I Celano, cap. 42, and *Legenda Antiqua*, 9.

sleep amazed and afraid. And rising up, the Blessed Francis said, 'Arise, brethren, and kindle the light.' And when the light was kindled he said, 'Who is he that said, "I am dying"?' And the brother made answer, 'I am he.' And he said unto him, 'What aileth thee, brother? How art thou dying?' But he said, 'I am dying of hunger.' Then the Blessed Francis forthwith had a table laid out, and, as a man full of charity and discretion, did eat with him lest he should be ashamed to eat alone; and by his will all the other brethren did eat with him likewise."[1]

The sojourn at Rivotorto ended strangely. One day when they were at prayer a peasant appeared before the hut with his ass. "Get in with you," he shouted to his beast, which he pushed before him; "get within; we shall do well in this place." Francis was disturbed, for though the peasant addressed his beast it was obviously at the occupants of the shelter he shouted. Francis does not seem to have thought of resistance. "In truth, my brethren," he said, "God hath not called us to entertain asses, but to pray and teach men the way of salvation." And he quitted the hut with his companions.[2]

[1] *Speculum Perf.*, XXXII. [2] *Tres Socii*, 55.

CHAPTER III

TO BASTIA

ONE may pass down under the great convent of San Francesco on the south side to Ponte San Vittorino on the way to Bastia into the sweet monotony of the plain, often looking back at the Sacro Convento on its hill, which from here appears, what it is, a great bastioned fortress. There is something in the serenity of this wide valley which I cannot explain, whatever it is *ipsi quoque in coelestibus*. I recall that it was here one bitter day as S. Francis was coming from Perugia to Santa Maria degli Angeli with Brother Leo that the most divine of all the lovely episodes recorded in the *Fioretti* befell. It was in the springtime and the very bitter cold grievously tormented them. S. Francis called to Brother Leo, that was going on before him, and said thus:

"Brother Leo, though the Brothers Minor throughout all the world were great ensamples of sanctity and true edifying, nevertheless write it down and take heed diligently that not therein is perfect joy." And going on a little further, S. Francis called a second time, "O Brother Leo, albeit the Brother Minor should give sight to the blind, make straight the crooked, cast out devils, make the deaf to hear, the lame to walk, the dumb to speak and (greater still) should raise them that have been dead a four days' space, write that not herein is perfect joy." And going on a little he cried aloud, "O Brother Leo, if the Brother Minor should know all tongues and all sciences and all the Scriptures, so that he could prophesy and reveal not only things to come, but also the secrets of consciences and souls, write that not herein is perfect joy." Going on yet a little further, S. Francis called aloud once more, "O Brother Leo, thou little sheep of God, albeit the Brother Minor should speak with the tongue of angels and know the courses of the stars and the virtues of herbs; and though all the treasures of the earth were revealed unto him and he understood the virtue of birds, and of fishes, and of all animals, and of men, and of trees, and of stones,

SSISI. Le Carceri.

BEVAGNA. San Michele, Portal.

and of roots, and of waters, write that not therein is perfect joy." And going on a little further, S. Francis cried aloud, "O Brother Leo, albeit the Brother Minor could preach so well as to turn all the infidels to the faith of Christ write that not therein is perfect joy."

And this manner of speech continuing for full two miles, Brother Leo with much marvel besought him saying, "Father, I pray in the name of God that thou tell me, wherein is perfect joy." And S. Francis thus made answer: 'When we come to S. Mary of the Angels, all soaked as we are with rain and numbed with cold and besmirched with mud and tormented with hunger, and knock at the door; and the porter comes in anger and says, 'Who are ye?' And we say, 'We be two of your brethren,' and he says, 'Ye be no true men; nay, ye be two rogues that gad about deceiving the world and robbing the alms of the poor; get ye gone,' and thereat he shuts to the door and makes us stand without in the snow and the rain, cold and a-hungered, till night-fall; if therewithal we patiently endure such wrong and such cruelty and such rebuffs without being disquieted and without murmuring against him; and with humbleness and charity bethink us that this porter knows us full well and that God makes him to speak against us; O Brother Leo, write that herein is perfect joy. And if we be instant in knocking and he come out full of wrath and drive us away as importunate knaves, with insults and buffetings, saying, 'Get ye gone hence, vilest of thieves, begone to the alms-house, for here ye shall find nor food nor lodging'; if we suffer this with patience and with gladness and with love, O Brother Leo, write that herein is perfect joy. And if we still constrained of hunger, cold and night, knock yet again and shout and with much weeping pray him for the love of God that he will but open and let us in: and he yet more enraged should say, 'These be importunate knaves, I will pay them well as they deserve,' and should rush out with a knotty stick and taking us by the hood, throw us upon the ground and send us rolling in the snow and beat us with all the knots of that stick: if with patience and with gladness we suffer all these things thinking on the pains of the blessed Christ, the which we ought to suffer for the love of Him: O Brother Leo, write that here and herein is perfect joy. Then hear the conclusion of the whole matter, Brother Leo.

4

Above all graces and gifts of the Holy Spirit that Christ granteth to His beloved, is to overcome oneself and willingly for the love of Christ endure pains and insults and shame and want: inasmuch as in all other gifts of God we may not glory since they are not ours but God's: but in the cross of tribulation and affliction we may boast, for this is ours: and therefore, saith the Apostle, I would not that I should glory save in the cross of our Lord Jesus Christ."[1]

Just where the main road, after crossing the Chiascio stream at the hamlet of Bastiola, turns sharp left to proceed through the industrial *borgo* of Bastia and so to Santa Maria degli Angeli, one sees, away on the right, a cemetery, the chapel of which is that of the ancient Benedictine convent of the nuns of San Paolo where S. Francis placed nineteen-year-old S. Clare for safety when she fled away in the night of Palm Sunday on March 18, 1212, across the spring fields from her father's house in Assisi to the Portiuncula where Francis awaited her, cut off her hair and received her into the Order. Here it was her father and her brothers pursued and found her, but could not persuade or force her to return home with them, as she clung to the altar and showed them her cropped head.

The ancient convent was abandoned before the end of the thirteenth century. The continual unrest and war which raged in the valley in the twelfth and thirteenth centuries forced the nuns to leave the place and take refuge within the walls of Assisi. Today the site of the convent has become the cemetery of Bastia, but the ancient monastic church with its beautiful apse, where S. Clare refused to return to her parents, remains and an inscription within records these things.

In Bastia, in the church of San Michele, is one of the last works of Niccolò da Foligno, a signed triptych dated 1499 of the Virgin enthroned with her little Son in the midst of angels, with SS. Sebastian and Michael and, above, the Annunciation with God the Father in benediction, and, below, some half-figures of saints on either side a Pietà. This, though belonging to his old age, is not the least vigorous of Niccolò's works. Paintings by his son and by Tiberio d'Assisi may be found here, in the churches of Bastia and in the town hall.

[1] *Fioretti*, VIII (Temple Classics).

Not far away beside the road to Perugia you see aloft on a hill on the left the tower of Collestrada, where in 1202, in one of the battles between Assisi and Perugia, when he was little more than a youth, Francis was taken prisoner, and where many years later he reconciled a poor man with his master.[1] A little nearer, beside the road, you see the great building called the Spedalaccio, where in the time of S. Francis there was a house for lepers and where in 1216, when he was returning with Frate Masseo to S. Mary of the Angels after obtaining confirmation of the Indulgence of the Portiuncula from Honorius III, he rested awhile, and as he prayed he heard a voice from heaven which said, "Francis, you are to know that even as this Indulgence has been given thee on earth so it is confirmed in heaven." And he cried out to his companion, "Frate Masseo, I tell thee from God that the Indulgence which the Supreme Pontiff has given me on earth is confirmed also in heaven." And thus consoled they set out for S. Mary of the Angels.

[1] II Celano, cap. 56.

CHAPTER IV

TO BETTONA, CANNARA AND BEVAGNA

THERE was one pilgrimage I was anxious to make in the footsteps of S. Francis. I mean to Cannara, where he established the Third Order, and to Bevagna, where he preached to the birds. Both towns lie under the heights between the Topino and the Tiber, the long ridge of mountain land on the south of the valley of Spoleto. No doubt S. Francis set out on his way to Cannara from the Portiuncula, past Rivotorto, and reached Cannara by the old road through Castelnuovo, but I was anxious to see Bettona, which, though it has no memories of S. Francis, is in itself worth the detour.

Bettona lies across the great valley from Assisi, where it divides, the western branch being the valley of the Tiber, the eastern the valley of Spoleto which the Topino waters. It is a little town on an olive-clad hill commanding wonderful views of all this Umbrian country of valley and mountain. Indeed, the far-stretched prospects it affords are enchanting and, with its Etruscan wall, its best attraction. Its churches, for the most part redecorated or rebuilt in the seventeenth and eighteenth centuries, still retain a few pictures of the earlier time. In Santa Maria Maggiore, over the first altar on the right, is a Gonfalone by Perugino one is convinced, with S. Anne, the Madonna and our little Lord in glory, with two saints, which, if it is by the great master, does not stand high among his innumerable works. More interesting is a Sienese panel on a gold ground of the Assumption by an artist close to Paolo di Giovanni Fei. A Pietà and a Crucifixion on either side the high altar (originally a Standard) are poor works of the school of Niccolò da Foligno.

The Municipio possesses a small picture-gallery. Here is a fresco of S. Michael, an early work by Fiorenzo di Lorenzo, and a signed and dated work by Perugino, a picture of S. Anthony of Padua with a donor (1512) and a Madonna della Misericordia with SS. Marinus, Jerome and donors from his workshop. Here, too, are some detached frescoes by Tiberio d'Assisi.

No, Bettona has nothing much in the way of works of art to offer, her glory lies in her wonderful views, the landscapes at her feet, from the Fosso Pagliano and vine-clad Monte Fratta across the far-stretched plain, and from Torgiano to Perugia, to Assisi, to Foligno.

I left Bettona, returning a little on my way, and then, over the folds of the Mountain of the Five Oaks, crossing many a barren torrent, I made my way to Cannara and there found S. Francis.

Cannara, with its beautiful round tower, gets its present name from the canes which grow in the marshy lands about it. Its interest lies almost solely in the fact that it was here S. Francis founded his Third Order for lay folk.

As recounted in the *Fioretti*, S. Francis was undecided in his mind whether he should devote himself to preaching or prayer; whether, that is, to an active or contemplative life, and he sent Frate Masseo to S. Clare to ask her to show him which was the will of God. Frate Masseo was also to go to Frate Silvestro; and Frate Silvestro, to whom Masseo came first, having prayed, replied that God had not called Francis for himself alone, but to the end that many through him should be saved. And S. Clare also made the same answer. And when S. Francis heard all this he rose and said to Frate Masseo, "Let us be going"; and he came to the Castello, or walled village, of Cannara and there he preached with so great a fervour that all, men and women, wished to leave their homes and follow S. Francis and enter his Order. But S. Francis would not suffer it, saying, "Make not ill haste nor leave your homes; and I will ordain for you what you should do for the salvation of your souls." And he resolved to found the Third Order for the salvation of the world. And he went on towards Bevagna and on the way he preached to the birds.

This was in 1216. It was not till 1221 that the new institution received its canonical statute, but many people had not waited for this. Among these were Orlando di Chiusi, who gave Monte La Verna to S. Francis, and the Lady Jacoba di Settesoli, who was with him when he died.

The establishment of the Third Order of S. Francis was a sensational, if not a revolutionary, act, for the Tertiaries took an oath to the Holy See and as the whole political edifice of the Middle Age reposed on such oaths taken to a suzerain lord or commune, the foundation of the Third Order meant that the Holy See was able to dispose of an unheard-of power against its enemies. If it opposed wars which it considered unjust, or favoured others, it could by means of the thousands who joined the Third Order break the resistance of the Communes, resist the civil power and even hold the emperor in check. As the Tertiaries very rapidly spread over all Italy, the Papacy had auxiliaries everywhere; for in some cities the citizens became Tertiaries *en masse*. The social consequences were also immense and the canonical immunity which detached the Tertiaries from lay jurisdiction diminished the feudal edifice and without doubt improved the lot of the poor.[1]

According to tradition, it was in the church of the Buona Morte in Cannara that S. Francis instituted the Third Order, giving there the habit to Blessed Lucio Modestini. Nothing remains of his time.

In the church of San Giovanni Battista, however, there is a painting by Niccolò da Foligno, dated 1482, of the Madonna and Child between SS. John Baptist and Sebastian, with a landscape in the background, but it is a mediocre work. The church of San Biagio has a fine Romanesque façade. That is all I could find of artistic interest in Cannara, for the small collection in the Municipio contains really nothing to delay the traveller.

Bevagna lies about four miles to the south of Cannara after returning to the road from Bettona. The way is lovely with the olive and the vine, and the views of Monte Subasio, with Assisi and Spello on its skirts, of Foligno in the plain and Montefalco on the hills before one, are full of enchantment and an ineffable peace. It was here on this road, in a place between Cannara and Bevagna, a place they call Pian d'Arca, that the famous and charming episode related in Chapter XVI of the *Fioretti* took place.

When S. Francis was coming from Cannara, where he had

---

[1] Cf. Fr. Cuthbert, *Life of St. Francis*, pp. 304 *et seq.*

that day promised the people to found an Order for them, which should allow them to remain in their homes with their families, he "came to a place between Cannara and Bevagna and as with great fervour he was going on his way he lifted up his eyes and beheld some trees hard by the road whereon sat a great company of birds, well-nigh without number; and said to his companions, 'Ye shall wait for me here upon the way and I will go to preach to my little sisters the birds.' And he went into a field and began to preach unto the birds there were on the ground; and immediately those that were on the trees flew down to him and they all of them remained still and quiet together until S. Francis made an end of preaching and not even then did they depart until he had given them his blessing."[1]

Though it is impossible to know the exact spot where this, perhaps the best-known episode in the life of S. Francis, took place,[2] one can be sure to pass over it as one goes on across the hill-side to Bevagna, above the green Umbrian plain watered here by many a stream.

Bevagna lies on a bend of the Topino, at the foot of hills covered with the olive and the vine. A rather dark and even gloomy little town, I, perhaps unfortunate, found it. In antiquity Mevania was famous for its bulls and its flocks, of which Virgil sings in the second Georgic, when having been drenched in the sacred stream of Clitumnus they were led to Rome to the temples of the Gods in a Roman Triumph. One may still see considerable remains of a Roman temple in Via Garibaldi and of a Roman mosaic in Via Porta Guelfa.

The place suffered throughout the Middle Age from war and outrage and was almost destroyed in 1375 by Corrado Trinci of Foligno, but, in 1439, came into the protection of the Church. It is still almost surrounded by its medieval walls with their towers and five gates. These, and the two wonderful Romanesque churches in the piazza, are the best things that remain to Bevagna.

The piazza is completely medieval (save for the fountain)

---

[1] *Fioretti*, XVI (Temple Classics).
[2] In the Salle d'Apollon in the Louvre is a small thirteenth-century Limoges enamel of this subject so exquisitely poetical in feeling that not even Giotto has excelled it.

and is enclosed by the Gothic Palazzo de' Consoli, with its fine
flight of steps, its arcade or loggia on the ground floor, and by
the lovely Romanesque church of San Silvestro, built by the
great artist of the place, Binellus, and signed and dated by him
in 1195; and by the church of San Michele, also of the end of
the twelfth century, built and decorated by the same master
and his associate Rudolphus, who have both signed their work
on the right of the magnificent central portal, which recalls in
grander fashion the minor portal of the cathedral of Foligno.
The two fine churches and the piazza in which they stand
are alone worth a visit to Bevagna.

But I came to Bevagna, after all, for the sake of S. Francis,
and the only reminder I could find of him was in the church
of San Francesco, which still retains its thirteenth-century
façade and where within is shown a stone on which he is said
to have stood when he preached to the birds. This was brought
from Pian d'Arca, and is inscribed:

> *Praedicat hic avibus Franciscus simplex et istum*
> *In pede Seraphico sanctificat lapidem.*

It is but a mile or two from Bevagna into Foligno, and thence
by the main road to Assisi, but I returned on my way over the
foot-hills, for it was pleasanter than the highway, noisy with
modern traffic and tarred for motors. And as I went I tried
to remember some of the many encounters S. Francis had with
birds. Certainly his preaching to them at Bevagna was not the
first. There was that occasion when there was such a clamour
of birds, as he would be preaching, that he could not hear
himself speak, so that he prayed them silence, which they
immediately procured for him by their departure *en masse*. He
once sang, too, against a nightingale and owned himself beaten.
And there was another occasion when a certain young man
had caught many turtle doves, and as he was carrying them for
sale, S. Francis, looking on them with pitying eyes, said to the
youth, "I pray thee give them me that birds so gentle may not
fall into the hands of cruel men that would kill them." Forthwith inspired by God, he gave them to S. Francis, who received
them into his bosom and began to speak to them tenderly,
"O my sisters, simple-minded turtle doves, innocent and chaste,

why have ye let yourselves be caught?" And S. Francis went and made nests for them all and they, abiding therein, began to lay their eggs and hatch them, and so tame were they, they might have been fowls, and never did they go away till S. Francis with his blessing gave them leave to go. "My little son," said S. Francis to him who had given them to him, "my little son, thou wilt yet be a brother of this Order."

Then there was the greeting the birds gave him on his first coming to La Verna, when at the foot of the rock of La Verna itself they came about him as he sat under an oak with singing and flapping of their wings for joy and gladness, and came about him so that some settled on his head, some on his shoulders, some on his arms, some in his lap and some round his feet. And when his companions marvelled, he said it was a sign that their coming was pleasing to Our Lord, since their little sisters and brothers the birds showed such joy at their presence.

And at last, as he died in the hut at S. Mary of the Angels, it is recorded that a multitude of crested larks, his favourites, flocked wheeling about the roof and for long with their said chirping bewailed the loss of their friend.

Certainly S. Francis had a wonderful way with animals, as witness his dealings with the Wolf of Gubbio. There was another Umbrian, too, who was friends with the beasts— Raphael Sanzio. Vasari records how "his sweet and gracious nature was so replete with excellence and so perfect in all the charities, that not only was he honoured by men, but even by the very animals which would constantly follow his steps and always loved him".

CHAPTER V

SPELLO

SPELLO is so near to Assisi, and the way thither by the old road out of Porta Nuova is so pleasant, that all save those who are desperate with hurry should walk or drive thither from the city of S. Francis. There is but little to be seen: a few Roman remains, an amphitheatre, a triumphal arch in ruin, two gateways, Porta Veneris and Porta Urbica, over which lean the heads of two men and a woman; and, save for a sculpture here and there, that is all that is left of the Roman Hispellum. It was not, however, to find Roman things that I came to Spello on her little hill, but to see the work of the great and exquisite sentimentalist, Pintoricchio. Nowhere save in Siena or Rome can you see him so well as in this small, clambering city, where in 1501—the year in which Perugino was painting in the Cambio—he was busy with his dainty modish stories, in the church of Santa Maria Maggiore. A painter who delighted in beauty, you might be tempted to say, as you look on his charming decorative work of 1501 in the Baglioni chapel here, with its original majolica pavement of Deruta tiles. Nor, after all, would you be wrong. Beauty, conceived as he conceived it, was his conscious aim. I do not know in all his work a woman who is not surpassing pretty. He pleases us by the lightness of his touch, the daintiness of his perfect handling, the nicety of his finish. He is so much greater in the Sistine Chapel than anywhere else that we are always startled to find so much promise, after all, merely talent. He seems to have been so susceptible to influence that in the company of great men he becomes almost one of them, just as when left to himself, or with the subtle and scornful Perugino, he becomes—well, just a painter of "out of doors", a "space composer", as Mr. Berenson has said, but so much less great than his master.

The church in its small piazza is not a very interesting building. The western façade is simple, and some Cosmatesque designs of animals and vines and flowers, together with reliefs, are on the doorway. They are possibly the work of the *mar-morari*, Rudolphus and Binellus of Bevagna, whose work is to be found there and in Foligno. They should be compared with the Romanesque bestiaries at Spoleto. In the Baglioni chapel, one sees on the left the Annunciation, in front the Nativity, and on the right Christ among the Doctors, with an elaborate Renaissance temple in the background. The best of these is, to my mind, the Annunciation. For once Pintoricchio seems to have been possessed, really captured, by the vision of Mary. She, that beautiful maid, blessed among women, wearied but listening to our devotion, is still in the dawn of her simplicity, reading her Book of Hours, when suddenly, before she can turn the page, God has sent His messenger, a kind of splendid knight, to tell her of her destiny. So it is in the midst of her dream that she is interrupted, and suddenly confronted with Love Himself, whose Mother, in a less happy way than in the old Greek world, but with a new tenderness and refinement, she, scarcely wakened to life as yet, is to be. Here is the story as it has been told to us in our childhood, not actually as it came to us then, but as we remember it now when we are older. In the Nativity, Pintoricchio is less fine, is, indeed, what we have come to regard him—a mere pupil of Perugino, without that master's magical spaciousness and splendour of proportion. It is the same with the Christ among the Doctors, and yet the picture strikes one. This man might surely have been a great painter had he been brought up in the intellectual Florentine tradition. But Umbria, with her light and space and gentle landscapes, soft hills and wide valleys full of sunshine, was too enervating for a personality so facile as to be susceptible to every influence. In contact with Rome, he achieved a kind of greatness, but here it was otherwise; if he understood the achievement of Perugino, he was yet unable to express himself through the same medium of perfect spaciousness and light.

In the sacristy here, now a small museum, among other things are a panel picture of the Virgin and Child enthroned, not a very attractive work, and a more charming fresco of the same subject, both by Pintoricchio, and a diptych by Cola di Petruccioli (1385) of the Crucifixion and the Coronation of Our Lady. Here, too, is a fine fourteenth-century Cross in silver

with enamels, and another Cross and chalice, also in silver, of
the fifteenth and sixteenth centuries. (Another enamelled Cross
of the fourteenth century is to be found in the sacristy of San
Lorenzo.) On the entry piers to the presbytery are two works
by Perugino in his extreme old age (1521), a Pietà and a Virgin
and Child enthroned with saints.

One wanders to the Gothic church of Sant' Andrea, where is
a large altarpiece by Pintoricchio of the Madonna and saints,
painted in 1508; the same qualities meet us in this work, only a
little more superficial in its exquisite pictorial prettiness, as in
the frescoes in the Duomo, though here there is a strong Peru-
ginesque influence everywhere, save in the enthroned Madonna
and Child and the little S. John. In the Municipio is a fine
picture by Niccolò da Foligno taken from the Convento di
Vallegloria, a Crucifix where beside the Cross stand the
Madonna and S. John Evangelist and a bishop, while at the
foot of the Cross S. Francis kneels. It was painted about 1460.

It is delightful to walk to San Girolamo under the olives
outside Porta Montanara with its frescoes, a Nativity by Perugino and others by followers of Pintoricchio and Mezzastris.
Or to wander out of Porta Fontevecchia to Santa Maria
della Rotonda, a fine Renaissance church, a Greek cross under
an octagonal dome dating from 1517. Or to go to San Claudio,
a small Romanesque and curiously asymmetrical church of
the twelfth century and to the Roman amphitheatre.

They say it was one day at Spello, when S. Francis and
S. Clare were walking together and came to some osteria or
other where they were given a morsel of bread, that as they sat
there on the stones the people began to point at them with
diffidenza and no little suggestion of evil and *bisbigli malevoli*,
indirect allusions and jokes.

They went away in silence.

It was a winter's day and the ground was covered with snow.
Evening came on under the grey sky as they went. Presently
S. Francis said:

"Sister Clare, hast thou understood what they were saying
of us?"

S. Clare did not reply, for her heart was sorrowful, and she
felt, if she had spoken, she could not have restrained her tears.

"We must never do this again," said S. Francis at last.

S. Clare knelt down in the path on the desolate mountainside.

"What, never, Father? When then shall we meet again?"

"When?" said S. Francis. "When the roses bloom in January."

Marvellous and divine miracle! In a moment, a second of time, the whole mountainside was covered with roses, so that the air was filled with their perfume.

CHAPTER VI

FOLIGNO AND MONTEFALCO

OLIGNO, in the broad valley of Spoleto, is known to
the world, if at all, as the city of the Blessed Angela,
or as the town of a few towers that hovers in the background of Raphael's picture, the Madonna di Foligno. A busy
enough place on a market-day, seeing that today, as ever, it is
the meeting-place of the roads from Arezzo, Perugia and the
north, and from Ancona and the Adriatic, for Rome; it has
not changed much, since the beginning of the sixteenth century, when Raphael put it into his picture. The inns are not
luxurious, but the place itself is alive, while Spello and Assisi
are dead or dying, concerned only with things long ago, but
Foligno is of a certain commercial importance and a military
station. It is not, however, these things that will bring the
traveller here on his way from Assisi to Spoleto, but perhaps a
desire to see the church where Blessed Angela heard the
preacher and confessed her sins, or it may be the paintings of
Ottaviano Nelli and Niccolò da Foligno, who was born here.

Going from the Piazza della Fiera into the Via Cavour,
where on the right one passes the inn, the Albergo della Posta,
a rather delightful hostelry, in no great while one comes to the
central piazza. On the far side of this piazza rises the Palazzo
Trinci, the dwelling-place of the family which ruled here in
medieval times.

The city was famous, during the last centuries of struggle
between the Italian burghers and their native despots, for its
peculiar ferocity in civil strife. "Some of the bloodiest pages in
medieval Italian history are those which relate the vicissitudes
of the Trinci family, the exhaustion of Foligno by internal
discord, and its final submission to the Papal power," says
Symonds. The Trinci family, it would seem, were practically
rulers of Foligno during the whole of the fourteenth century,
and in the early part of the fifteenth century until the Pope
expelled the house. Siding with the Church as they did in the

struggle of Guelph and Ghibelline, it seems that they always had their power from the Pope, so that when in 1439 they quarrelled with Eugenius IV, they fell never to rise again. It was, however, in 1424 that they employed Ottaviano Nelli of Gubbio to paint their chapel for them, attaining thereby an immortality, at least among us travellers, that none of their other deeds would have given them unless, indeed, we recall that Paoluccio Trinci who restored the Observants to the Order of S. Francis.

The palace itself, with its windows and finely sculptured arms of Sixtus IV, is worth more than a glance. The chapel is built on the upper floor of the palace, and is painted in fresco with the story of the Blessed Virgin. On the roof Ottaviano has told the beginning of that story, of S. Joachim and S. Anne, the mother and father of Mary. For, as it happened, they loved one another and were wedded, but they had no child. For this cause they made their offerings in the Temple, and, being childless, they were suspected of some evil and turned adrift from the Temple where they served. S. Joachim in his wretchedness went into the desert, and there, after many years, an angel found him and told him to go to the Golden Gate of the Temple, nothing doubting, to meet S. Anne. And in truth it all happened as the angel said, and soon a child was born to them, the Blessed Virgin herself—*Rosa Mystica, Lilium Convallium.* Soon Mary is presented in the Temple and marries Joseph, whose rod alone among those many others blossomed; she hears the message of the angel and Christ is born, and the kings come from the East to worship Him. He is crucified and ascends into heaven. The Apostles, as was most fitting, come to the Blessed Virgin before they go into all the world, as the Prince of Life had said. Suddenly they are recalled and see that most sweet Rose fall on sleep, and pass into the heaven of her Son.

Above the altar are scenes showing the Crucifixion, S. Francis receiving the Stigmata, SS. Dominic, Antony Abbot and the Baptist, together with the signature and the date 1424. These are works of Nelli's old age and have not the refinement of the Belvedere Madonna and Child at Gubbio, or even of his fresco in San Francesco at Assisi.

The cathedral of San Feliciano, on the eastern side of the piazza, is an almost entirely modernised building. · The Romanesque façade has been outrageously restored; but not the lateral Porta minore, a work of the twelfth century, probably by Binellus and Rudolphus of Bevagna, where they signed the portal of San Michele. S. Feliciano, to whom the church is dedicated, was a bishop, it is said, of this city in the third century. But it is not for him that we come to it today, without fresco, or precious object, except for the Crucifix beside which Niccolò da Foligno has painted the figures of the Virgin and S. John, and the magnificent Baroque statue of the patron saint in silver in the sacristy. It is for Blessed Angela's sake we come and meditate for a moment here.

Blessed Angela of Foligno is one of the greatest mystics of Italy, perhaps the greatest of the Italian thirteenth century. Very little is known of her life apart from the account of her visions which she at the request of her confessor dictated to him.[1] She was born at Foligno about the middle of the thirteenth century of a wealthy family owning various castles and other properties. She married and had several sons, but lived an irregular and even vicious life till, touched by grace, she suddenly made up her mind to go to confession. However, when she came to the point her courage failed her, and from shame she felt unable to mention the more grievous of her sins. She then communicated, adding sacrilege to her other faults. At length, tortured by remorse, she invoked the aid of S. Francis, who in the following night appeared to her. "My sister," said he, "if you had called on me sooner I should have granted your prayer before this." She herself tells us what then befell. "In the morning I went therefore to the church of San Francesco, but on my way I found a friar who was preaching at San Feliciano and this friar was chaplain to the bishop. And so I determined, thanks to Our Lord, fully to confess to this friar, and so I did. And having heard my confession, he said that if I would allow it he would tell my sins to the bishop and, he added, the penitence that the bishop will impose I will report to thee, though I could

<hr />

[1] The best edition in the vernacular of Blessed Angela's book is that of P. Paul Doncoeur, *La Livre de la B. Soeur Angèle de Foligno. Documents originaux édités et traduits* (Paris, 1926).

OLIGNO. Cathedral: Niccolò da Foligno, Head of S. John (detail).

SPOLETO. Duomo.

absolve thee without the bishop. In this confession I felt no love, only bitterness, shame and grief."

Blessed Angela became a Franciscan Tertiary and the leader of a large number of penitents. She was subject to extraordinary visions, some of which she recounted to her confessor, Frate Arnoldo, who wrote them down at her dictation, and it is this that has come down to us. After much suffering she died in great peace on January 4, 1309, and was buried in San Francesco in Foligno, once a beautiful building of the thirteenth century, but now rebuilt in modern times. It is there we may venerate her relics. The beautiful *cassa* with her effigy of the fourteenth century remains.

From the Cathedral one passes to the church of the Annunziatella where there is a ruined work by Perugino—the Baptism of Christ (1507). To get to it one passes through the shop of a carpenter, which to the traveller who is something of a symbolist will surely not be displeasing. But it is perhaps in the church of San Niccolò, where Niccolò da Foligno has painted a magnificent altarpiece, that one finds one's best excuse for having come to Foligno at all.

For this is the city of Niccolò da Foligno, who was born here about 1430, married here in 1452, painted many frescoes here and in the neighbouring cities and as far afield as the Marche and died here in 1502. He was perhaps the pupil of Bartolommeo di Tommaso whose altarpiece of the Madonna and Child enthroned between two saints is in the church of San Salvatore here, and then of Benozzo Gozzoli, the Florentine pupil of Fra Angelico whose frescoes fill the choir of San Francesco close by in Montefalco, and finally came under the influence of Carlo Crivelli. Niccolò's earliest dated work (1456) is a fresco in S. Maria in Campis outside Foligno, but four years later he painted the Madonna and S. John about the sculptured Crucifix in the Cathedral—the head of the S. John is particularly fine and characteristic of the master; and then in the church of San Niccolò we find this magnificent altarpiece signed and dated 1492, when he was more than sixty years old.

In the central panel the Blessed Virgin and S. Joseph adore the Bambino; behind, not far away, the shepherds, impatient to see the promised Saviour who is Christ the Lord, run towards

Bethlehem; far away the three kings journey through a strange landscape to find the place where the Child lay. Above, Niccolò has painted the Resurrection, while at the sides are S. John Baptist, S. Nicholas and S. Sebastian, with two others, and S. Nicholas of Tolentino, S. Jerome, S. John Evangelist and S. Michael, with two others. The Coronation, in a side-chapel, is less worthy of this often melancholy painter, though the landscape is exquisite, but the triptych, with its predella of the Passion, is, I think, his last masterpiece, and if it shows signs of his decadence, especially in the figures of saints, it is still largely free of his later mannerisms.

In the sacristy is a splendid *armadio* with paintings and a Virgin and Child by Luca di Tommé.

From San Niccolò I passed down the Via della Scuola and, turning to the right, found the Piazza Giordano Bruno wherein are the two churches, San Domenico, with a fresco of the Crucifixion by Mezzastris, and Santa Maria infra portas. The latter is a very ancient building, containing ruined frescoes. Many curious legends surround it with a kind of fascination which attracts one as much as the obvious beauty of the place. Once, so we are told, it was a temple of Diana; and then again, that S. Peter celebrated Mass there in the little chapel on the right. However this may be, it is worthy of a visit, chiefly because of its picturesque doorway, I suppose; though, indeed, I found the church itself delightful. Moreover, here are frescoes of S. Roch and S. Jerome by a fellow pupil of Niccolò da Foligno, Pier Antonio Mezzastris, whose work is so charming in the Cappella dei Pellegrini in Assisi.

In San Salvatore in Piazza Garibaldi on the other side of the city, with its fine portals and charming tower, there is the great panel picture of the Madonna and Child enthroned with angels between the Baptist and Beato Pietro Crisci, with the donor, Ronaldo Corrado Trinci, painted in 1437 by Bartolommeo di Tommaso, perhaps the master of Niccolò da Foligno, a remarkable work. Other churches, too, have some fine features, such as San Giacomo, a noble portal and tower, and Santa Caterina, again a fine portal with a rose over it, and Sant' Agostino had a charming tower destroyed in the last war.

The Pinacoteca in the Palazzo Comunale with its tower of

the fifteenth century, but otherwise spoiled by rebuilding, has a
work by Niccolò, S. Francis receiving the Stigmata, and a
detached fresco by Bartolommeo di Tommaso of the Madonna
of Loreto, S. Anthony of Padua preaching and the Martyrdom
of S. Barbara, and many detached frescoes by Mezzastris,
other works by whom are in Santa Lucia and Sant' Anna.

Outside the city in the environs there are several places of
beauty and interest. A good mile outside Porta Romana is the
church of Santa Maria in Campis with a fresco by Niccolò da
Foligno of the Crucifixion, with the Madonna, the Baptist and
the Magdalen at the foot of the Cross, and above four sorrowful
angels, the earliest of his dated works (1456).

And then three miles outside Porta di Firenze is the very
interesting church of San Giovanni Profiamma. This name, it
seems, is a corruption of Forfiamma, which records the Roman
town of Forum Flaminii. The church has a lovely portal with
round arch and symbolic figures and dates from 1239. It was
restored some years ago, too much indeed, but is still beautiful
with its fine crypt, built up over which, and much higher than
the nave, is the sanctuary reached by a central flight of steps.
The ciborio, a replica of that of the thirteenth century, stands
over the altar, which is supported by part of an antique granite
column, and the round-arched arcade on either side is charming.

The days passed thus delightfully at the Albergo della Posta
in making little journeys to the neighbouring places and their
churches.

Some two miles outside Porta Ancona is the church of
San Bartolommeo with a beautiful façade of the fifteenth
century. Within, the church has been remade in the sixteenth
century, but in a chapel on the left is the last work of Niccolò
da Foligno, the Martyrdom of S. Bartholomew, which he
directed his son Lattanzio to finish.

From San Bartolommeo one follows up the valley some two
miles to the ancient abbey of Sassovivo under Monte
Serrone. The flourishing days of this Benedictine house were
those of the thirteenth century, when the Roman marble crafts-
man Petrus de Maria built and decorated in mosaic the
exquisite cloister, to the order of Abbot Angelus (1229), as the
inscription records. This cloister is, I think, unique in its

grace and beauty in this valley of Spoleto, otherwise so rich in works of architectural beauty. The abbey is now an ecclesiastical seminary. It is delightful to spend an afternoon there with the *Fioretti* in the shade and to return down the beautiful valley at evening.

So the summer days passed, and when it was too hot in the valley I went up to Montefalco and found there coolness and silence.

The road to Montefalco is beautiful with views of the ever-changing valley and the mountains; and the little city herself stands high on her hill. Her unfrequented streets are still as of old, and she seems to look across the wide valley to Assisi as a daughter towards her mother. It is not Giotto who has clothed her with glory while telling the legend of S. Francis, but Benozzo Gozzoli, the pupil of Fra Angelico, with his simple literalism and delightful sense of the loveliness of such natural things as flowers and animals, who has painted for her the same immortal story—not in vain, for his influence is found again and again in such men as Bonfigli, Niccolò da Foligno, whose work one has learned to care for in Foligno and Assisi, and in Fiorenzo di Lorenzo. Nor, as it seems to me, did Pintoricchio wholly escape his charm; much of his delight in those natural beauties which crowd his pictures is, it may well be, owing to the work of this Tuscan painter.

It is in the little church of San Francesco—desecrated now and used as a picture-gallery—in what was once the choir, that we find the frescoes of the life of S. Francis, painted in the middle of the fifteenth century by Benozzo Gozzoli. It is here for the first time almost we come upon that growth, that development into some half-apprehended ideal, which every legend seems to follow. S. Francis was a man so like to Christ as almost to be mistaken for Him; it is therefore certain that he too, like the Prince of Life, was born in a stable. And even as old Simeon and Anna had prophesied of Christ, so a pilgrim tells of S. Francis, and a poor man spreads his coat for the saint to tread on. Thus gradually in the minds of men S. Francis became, even in lesser things, a kind of imitation of Jesus of Nazareth. The first words of the *Fioretti* are proof of this, for it is there written that "At first, needs must we consider how the

glorious Saint Francis in all the acts of his life was conformed
unto Christ the Blessed One: how even as Christ in the beginning
of His preaching chose twelve apostles to contemn all earthly
things, to follow Him in poverty and other virtues, so S. Francis
in the beginning chose out for the founding of the Order twelve
companions, possessors of the deepest poverty." Thus, as the
legend developed we see how men's minds were impressed by
the strange and beautiful likeness of the Poverello to the Saviour
of the World. The frescoes continue the life of the saint almost
as in the upper church at Assisi, where the traditional works of
Giotto were doubtless known to Benozzo Gozzoli. These
Montefalco frescoes are particularly interesting as the early work
of a man who, brought by Fra Angelico to Rome and Orvieto
—where, as here, his work is really an imitation of his master—
was later to develop a more individual style, as in the frescoes
in the Riccardi chapel, or at San Gimignano, or in his ruined
masterpieces at Pisa, where he painted from 1469 to 1487. Here
in Montefalco he is strictly the pupil of Fra Angelico. But
in that attitude of the scholar to one who was so worthy of
his allegiance, it may well be, we find his work really finer
than when he had become himself a little master. Of far more
importance, it seems to me, in Umbrian than in Florentine art
—where he is really a mediocrity—he was, in Central Italy
certainly, the means of awakening much thought and energy
in painting. Born near to Florence in 1420, he was, as indeed
were other artists, apprenticed to some metal-worker, and even
helped Ghiberti to forge the Gates of Paradise. In his early
work, however, under the influence of Angelico, he, having had
a glimpse of heaven, turning to the earth, found it every whit as
fair. And it is, I think, while still under the spell of Angelico
that he is valuable to us, rather than in his far more popular
frescoes in the Riccardi chapel. He tells the story of S. Francis,
here in Montefalco, like a romance almost, in which the spirit
of adventure, the call of the road, the magical persistence of
tomorrow blend very happily with the lovely life of the little
poor man. Looking on these frescoes, the splendour of the
Journey of the Three Kings in Florence seems tawdry, the
gorgeous works at Pisa superficial. Here his work is so boyish,
as it were, as almost to disarm criticism, and in that very

freshness, without ulterior ideas about art, he comes nearer perhaps than Giotto to realising for us the romantic beauty of S. Francis's life. He certainly realises that, and strives to make us realise it as no other painter of the Franciscan legend has been able to do, before the far more exquisite and spiritual work of Sassetta. And so, though for no other cause yet for this, I return to Montefalco again and again.

There is more of his work still to be seen in the chapels of the north aisle, of which the angels still keep something of their former beauty, and tell us not a little of his pupil Bonfigli.

Perugino too has left us a remembrance of his genius close to the west door—a lovely fresco of the Adoration of the Shepherds, whose landscape, with that wide Umbrian sky full of light and space, tells us as much of Italia Mistica as any picture I remember. For with Perugino there is at least this much saved from the wreck of time—to wit, his marvellous apprehension of space, of serene light, and the spiritual effect of just that. It is as though he had contrived to seize the poetry of a clear, serene sky and ample landscape, and to place in that apprehension all his treasure, so that in spite of his sentimentality and insincerity and scornfulness he is a great spiritual poet, composing out of just light and space wonderful dreams.

No one should leave Montefalco without visiting the church of Santa Chiara, not the S. Clare of Assisi, but a little daughter of S. Francis nevertheless, a contemporary of Blessed Angela of Foligno and, like her, a tertiary of the Franciscan Order, a mystic and a visionary. Her convent, once dedicated in honour of the Holy Cross, was built in 1290, and though now entirely modernised, it still contains her shrine and the incorrupt body of the little saint. There she lies, the exquisite pale face, with closed eyes, and her delicate hands still visible. "If you seek the cross of Christ," she said to her sister Giovanna, "take my heart: there you will find our suffering Lord." When her heart was examined after her death in 1308, the image of the Crucifix and the instruments of the Passion were seen to be formed solidly in some sort of tissue within her heart. Her blood, too, is said to liquefy. She was a tertiary of S. Francis, but towards the end of the fifteenth century[1] her nuns forsook the Rule of S. Francis and were given that of S. Augustine, so that S. Clare of Montefalco is claimed by both the Augustinian and the Franciscan Orders.

The Franciscan convent of San Fortunato, outside the city towards Spoleto, possesses one of the best frescoes by Benozzo Gozzoli. The quiet country master Tiberio d'Assisi, too, has painted there with all his charming serenity the story of S. Francis and the roses; and, indeed, the chapel where his frescoes shine is the chapel of the Rosary, a cool and lovely place in which to meditate awhile on a summer afternoon. The present buildings date from 1446, and it was thus in a new church that Benozzo painted in 1450 his Adoration of the Child amid those musical angels.

[1] Cf. P. Bonaventura Marinangeli in *Miscellanea Francescana* (Foligno, 1913), Vol. XIV, pp. 129 *et seq.*

CHAPTER VII

NOCERA AND UMBRA GUALDO TADINO

I T was so hot in the valley that while I was in Foligno I thought I would go up to Nocera and Gualdo Tadino for a few days and enjoy the freshness there among the mountains. Yes it was hot, a magnificent early summer:

> *Et nunc omnis ager, nunc omnis parturit arbos,*
> *Nunc frondent silvae, nunc formosissimus annus. . . .*

Besides, I wanted to see the great altarpieces of Niccolò da Foligno at Nocera and Gualdo and to view the battlefield at Gualdo where Narses slew Totila and brought the Goths to an end in Italy—a famous victory.

It is an easy run of little more than twenty minutes in the train from Foligno to Nocera Umbra. The line ascends the ever-narrowing valley of the Topino, and the ancient city, in a wonderfully beautiful situation above the stream, is surrounded by mountains. Famous today for its waters which are bottled and sent all over Italy, it was in Roman times a notable station on the Flaminian Way and as celebrated then for its wooden vessels for household use as it is now for its waters.

One enters by the Porta Vecchia and presently comes in the Piazza Caprera to the church of San Francesco. It is possible that S. Francis was here as early as 1215, but it is generally thought that it was S. Rinaldo, Bishop of Nocera, who in 1221 invited Francis to set up a convent of *frati* here. This stood in the Piazza del Mercato, but it was destroyed by the Saracens of Frederic II in 1248, and it was not till 1336 that the present church was built. Half abandoned as it seems, there is nothing of interest within but a fresco by Matteo da Gualdo in a chapel on the right, of the Virgin and Child, dated 1498—not a very attractive work.

Close by in what was once the church of the Madonnina is the small Pinacoteca. This possesses two important paintings. The first in date is a remarkable Crucifix of the school of

Giunta Pisano; it was once in the sacristy of the Cathedral. The other is the magnificent polyptych by Niccolò da Foligno, signed and dated 1483. In the midst, under a pavilion, the Madonna kneels in worship of her little Son, while behind, angels from the nurseries of heaven sing *Gloria in excelsis*. At the sides stand S. Lorenzo, S. Rinaldo, S. Feliciano and S. Francis. Above, the Virgin is crowned Queen of Angels: beneath in the predella are the twelve Apostles and four small angels. At the sides of the frame are ten little figures of saints. Above, on either side the Coronation, are half-figures of the four Doctors of the Church. It is that rather rare thing, at once an elaborate and a complete polyptych—unless, indeed, the five small arches beneath the main panels originally contained paintings. Niccolò seems to have painted this large altarpiece under the influence of Carlo Crivelli. It is somewhat hard and has lost the charm of his earlier works; for instance, the altarpiece in the Cathedral of Assisi.

Among other pictures here are Matteo da Gualdo's S. Joachim and S. Anna at the Golden Gate—a late work; and a Tuscan Marriage of S. Catherine by some follower of Neri di Bicci.

The Duomo crowns the little city, but though it dates from the eleventh century, it was rebuilt in 1450 and redecorated later.

About an hour's walk to the east of Nocera, on the way to the famous Acque Angeliche, is a small group of buildings on a hill-top called the Convento della Romita. It is now in a state of ruin, but according to local tradition it was here S. Francis stayed when, already mortally sick, on his last journey he paid his last visit to Nocera in 1226.[1] He had been carried from Siena, whither he had been taken from Rieti, to consult the doctors there, and thence to Cortona on the way to Assisi. In order to avoid the territory of Perugia, for it was feared the Perugians would seize and hold him on account of the fame of

---

[1] On this or some previous visit Thomas of Celano records (*Tract. de Miraculis*, Quaracchi, 1928, cap. 43, p. 37) how S. Francis raised a certain youth Gapharus from the dead. Having come to life again, Gapharus gives an account of how S. Francis came to him as he lay dead and led him along an obscure and long path, showed him Paradise and then led him back by the same way to earth, saying, "Return to thy father and mother, for I do not wish to retain you longer." And so, said Gapharus, "as it pleased him I am returned".

his sanctity, a long detour was made through Gubbio and Nocera. At Bagnara under Monte Pennino, some five miles east of Nocera at the source of the Topino, where there was a hermitage of the Order, he was met by an armed escort sent by the Commune of Assisi, which escorted him for the rest of the way.

I left Nocera with reluctance. It is true there is not much to see there, but it is a beautiful and quiet place, most delightful in the summer heat. I went on to Gualdo Tadino, crossing the Caldognola torrent again and again, under the ruins of the Rocca di Postignano, into the open plateau of Gualdo under Monte Penna.

S. Francis seems to have come to Gualdo with his brethren fairly early, according to a chronicle published by Faloci Pulignani in the *Miscellanea Francescana*.[1] He was vilified and stoned, and is said to have left the place washing its dust from his feet in the Rasina stream, according to the precept in the Gospel. But the second time he came this way he was enthusiastically welcomed and a small convent or hermitage was erected for him and his brethren. This *conventino* is said to have been in the bare and rocky valley, a ten-minute walk to the west of the town, through which the Rasina runs. Nothing of this remains.

Gualdo Tadino, under its romantic Rocca Flea, is set high above the plain of the Rasina and still preserves not far away to the south a few ruins of the ancient Tadinum through which the Via Flaminia passed southward after the passage of the Apennine. And it was here or hereabouts that Totila was met, defeated and killed by Justinian's general, the eunuch Narses. This befell in July A.D. 552. Italy was then in confusion and half-starved and in agonising process of being reconquered for the Empire. Theodoric the Goth had conferred undoubted benefits upon the Italian people, and it was on these that Totila, a formidable chieftain, who had come to the front on the death of the Gothic king, based his appeal to the Roman Senate. "Surely," he said, "you must remember sometimes in these evil days the benefits you received not so very long ago at the hands of Theodoric and Amalasuntha." Totila, in fact, based his

[1] IX, pp. 185 *et seq.*

appeal upon the material well-being of the people. It was a powerful appeal and it nearly succeeded. That it did not succeed, though it had so much in its favour, is the best testimony we could have to the real nature of the war, which was not a struggle between two races or even primarily between barbarism and civilisation, but something even greater and more fundamental—a fight to the death between two religions, Arianism and Catholicism, upon the result of which the whole future of Europe depended.

Totila, by the year 544, held all Italy with the exception of Ravenna, Rome, Spoleto, Perugia, Piacenza and a few other strongholds. In the course of the struggle, in which Belisarius was still the Imperial General, Rome was occupied and re-occupied no less than four times, and in 546 was left utterly desolate. In 548 Belisarius was recalled, but before he arrived in Constantinople, Perugia had fallen; in the next year, 549, a mutiny in Rome gave the city to the Goths and Rimini was betrayed. In 551 Narses was appointed General-in-Chief in Italy, but in that year only Ravenna, Ancona, Otranto and Crotona remained to the Empire.

Meanwhile, in Illyricum Narses gathered his army. He came through Venetia round the head of the Adriatic, close to the sea—for a formidable Frankish host held the great road—crossing, with what anxiety we may guess, the mouths of the Piave, the Brenta, the Adige and the Po by means of his ships; and having thus turned the flank of the Frankish armies, he triumphantly entered Ravenna. There he remained nine days, as it were, another Caesar about to cross the Rubicon.

While he waited in Ravenna an insulting challenge reached him from the barbarian Usdrilas, who held Rimini. "After your boasted preparations which have kept all Italy in a ferment, and after striking terror into all hearts by knitting your brows and looking more awful than mortal men, you have crept into Ravenna and are skulking there afraid of the very name of the Goths. Come out with all that mongrel host to whom you would deliver Italy and let us behold you, for the eyes of the Goths hunger for the sight of you."[1]

And Narses laughed at the insolence of the Goth, and

[1] Procopius, *Gothic War*, VIII, cap. 28.

presently set forward, with the army he had made, upon the
great road through Classis for Rimini till he came to the bridge
over the Marecchia which Augustus had built and which was
held by the enemy. There in the fight which followed—little
more than a skirmish—the barbarian Usdrilas came to his
end; but Narses, ignoring Rimini, marched on, his great object
before him, Totila and his army, whom and which he meant
before all else to seek out and to destroy.

So he went on up the Flaminian Way to Fano and there
presently left it for a by-way upon the left, rejoining the great
Roman road some miles beyond the fortress of Petra Pertusa,
held by the enemy, which he disregarded as he had done that
of Rimini. He marched on till he came to the very crest of the
Apennine, which he crossed, and camped upon the west and
south under the great heights, at a place then called Ad Ensem
and today Scheggia.

Meanwhile Totila had come to meet him from Rome, and had
reached Tadinum, Gualdo Tadino, where he found Narses
unexpectedly, for he thought the way over the mountains
securely barred by the fortress of Petra Pertusa upon the great
road before him.

Narses sent an embassy to Totila to offer "not peace but
pardon". This the barbarian refused. Asked when he would
fight, Totila answered, "In eight days from this day." But
Narses, knowing what manner of man he was, made all ready
for the morrow and at once occupied the great hill upon his
left which overlooked both camps.

And on the morrow Totila, having been reinforced with two
thousand men, rode forth before the two armies and "exhibited
in a narrow space the strength and agility of a warrior. His
armour was enchased with gold, his purple banner floated with
the wind; he cast his lance into the air, caught it himself
backwards, recovered his seat and managed a fiery steed in all
the paces and evolutions of the equestrian school."[1]

Narses the eunuch smiled.

When Totila had finished his display the two armies faced
one another. At noon the battle was joined. The Gothic
charge failed. Narses drew his straight line into a crescent and

---

[1] Gibbon's free translation of Procopius.

the short battle ended in the utter rout of the Goths, Totila flying from the field. In that flight, one, Ashbad a Gepid, struck at him and fatally wounded him. He was borne by his companions to the village of Capra, more than twelve miles away, and there he died.

Thus ended Totila the Goth, here near Gualdo Tadino, and with him the Gothic cause in Italy, which was once more gathered into the government of the Empire.

This very famous encounter, too ephemeral though it was, is, of course, by far the most important, if not the only outstanding, event in the history of this little lonely city, and even that she can scarcely point to, for no one knows the exact situation of the field of battle.[1] The traveller who, like me, comes to Gualdo in memory of that dramatic encounter, will remain, as I did, for quite other reasons in the little town, for it has its own charms to offer us.

The churches of Gualdo are not of much interest. The Duomo, which dates from 1250, has, however, a fine central portal with rose above, but the interior has been altogether modernised. There is a fine fourteenth-century silver abbot's cross in the sacristy.

The church of San Francesco, built in 1315, contains some interesting if fragmentary frescoes by Matteo da Gualdo. Matteo was born here about 1430, and is thus a contemporary of Niccolò da Foligno. His earliest dated work is in the Pinacoteca here, in a house of the thirteenth century in Via Roberto Calai. It comes from the church of Santa Margherita and is dated 1462. He there appears as under the influence of Crivelli. This rather affected but beautiful altarpiece represents the Virgin and Child enthroned on an elaborate throne on the arms of which kneel two small angels. On either side are S. Francis and S. Bernardino, S. Margaret and S. Helen, and in two rounds above, two half-figures of saints. This is perhaps Matteo's most charming work, though the more majestic Madonna and Child enthroned among angels on the roadside Pellegrini chapel in Assisi, painted in 1468, is, as a decoration at any rate, his masterpiece.

[1] The battle of Gualdo was, alas, not in any way decisive for only a few years later Italy was overrun more effectively than ever before by a new tide of barbarians, the Lombards who were far more barbarous than the Ostrogoths.

In the triptych which he painted in 1471 for the church of San Niccolò here in Gualdo, and now also in the Pinacoteca, we see the Virgin and Child enthroned under a canopy between S. John Baptist and S. John Evangelist; and the three scenes of the predella represent two scenes from their lives and the Last Supper. Two angels kneel at the feet of the Virgin.

In another triptych dated 1477, again with the Virgin and Child enthroned and here between S. Facundius, S. Sebastian, S. Pancrazio and S. Antony Abbot, we cannot but feel a certain exaggeration, almost a grimace in the figures.

The later panel of the Tree of Jesse, painted for the church of Santa Maria, here too in the Pinacoteca, is also lacking in charm. The crowned Virgin with hands clasped in prayer stands in the midst of her genealogical tree, the branches of which are adorned as with fruit with her ancestors. The tree is rooted in the body of Adam, and above, God the Father looks down in benediction.

These works by Matteo da Gualdo are, of course, the reason for the Pinacoteca, but its real glory is the great polyptych by Niccolò da Foligno painted in 1471. This great altarpiece is twelve years earlier than the equally elaborate polyptych at Nocera and not so brilliant a masterpiece, yet it has much charm. The Virgin is more primitive, the Jesus parvulus who takes some cherries from a tiny basket held by one of the angels is more human. At the sides are full-length figures of SS. Peter, Paul, Francis and Bernardino. I don't know but that I prefer this to the other work. The truth is, the more one sees of Niccolò's work the more one likes it. It surprises one to come upon these elaborate polyptychs of his, here in Umbria; they are almost Venetian and, I suppose, are part of the influence of Carlo Crivelli upon Niccolò.

As at Deruta, Gualdo has a well-known majolica factory where the once celebrated Gualdo ware is reproduced.

There is little beside to see in Gualdo Tadino, and yet one is loath to leave this quiet country of hills, where the mountains begin to humble themselves to the sweetness of the valley. But here, as elsewhere, one sees what is in one's heart. They are not the best of us, perhaps, who will hurry away down the narrow valley back to Foligno.

CHAPTER VIII

TREVI AND THE TEMPLE OF CLITUMNUS

THE way from Foligno to Trevi takes one at once almost into Virgilian country, the valley of the Clitumnus. If the night is spent at Montefalco—not so daring an adventure as it seems—one may drive to Trevi by a way as pleasant as any in the world, following the river as it flows, and crossing both river and railway to climb up to Trevi. But the way by San Martino is beautiful exceedingly, and the torrents after the rain only add to the charm of the road. All travellers have wondered at Trevi since she perched herself on the top of her precipitous hill, and though few of them visited her on her lonely height, she impressed her memory upon them even from a distance. "I am so very tired and sleepy," writes one of the most charming travellers that ever followed where the road led —to wit, Nathaniel Hawthorne:

> I am so very tired and sleepy that I mean to mention nothing else tonight except the city of Trevi, which, on the approach from Spoleto, seems so completely to cover a high-peaked hill from its pyramidal tip to its base. It was the strangest situation in which to build a town, where I suppose no horse can climb, and whence no inhabitant would think of descending into the world after the approach of age should begin to stiffen his joints. Looking back on this most picturesque of towns (which the road, of course, did not enter, as evidently no road could), I saw that the highest part of the hill was quite covered with a crown of edifices, terminating in a church tower; while a part of the northern side was apparently too steep for building, and a cataract of houses flowed down the western and southern slopes. There seemed to be palaces, churches, everything that a city should have; but my eyes are heavy and I can write no more about them, only that I suppose the summit of the hill was artificially terraced, so as to prevent its crumbling down, and to enable it to support the platform of edifices which crowns it.

Well, I was tired, too, when I came to Trevi at sunset, and the inn was poor even for an Umbrian albergo. But I forgot the poverty of my room in the relief of being able to sleep; and, indeed, the bed was soft and clean, things common in Italy even in the poorest places.

There is nothing but a fine Perugino and the strange situation of the place itself to bring one to Trevi. Half-way down the hill, in the church of La Madonna delle Lagrime, is a large fresco of the Adoration of the Magi, set in 4 beautiful landscape, which Perugino painted when he was seventy-five years' old.

In the outer chapel half a mile away of San Martino is a fresco by Lo Spagna of the Assumption with a lovely landscape; and within San Martino two frescoes of uncertain authorship. In the gallery in the Palazzo Comunale there is a picture of the Madonna of Mercy which is ascribed to Niccolò da Foligno; a simple picture of the Virgin and Child by Pintoricchio, and a replica of his Coronation of the Virgin, in Todi, by Lo Spagna. In a fresco here by Lo Spagna of the Entombment, we see a copy of Raphael's picture in Rome.

But this is Virgilian country, and it is surely of him we should think when we first set foot in it. Could it have been of any other city that he sang, than Trebia of old, when in the second Georgic he writes:

> *Haec loca non tauri spirantes naribus ignem*
> *invertere satis inmanis dentibus hydri;*
> *nec galeis densisque virum seges horruit hastis:*
> *sed gravidae fruges, et Bacchi Massicus humor*
> *implevere; tenent oleae armentaque laeta.*
> *Hinc bellator equus campo sese arduus infert;*
> *hinc albi, Clitumne, greges, et maxima taurus*
> *victima, saepe tuo perfusi flumine sacro,*
> *Romanos ad templa deum duxere triumphos.*[1]

The white, the snowy flocks of Clitumnus, where are they now? And the bull that bathed in the sacred stream before it was

[1] "This land no bulls with nostrils breathing flame ever ploughed for sowing monstrous dragon's teeth; no human crop ever bristled with helms and serried lances; but teeming fruits have filled her and the Vine god's Massic juice; she is the home of the olive and of joyful herds. Hence comes the war-horse proudly stepping the plain, hence thy snowy flocks, Clitumnus and the bull, noblest victim so often steeped in thy sacred stream—have led to the Temples of the gods the Triumphs of Rome."

led the chiefest victim to the temples of the gods, the triumphs of Rome; and those temples, are they quite gone from our world? Let us see.

As you set out for Spoleto, if you are wise enough to go by road—it is but twelve miles—when you have passed a third of the way you come to a tiny Temple high over the stream, which here among the trees and the grass has its source. And it is the Temple of the river god that you look on, in all its little splendour of silence and ruin. At least, I hope it is; but some speak of a Christian building and will not listen to Pliny. But however that may be, it is a place too beautiful for any to pass by.[1] I confess that, following the advice of the younger Pliny, I bathed there beneath the glancing, whispering poplars, and found, as he had said, the water as cold as snow. But in vain, in vain, I looked for the god Clitumnus and could not find him, though Pliny said that he was there, "not naked but adorned with the toga". And then in the shade, within sound of the beautiful river, I read again in Virgil. Is it not thus one might desire to spend endless days?

But for the traveller by road the sun is ever something of a god; imperious as he is he commands our days. He was slanting down the sky, reminding me that Spoleto was still far and I alone, and night would follow him. So I set out at last with regret; and later I came to San Giacomo in Poseta, where I saw some of the finest Lo Spagnas in Italy, especially a Coronation of the Blessed Virgin, his masterpiece, though stolen from Filippo Lippi. And so I came to the gates of Spoleto.

---

[1] Within the temple, if temple it be, are very early (? seventh century) paintings of Christ and SS. Peter and Paul—the earliest it is said in Umbria. Most authorities place the temple as a building of the fourth century.

CHAPTER IX

SPOLETO

SPOLETO is a beautiful city of rose colour set on the slope of Monteluco, in a bend of the Tissino torrent, amid a cluster of mountains which crown her with their exquisite grace. In her silent streets I began to understand her beauty and her joy, and, indeed, it is in a kind of sudden and overwhelming joy that her towers pierce up into the sky—those rosy towers that at dawn and midday and sunset are musical with soft bells, and that fade away into the night from rose colour to violet and deep purple under a heaven of innumerable stars. Behind her rise, higher and higher, forests of primeval ilex, the sacred tree of the Latin race, shrouding her, as it were, in a mantle most rare of darkest green. Over her head, far away above the forests, a Franciscan convent soars like a brown bird floating on the wind, whose bells are not heard, but only seen to ring, or heard only in the most fortunate days when their sound is little more than the piping of those crested larks that sang S. Francis up to heaven.

> *Qual lodoletta che 'n aere si spazia*
> *Prima cantando, e poi tace contenta*
> *Dell' ultima dolcezza che la sazia.*

It was here in this valley, luminous beyond our northern dreams, that Blessed Angela of Foligno heard those breathless words of Christ: "I love thee more than any woman in the valley of Spoleto." So in the vineyards and the valleys of Umbria of old, men and women talked with God, and indeed the whole land, even to the most superficial observer, seems blessed. Climb up to the great aqueduct that spans the profound ravine which isolates Spoleto on her round hill, and at evening look across the valleys to the hills and the mountains; that luminous softness, a delicacy so magical that you had thought only the genius of Raphael or Perugino could imagine and express it, is just reality. With light, with fragile glory, with the wide and

tender glance of the sky, every delicate form of hill and cloud
and mountain is embraced. It is amidst these perfect hills that
Spoleto sings for joy.

Yet she, too, like Assisi and Perugia and all the cities of
Umbria, has her terrible aspect. She, too, in her day has faced
insolent armies, and, grimly crouched beneath her fortezza,
awaited the signal, holding her heart for fear. Even now in
days of still sunshine—days so mysterious in Italy, that produced, doubtless, something of the mysticism of her countless
saints—La Rocca, her fortress, holds all the terror of the Middle
Age, all the fierce and cruel joy of the Renaissance, that saw the
streets of these cities, now so quiet, run with blood, that looked
for sudden and fierce encounters at the street corner in the
sunshine or the moonlight, at the same time as it produced the
serene work of Perugino and the curiously impersonal and dry
paintings of Piero della Francesca. Still La Rocca watches for
the foe, and does she not see him advancing surely down the
valleys of Umbria? For the mass age will make but little
of ridding her of her precious possessions, her maze-like ways,
her dreams, her quiet and, above all, her joy.

Very ancient is Spoleto and her position at the head of the
great valley which has always borne her name was formidable.
For from the time when in 220 B.C. Caius Flaminius built the
great north road from Rome, the Via Flaminia, and Spoleto was
then already old, she has commanded the entrance and exit of
the eastern branch of that great highway which just above her
to the south crossed the mountain pass of the Somma. For the
Via Flaminia at Narni divided in a loop, the western branch
passing directly to Mevania (Bevagna); the eastern branch,
passing up the valley of the Nar and crossing the mountains
to Spoletium, joined the other branch at Forum Flaminii
(San Giovanni Profiamma) near Foligno.[1] Thus Spoleto was
able to bar the march of Hannibal upon Rome and successfully
resisted his siege. After the Roman disaster at Cannae she
sent an embassy to the Roman Senate to confirm her allegiance
and later at the end of the Social war was rewarded with
Roman citizenship and became a Municipium. Sulla, however,
sacked her, but she was restored and became the headquarters

[1] Cf. *supra*, p. 55.

of the young Octavianus in his victorious Perugian war.
During the long peace of the Empire little is heard of her, but
her strength and the importance of her position were manifest
at the decline, when Vitiges only took her by stratagem and
she was garrisoned by Narses.

The most interesting period of her history is that of the
Ducato, which began with the Lombard conquest and only
ended when she and her territory became the possession of the
Church. The first Lombard duke was Faroaldo I (569); his
successor extended the duchy from the Pentapolis to Benevento,
including the neighbourhood of Rome. The duchy passed to
the Franks, but after their fall came Barbarossa, whom she
resisted on behalf of the Church and was destroyed. It was
the end of her eminence; Innocent III and Gregory IX
definitely made her part of the Ecclesiastical States, which in
the exile of the Papacy in Avignon were half ruined in the
quarrel of Guelph and Ghibelline. Cardinal Albornoz came on
his victorious way on behalf of the Papacy, pacified her, and in
1364 rebuilt the great Rocca which was completed a century
later by Nicholas V. Papal governors were established there,
and among them was Lucrezia Borgia in 1499. She was the
last eminent person to appear and lord it in Spoleto.

Several monuments or vestiges remain today of this long,
violent and varied history. I have sometimes amused myself
in the long summer days by visiting them in their historical
order. Little save the bases of the walls and the gates—the
Arco di Monterone and the Arco delle Felici, for instance—
remains from the pre-Roman times, but the Roman monuments
are numerous, if ruinous, in temple, theatre, crypt, amphitheatre and, most splendid and conspicuous, the Ponte San-
guinario, some eighty feet long and thirty-three feet high, with
its three arches outside the old Porta Leonina (Porta Garibaldi) by which one enters the city. There is a portico too,
near Piazza del Mercato the ancient Forum, and the arch
dedicated in honour of Drusus and Germanicus in A.D. 21 near
Sant' Ansano, and close by, a Roman temple with two columns
and part of the cella and a Christian sanctuary or crypt. There
are, too, remains of the theatre and of the second-century
amphitheatre. A Roman house with fine mosaic pavements,

which belonged to the mother of the Emperor Vespasian, lies below the terrace in front of the Municipal Palace.

Of the early Christian time, San Salvatore beyond the cemetery outside Porta Garibaldi, in spite of various restorations, is with its three naves a rare example of an early Christian building of the fourth century. The façade, which is almost intact, still possesses in great part its marble ornament in the classical Byzantine style, and is in two parts, with three solemn portals decorated with sculptures and, above, three fine windows. It always reminds me curiously of the Temple of Clitumnus. Within, the beautiful frescoed apse and columned presbytery always delight me beyond any other architectural monument in Spoleto. The whole church is a most precious work of art of the early and still classical Christianity.

San Marco, too, which is mentioned by S. Gregory the Great, and San Giuliano have the one a crypt and the other foundations of the sixth century, though the latter was completely rebuilt in the eleventh century, to which time San Gregorio Maggiore in Piazza Garibaldi belongs, while Santa Eufemia in the cortile of the Palazzo Arcivescovile goes back to the tenth century.

It was in 1155 that Barbarossa destroyed the city, which arose more beautiful than ever under the protection of Innocent III. The Duomo was then rebuilt with its lovely portal, only the tower remaining from the older building. San Pietro, too, outside Porta Monterone beyond the Tessino rose again, after its destruction in 1322, on the ruin of the older structure of which only the façade remains, a masterpiece of the eleventh–twelfth centuries, though as a piece of architecture this façade is not so imposing as that of San Rufino in Assisi. Of about the same time are the sculptures on the façade of San Ponziano outside Porta Ponzianina on the farther side of the Tessino to the north-east of the city.

From the thirteenth century there is the Gothic façade of San Domenico; the lovely portal with its lunette of San Niccolò; all that remains of the church, burnt in 1849, is somewhat later (1402).

The most memorable achievement here of the fourteenth century is the magnificent Rocca which crowns the city and

was built by Cardinal Albornoz in 1362, but was transformed
in the fifteenth century, it is said, by Bernardo Rossellino of
Florence. The original architect was the great Matteo Gattapone of Gubbio, who is said to have built the Palazzo della
Signoria, now the Museo Civico, near the Cathedral, as well
as the mighty Ponte delle Torri at once an aqueduct and a
viaduct.

To the Renaissance Spoleto owes the beautiful portico of
her Cathedral and among other buildings the church of Manna
d'Oro, an octagonal building which might have been designed
by Bramante and is now the baptistery of the Cathedral. The
transformation of the Cathedral in the seventeenth century is
by local tradition ascribed to Bernini, as is the Baroque church
of San Filippo in Piazza Mentana.

But on first coming to Spoleto it is to the Cathedral we
climb, breathless, for her ways are steep and rough, to see the
frescoes of one of the most delightful of the Florentine painters,
Filippo Lippi. They are his last masterpieces, and tell the story
in brief of the Blessed Virgin in her own Cathedral, Santa Maria
Assunta. The chief fresco is that of her Coronation. Pale from
the encounter with death, in which but a moment ago she has
proved victorious, tall and slight, Regina Angelorum is
crowned, not by Christ her Son, but by God the Father, in a
heaven delicate as the petals of the flags in the valleys full of
corn, powdered with stars that seem to have risen just out of the
sea. The sun and the moon beneath her feet are lesser glories
where she is. About her a company of angels sings and dances
for joy, since heaven is by so much richer than our earth. A few
with a shy and timid grace, magically charming, hand her a few
flowers from the meadows or the woods of heaven, as though
to ask her if they might be sweeter than the lilies she loved as a
girl, or the wild flowers of Palestine. The rest of the frescoes—
the Annunciation, in which she stands so surprised, so agitated,
that she twists her fingers together and is not sure how to
answer; the Nativity, a magnificent composition, now but a
shadow; and the Death of the Virgin, where Christ Himself
with a tenderness, but with a tenderness and love, bears His
Mother to heaven—are much over-painted, and by a lesser
hand, yet we catch some shadow of Filippo in them all, so

POLETO. San Salvatore.

SPOLETO. Duomo: Fra Lippo Lippi, Coronation of the Blessed Virgin (detail).

that even in their ruin they are not the least among the precious
things of Spoleto.

In a quiet and sunny chapel of the great church, the dust of
Filippo Lippi, that vagabond and joyous painter, was laid by
the jealous people of Spoleto in 1489. Lorenzo de' Medici,
who seems to have loved him, tried in vain to secure his ashes
so that they might lie in Florence, but Spoleto, proud and
poor, with but little that was very precious in her possession,
would not have it so. You are rich and we are poor, she seems
to have said; excuse us, then, if we keep the bones of this one
great man, which you can well afford to leave in our keeping.
Lorenzo appears to have consented, perhaps a little reluctantly,
contenting himself with building a noble tomb for the painter
here in Santa Maria Assunta from a design by Filippino Lippi
and with asking Poliziano to compose a long Latin inscription.

The strangely adventurous life that came to an end here in
Spoleto is very typical of certain aspects of the Renaissance: its
profound passion for liberty, its experiment in romance and
sentiment, its desire above everything for vitality. And it is
curious that it is not in the exciting and creative earth of
Tuscany that Filippo Lippi, the fatal and erring son of the
most beautiful of cities, is laid to rest, but amongst the quiet
and blessed hills of Umbria, that mystical land that produced
no great intelligence, only a spirit that might have saved the
world.

On the opposite wall of the chapel, where Fra Filippo's tomb
stands in the right transept, is the mural monument of Giovanni
Francesco Orsini by Ambrogio da Milano (1499), but it has
been spoiled and rebuilt. Pintoricchio painted the frescoes, now
only fragmentary, in the Cappella Eboli to the right of the
entry. The Crucifix now in the left transept used to hang here.
It is signed and dated by Alberto Sotio, 1187, and comes from
the small church of SS. Giovanni e Paolo, where there are still
frescoes by this painter who seems rather Roman than Byzantine. This Crucifix is painted on parchment attached to the
wooden Cross; the Christ is shown alive with open eyes and
there are two small figures of the Virgin and S. John at the
sides.

The interior of the Cathedral was remodelled, perhaps by

Bernini in 1634–44, and it was he who made the beautiful bronze bust of Urban VIII over the central doorway. Happily he left the façade, the Solsternus mosaic and the lovely Renaissance portico alone.

The Cathedral possesses a precious relic of S. Francis, an autograph letter to Brother Leo. This is preserved in the sacristy and consists of a sheet of parchment about 5 by 2½ inches, on which S. Francis has written his letter in Latin, which may be translated as follows:

> Brother Leo, the Brother Francis sends thee greetings of peace. I call thee my son as would a mother, seeing that all that we spoke together on the way I sum up in that single word. If later thou hast need to ask counsel of me, this is the advice I give thee. In whatever way it pleases thee to please Our Lord God for following His rule of poverty, do so in thine own way with the Lord's blessing and in my obedience. And if it be necessary for thee on account of thy soul or other consolation and thou wishest, Leo, to come to me, come. I salute thee in the name of Christ.

The authenticity of this letter cannot be questioned. In Wadding's time it was kept in the conventual church of San Simone, which in 1893 was alienated from the Order and became an institute for the orphans of State officials. The church still exists close under the Rocca; it is of the thirteenth century and has a good Gothic portal. San Simone, however, was not the first church of the Franciscans in Spoleto. Beside the convent of Monteluco outside the city, they early possessed the little church of Sant' Elia which has disappeared, but even before that they had been the guests of the Benedictines, who had given or lent them the church of Sant' Apollinare; this too no longer exists.[1] The most famous event connecting S. Francis with Spoleto is that which befell him when he set out with the poor Knight of Assisi to join the Pontifical army in Apulia, and on the night before his setting out, as he lay sleeping he saw in a dream a marvellous palace full of arms, accoutrements and banners, and was told that all these were for him and his knights. Arrived in Spoleto, the voice of his vision spoke to

[1] See Faloci Pulignani, *Il B. Simone da Collazzone* in *Miscellanea Francescana*, Vol. XII (1910), pp. 97 *et seq.*

him again and asked him who could do better for him, the servant or the lord. "The lord," said Francis. "Why then," said the voice, "art thou seeking the servant instead of the Lord?" Then S. Francis said, "Lord, what wilt Thou that I should do?" And the Lord said to him, "Return to the place of thy birth, for thy vision shall through Me have a spiritual fulfilment." So S. Francis returned to Assisi and presently the Crucifix of San Damiano spoke to him and told him what he should do. S. Francis was then about twenty-five years' old.

More paintings by Sotio of the twelfth century are to be found in SS. Giovanni e Paolo, among them the Martyrdom of S. Thomas Becket and the Dance of Salome. Outside this small church are some thirteenth-century frescoes and, within, others of S. Margaret with SS. Michael and Thaddeus, an Assumption with S. Thomas receiving the girdle and an important portrait of S. Francis, among the earliest known. Other paintings of this time are to be seen in Sant' Ansano, and in San Gregorio Maggiore, which has a façade of the twelfth century.

It is, however, something quite different we find in San Salvatore,[1] which has been built from the ruins of a Roman temple. From a picturesque and historical point of view, it delights me, as I have said, beyond any other piece of architecture in Spoleto. Today its façade guards the Campo Santo, with its hard white crosses and beady flowers, and all the frippery of modern death. Magnificent columns, Roman and pagan, group themselves round the choir and chancel; and the nave is ennobled by the remains of other shafts, now ruinous, that once bore the weight of some splendid roof. Pagan gods, not dead but living in exile, perhaps in the ilex woods that crown the city and envelop her in their sombre mantle, seem to creep into the warm sunshine that floods the church from the open door. They knock at our hearts; and gazing at the feeble and terrible "decorations" of the Christian altar between the majestic pillars of an alien religion, it is rather of the nobility of the past, which is so present everywhere in Italy—of its beauty and its sufficiency—that we think, than of its Christian successor.

[1] On San Salvatore, see M. Salmi, *La Basilica di San Salvatore di Spoleto* (Olschki, Florence, 1951).

And yet who here in Spoleto can resist the touching appeal
of that little ugly shrine that greets the traveller on his way to
San Paolo, that old thirteenth-century church? It is a picture
of S. Maria Immacolata, and bears the legend: *Et macula
originalis non est in Te.* As I passed by at evening some children
were decking the shrine with wild flowers, gathered on the
Umbrian hills. The cage that guarded the picture was starred
with buttercups as lovely in their shining yellow as those which
doubtless in old days sprang up beneath the white footsteps
of Persephone as she crossed the rivers of Sicily on her way to
Demeter, after her unwilling exile from our world. Will she
not know and smile and understand, this Virgin that is the one
goddess left to a sorrowful world? Be sure, if she is not mindful
of the flowers of the maidens and children, if in that heaven
where she is she does not smile to her Son upon His Throne of
chrysoprase and jasper to see these, simple of heart, bringing
the flowers of the field for her Festa—then Persephone never
trod our world, nor was Demeter bereft and sorrowful; all is a
lie—the beautiful, austere gods, the terrible love of Christ, the
very Fatherhood of God, since even these so simple of heart
may deceive themselves on their lovely way to death.

The convent of San Paolo is now used as a poor-house round
whose walls is pictured, not inappropriately perhaps, the Way
of the Cross. In so peaceful a spot amid the cypresses and
olives, those who have been a little defeated in a world once so
wonderful contemplate the way to heaven. Here is a series of
important frescoes of the twelfth century, pictures from Genesis
of the Creation.

San Pietro is a magnificent fragment of Romanesque architecture overlooking the ravine. Behind the church rises the
wooded Monteluco, and on a platform, reached by a series of
antique steps, this church, one of the most striking Romanesque
buildings in Italy, has stood for more than a thouand years.
Its façade is sculptured in reliefs with moral fables, partly from
the Bestiaries. Here the wolf feigns penitence in order to capture
the lamb; the fox lies on his back, to all appearance dead, in
order to seize the more surely the foolish doves. But it is only
in this splendid and simple façade that the lover of beauty, for
whom, after all, all architecture and painting and sculpture and

literature really exist, will find delight; the church itself is but the mediocre whitewashed *rifacimento* we have grown so accustomed to, with nothing really to recommend it, existing as it does without the mysticism and beauty of the Gothic building, or the sense of space and light to be found in the buildings of the Renaissance.

In the Pinacoteca in the Palazzo Comunale one finds another Crucifix, perhaps a copy of one by Sotio, and a small and rather dark Crucifix of the thirteenth century with Our Lord in agony and with small scenes of the Passion about it. Above, the body of Our Lord is borne by Angels, a unique composition, so I am told. Here, too, is a polyptych by Luca di Tommé of Siena, with half-figures of the Virgin and Child, the Baptist, SS. Peter and Paul, Apollinare, and above, Our Lord in the centre with SS. Catherine, Antony Abbot, Leonard and another. It is not a very attractive work. Far more interesting are the three panels here by Niccolò da Foligno: the Virgin, a Saint praying and a S. John Baptist, all of which come from the church of Santa Maria delle Grazie on Monteluco, and a late drawing for a Pietà. The Raphaelesque fresco by Lo Spagna of the Madonna and Child with S. Jerome, S. Augustine, SS. Catherine and Anthony is perhaps the painter's masterpiece, lovely alike in colour and refinement. Another fresco represents some allegorical subject.

The most grandiose of Lo Spagna's works is to be found here in Spoleto in the church of San Giacomo, where in the apse he has imitated Fra Filippo in painting the Coronation of the Virgin. Below is a series of scenes from the legend of S. James. The fresco of the Madonna and Child and two angels in Sant' Ansano is rather the work of his pupils than his own. But after Fra Filippo's frescoes in the Cathedral, perhaps the loveliest painting in Spoleto is the triptych in the Episcopal Palace by an unknown master, of the Assumption, between S. Giovanni, Bishop of Spoleto, and S. Lucia with a predella. This is a work of great beauty and charm.

It was Holy Week when for the first time I came to Spoleto; a certain silence and wistful sadness, I remember, seemed to invest the city; the streets were very quiet, the churches sombre. At evening I watched the processions, with their torches and innumerable tapers, wind along the roads; all night as I lay in my bed I seemed to hear the melancholy chants that accompanied them up an endless Via Crucis. In reality it would seem Christ had died that afternoon; now at last mankind was desolate. The tones of the *Vexilla Regis* seemed to wave like long streamers from the church towers, and one heard the Mother, heart-broken and weeping, sigh to the world spread at our feet:

O vos omnes qui transitis per viam, attendite
et videte, si est dolor sicut dolor meus.

Then there was silence. Spoleto, with finger on her lip, awaited the dawn of Easter. At last it broke, very cool and sweet and full of promises. An immense hope seemed to have swept over the world. In the churches they sang again *Alleluia*, and I, with the whole city, went to the Cathedral to greet the Christ, new risen from the tomb, in the Easter Mass.

Out of my window, as I write, I can see S. Mary of the Angels gleaming in the sunlight beneath the mass of Subasio. It is only the mountains that hide Orvieto from me, and even perhaps Rome herself. Innumerable roads wind over plain and mountain to half a hundred cities that the world has forgotten. I seem to see them all in the soft lucidity of evening, that is the most precious part of the day in this land where, every evening, God paints for us those pictures which taught Perugino all he knew—his magnificent spaciousness, his sense of luminous light. Before the sunset Spoleto, like a tall and sweet maiden, kneels on her hill and seems to pray. Ever she has the attitude of prayer; and after dark when her little lights gleam far over the plain, I seem to know that they burn before the shrines of many saints whose prayers she has desired, simple of heart as she is, kneeling at the head of her long valley under the soft sky.

CHAPTER X

THE ROAD TO NORCIA

As the summer waxed in the valley of Spoleto, with Sol in Leone, I found the heat unbearable and determined to go up to Norcia under the Monti Sibillini in search of coolness. This proved a mistake. *Frigida Nursia,* Virgil calls it: I was not to find it so. There is now an electric railway but I decided to hire an automobile and go by road (it is not much more than thirty miles), as there were several small places I wished to see on the way. So very early one morning I left Spoleto and we were soon climbing up out of the Tissino valley through a charming and picturesque country, to descend presently into the upper Val di Nera at Piedipaterno.

Here we turned back on the Terni road for a couple of miles in order to see Castel San Felice, a small medieval place where just outside the village is the Romanesque church of San Felice di Narco, with a fine façade and a rose window in a square frame, sculptured with stars, and in the angles the symbols of the four Evangelists. Two charming windows with twisted columns and fine capitals are on either side. Across the façade beneath runs a marble band with sculptured reliefs of San Felice slaying a dragon and raising a man from the dead. The mosaic arches and the tympanum with the Lamb suggest the work of the Roman marble workers, who were certainly at work at Narni. Within, is a single nave, and on the walls several frescoes—the Adoration of the Magi by some local and late follower of the Lorenzetti, while in the apse is a painting of God the Father between two angels, and, below to the left, the Virgin, S. Sebastian and other figures which are now obliterated. These must date about 1450, and the S. Michele and S. Felice slaying a dragon somewhat earlier.

The *transenne* screens, which close the sanctuary, are decorated with mosaic and again suggest the Cosmatesque work of the Roman *marmorari.*

On the way back to Piedipaterno I turned aside to visit

Vallo di Nera on its hill, a picturesque place surrounded by
walls with polygonal towers, in fact a Castello. Here in the
lower part is the Gothic church of San Francesco, still of the
thirteenth century, with fine portal and rose and, within, a
fresco of a procession signed and dated 1401, by Cola di Pietro
da Camerino. This not very interesting provincial master has
also painted here the Last Judgment. I did not go up to the
upper part of the Castello.

Here or hereabouts have been found many of the Etruscan
figurines and bronzes which are now in the Etruscan Museum
in Florence. And as we proceeded on our way I began to
wonder who it was who first began to dig up and to treasure
the works of a dead and past civilisation. The history of the
most romantic of the sciences has yet to be written. The Greeks
knew little and seem to have cared less for the ruins of Troy,
though the deathless story of the war is the foundation of so
much of their poetry and drama. The Romans were curious
of antiquity, but casually. Cicero collected furniture and paid
enormous prices for old and beautiful pieces, and books of
course have always been collected. Yet it was not the Romans
but ourselves who discovered the marvellous statues buried by
the Athenians of the fifth century on the Acropolis after the
Persians had sacked the city 480 years before Christ.

But after the fall of the Empire and the more than five
hundred years of barbarism which followed it, one of the first
things to emerge in the earliest Renaissance was archaeology,
though it was little enough of a science then.

Ghiberti, the sculptor of the Paradise Gates of the Baptistery
at Florence, records in his *Commentari* that in the time of the
wars between Florence and Siena, in the city of Siena there
was dug up a statue of Venus, which bore the name of the
Greek sculptor Lysippos, and it was erected beside the Fonte
Gaia in the Campo. The people came in crowds to admire it,
but one of the governors stood up in the Council and said,
"Citizens, the Church forbids, and rightly, the cult of idols.
I judge, then, that our army suffers defeat at the hands of the
Florentines by the fault of this Venus that we have erected in
the chief piazza of our city. The curse of God is upon us. I
counsel you therefore to break the idol and to bury it in

Florentine territory, so as to draw upon our enemies the wrath of heaven." And thus did the citizens of Siena.

In the fifteenth and sixteenth centuries, however, the enthusiasm for antiquity was great in Italy. The Medici vied with the Popes for the possession of any works of art that were found. But for the most part all that was found was by chance. In spite of the eagerness not only of great princes, but of great artists, of Raphael, for instance, and the architect Bramante, the mighty temples of Paestum, the most enormous and complete Greek remains in the world, though only four miles from an episcopal city and but twenty-five miles from the university city of Salerno, were quite unknown till they were "discovered" by Conte Gazolo in 1740; while Henry Swinburne was the first to describe them, in 1779, and they were first mapped by Wilkins in 1807.

While I was thinking thus, we had crossed the Nera and entered a naked gorge, on coming out of which we had a view down the Val del Tissino; then on the right Cerreto rose up with its bastioned towers, and here was Ponte founded as a strong place by the Contessa di Celano. At Ponte there is a lovely church, Romanesque of the twelfth century, on the façade of which the Roman mosaicists have left their mark. At the angles of the rose window are the symbols of the Evangelists.

At Cerreto di Spoleto, Jovianus Pontanus was born in 1426. I do not suppose he means very much to any of us today, but he was a famous humanist and the friend of Sannazaro and Beccadelli, and anyone who has dipped into the Latin poetry of the Renaissance must remember his *Urania* with interest, because of its lament for his daughter Lucia; and besides, it embodies the astronomical knowledge of his pre-Galileo age. His voluptuous love poems too are quite pagan and worth a glance. He became a classic while he was alive, but has now wandered off Parnassus. It is true he was born in Cerreto, but when his father was murdered here in a brawl, his mother escaped with him to Perugia, where he was educated. But it was in Naples he made his fame and his career. There he met Beccadelli and Sannazaro and, entering Naples as a penniless scholar, became the companion and trusted friend of its sovereign, who loaded him with honours, lodged him in a fine house and enrolled him among the nobles of the Kingdom. Nevertheless he welcomed Charles VIII of France when he entered Naples in 1495, an example of ingratitude outstanding in the history of Italian humanism. He died in Naples in 1503, and you may still see there at Monte Oliveto his amazing tomb with its life-size terra-cotta figures, of himself, his friend Sanna-zaro and his patron Alfonso kneeling before the dead Christ.

Beyond Cerreto the narrow valley, dark with ilex, opens a little and one passes from the Val di Nera into the Val di Corno, and the village of Triponzo marks the place where the two streams meet. Triponzo surrounded by its turreted walls is dominated by a huge tower. Its churches have little to offer one, but close by is a great rock, with an inscription, hewn into shape by the Romans.

The narrow valley of the Corno with its sheer and rocky sides soon narrows still more, and becomes more and more wild as far as Serravalle, with its thirteenth-century church of San Claudio, where the road for Cascia leaves the highway. Here the Corno and the Sordo, the river of Norcia, meet. The road passes into the Sordo valley as slowly it widens, one sees a great mountain crest and presently there appears not as one expected perhaps, Monte Vettore of the Sibillini, but first Monte Fusconi, some 5,000 feet high, and then Monte Vetica, not far short of it. A great plain surrounded by mountains opens before one, the Piano Santa Scolastica, and there at the rear and northern end of it is the little city of Norcia where S. Benedict was born.

CHAPTER XI

NORCIA AND CASCIA

I FOUND a possible lodging in Norcia in the house of a couple whose nephew, a young boy, was paying them a visit from his home in Dolcedorme, and he became my daily companion. We explored Norcia and the surrounding country together, wandered in the woods, penetrated into the mountains and visited Cascia. He was, I suppose, in some sort my servant, but no one could have had a better or more charming companion. His name was Ulisse.

It was scarcely cooler at Norcia than it had been at Spoleto, and indeed very hot. Even the snow on the Monti Sibillini had disappeared, even Monte Vettore, over 7,000 feet high, had but a patch or two. The little city in an amphitheatre of their wooded foot-hills lies on the edge of a great and fertile pasture, watered by the Sordo and Torbidone streams and the sources of San Martino. Owing to numerous earthquakes it is completely modern in appearance and regular in plan, but there remain a few buildings more or less transformed. The Palazzo Comunale still retains a portico of the twelfth century, and the church of San Benedetto is, without, a fine example of Italian Gothic of the thirteenth century, but, within, it has been completely remade. Beside the crypt are the remains of a late Roman house which, of course, local tradition insists is the home in which S. Benedict and S. Scholastica, his sister, were born; and this may be true, since the church is certainly built over a house. Norcia was the seat of their mother's family.

S. Benedict and S. Francis are not only the most famous of Umbrian saints, they are the most famous of Umbrians, and their achievements are curiously similar, for both saved the Church and civilisation, the one in the sixth, the other in the thirteenth century. We are unfortunately almost entirely ignorant of the early life of S. Benedict, who was educated in Rome, according to S. Gregory, whose *Dialogues* are in fact the source for what we know of the founder of Western monachism. Perhaps, however, S. Benedict passed his childhood and his youthful vacations in Norcia, and it may well be that the landscape about his home under the solemnity of the Monti Sibillini influenced him as fundamentally as the landscape of the valley of Spoleto about Assisi seems to have influenced S. Francis. Both these overwhelming creative personalities brought the remedy of common sense and service to a world no less distracted by anarchy, fantastic nonsense and egoistic ideologies than our own; both established world-wide organisations which are flourishing to this day. For if S. Benedict founded the Rule which was to be that of all Western monachism through all the ages since, S. Francis founded the Order, a new thing completely international, in which the friar did not belong to an abbey or convent in a certain place, in a certain country, like the monk, but to the Order, so that he could be sent and was at home anywhere in the world. It is curious that both these great saints, the one a statesman, the other a poet, should have been born in the valleys of Umbria.

The other churches of Norcia have little to offer; San Francesco, Sant' Agostino, where there are some frescoes of the end of the fifteenth century, San Giovanni and the curious "Tempietto" built by Vanni Tuzi are all of the fifteenth century. The Duomo is of the eighteenth century.

In the Palazzo Comunale is preserved the fine fifteenth-century Reliquary of S. Benedict in silver gilt with enamels; it is about a metre in height. It comes from San Benedetto. Here too is a fifteenth-century Codex in the vulgar tongue, with miniatures, called *Lo Specchio dell' Ordine Minore* or *La Franceschina*.

The best monument left in Norcia is the Castellina, a rather small but solid building, four-square with four towers with bastions at the angles, originally built by Vignola in 1554 by order of Pope Julius III (Del Monte).

When we had seen all there was to be seen in Norcia, Ulisse and I would wander about the countryside whose pastures were full of beasts—sheep, oxen, cows and pigs—or explore the woods or in the cool of the day walk to Santa Scolastica along the straight road through the *piano* or go to Valcaldara or to San

Pellegrino or climb the flank of Monte Vetica. But it was still very hot.

One day we made a more serious expedition to Castelluccio, a very high village with an inn above the Piano Grande, at the base of the Monti Sibillini, right under towering Monte Vettore. It was cooler up there at over 4,000 feet.

Then there was the journey to Cascia, which we managed by taking the electric train from Norcia to Serravalle and proceeding from there by bus.

Cascia is over 2,000 feet above the sea and stands on the slope of a hill over the Corno stream. It is a remarkable little place with a few hundred inhabitants, and entirely given over to Santa Rita, who is its whole existence. And no wonder, for as Ulisse impressed upon me again and again, Santa Rita is the saint *dell' impossibile*. "If you are in despair, if you are at your wits' end, if everything seems lost *e buona notte*, and only a miracle—but not an ordinary miracle, an 'impossible' miracle —can save you, go to Santa Rita. Or, if that is impossible, then make your petition to her, however extraordinary, unheard of, impossible of fulfilment it may be, and you will see!"

"Yes," said I, "I think I see. If you have lost the love of your life, if you are in such a position that only the end of the world can save you, if you are absolutely broke and in more than desperate need of money——"

"Ah," said Ulisse, "*momentino*, signore. *Tutti i santi* and even Santa Rita are difficult about money. *Si*, signore. Although she will do the impossible for you, she seems to have the same feelings about money, signore, as S. Francesco had, who, as the signore will remember, refused to touch it except with a stick."

"Yes," said I, "I was forgetting. Santa Rita was an Augustinian nun and had a high opinion of poverty and certainly thought, and it might almost seem still thinks, it good for one."

"Signore," said Ulisse, "the only saint who is good for money is Sangiuseppe, who was a family man and understood the difficulties one meets with in the world. And even he——"

Santa Rita was born in 1381 in a humble peasant home at Roccaporena, a mountain village about an hour's walk to the west of Cascia through the narrow Corno valley, under Monte

Sciudri, where the sugar-loaf Scoglio di Santa Rita over the Fosso del Mechiglio and the house of her nativity, now covered by a church, with a picture of her in prayer by Luca Giordano over the altar, are her memorials. She was the child of her parents' old age, and from her earliest years was extraordinarily pious and presently wished to become a nun in the Augustinian convent at Cascia. But her parents wished to marry her, and she, an exemplary daughter, submitted. The man her parents had chosen proved, however, to be of so violent a character that he became not only the terror of his wife, but of the whole neighbourhood. Rita bore with him most patiently for eighteen years, gave him two sons, who followed in the ways of their father. He, however, repented at last and begged her pardon, but shortly after was carried home dead and covered with wounds after a brawl. The sons wished to avenge him, but Rita prayed that they might die rather than commit murder, and her prayer was answered, for shortly after their father's death they caught an illness which proved fatal.

Alone in the world, she now turned to the Augustinian nuns of Cascia; but their constitutions forbade them to receive a widow. She renewed her request, but was always reluctantly refused. Whereupon she turned to her three heavenly patrons, S. John Baptist, S. Augustine and S. Nicholas, who brought about the impossible, for the Rule was relaxed in her favour. She was received into the Order in 1413.

In the convent, submissive as ever, she was perfectly observant of the Rule, and even watered a dead vine, day after day, when, to try her, the Mother Superior bade her do so. She practised the harshest austerities, wore a hair-shirt, scourged herself thrice a day, cared for her fellow religious in illness; doing all for the love of God. She was often caught into ecstasy in contemplation of the Passion of Our Lord. And one day, when she was listening to a sermon on the Crown of Thorns, preached by S. Giacomo della Marca, she became conscious of a pain as if a thorn were embedded in her forehead. An open wound appeared and suppurated, so that she had to be confined to her cell and had to live the life of a recluse. Presently, too, she began to waste away and her end came on May 22, 1457. May 22 is her feast and the day of the chief of the many pilgrimages from

all over the world made to the shrine in which her now mummified body lies.[1] The rose is her symbol, and roses are blessed in
Augustinian churches on her feast day. It seems that when
she was dying she asked for a rose from her old childhood's
garden at Roccaporena. As it was so early in the season in these
high and rough parts, there seemed little hope of being able to
find one for her. However, on entering the garden, her friend,
to her great surprise, saw on a bush a rose in full bloom, and
brought it to Santa Rita. That is why the rose is her symbol.
She was canonised as lately as 1900.

A terrible earthquake in 1599 destroyed Cascia, so that the
buildings in the town are for the most part very late. Some,
however, escaped destruction even in the earthquake of 1703,
which again destroyed the place and killed over 700 people.
Among these buildings is the narrow sanctuary of Santa Rita,
which is now to be replaced by a great modern church.
The mummified body of the saint is preserved in a crystal
urn mounted in silver. The convent too may be visited where
she died, and the beautiful original sarcophagus with her
painted effigy in which she was first laid may be seen.

Older than this *santuario* is the church of San Francesco, a
building of the fifteenth century, still Gothic, with a fine portal
and frescoes within, and good choir stalls. In the collegiata
of Santa Maria and in the church of Sant' Agostino are
frescoes of the Perugian school of the fifteenth and sixteenth
centuries.

But the glory of Cascia is the shrine of Santa Rita, the
Santa dell' Impossibile. There I made my petition, but I did not
tell Ulisse what it was.

So we passed the summer days, moving about the countryside. We went to the Madonna della Neve, before which rises
the majesty of Monte Vettore. It is a Renaissance church
covered with frescoes of no great merit of the last quarter of the
sixteenth century. We visited, too, the Abbazia di Sant'
Eutizio, a Romanesque church built at the end of the twelfth
century, with a fine portal and rose dated 1236, a campanile
and polygonal apse.

[1] The body of S. Rita is said to have remained incorrupt for some 300 years,
but was reduced to its present mummified state after a fire in the middle of the
eighteenth century.

It was as we returned one perfect night from the Cappuccini, and the mountains seemed more wonderful than ever under the full moon, that I remarked on the marvel of this to Ulisse. "O signore," said he, "but the signore should see our moon at Dolcedorme."

A strange answer surely, connoting I know not what, pointing beyond the Middle Age, beyond all recorded ages. But men have always believed strange things of the moon, the planets and the stars. Dante thought that the earth was the centre of the universe, that hell stirred under his feet, that the seven spheres over his head hung like lamps to enlighten mankind, and that beyond them stretched the stellar Paradise, the *Primum mobile* and the Empyrean. And his notion of all things, logical and exact, endured till Copernicus and Galileo upset it, and Fontenelle, teaching his blonde marquise astronomy, wickedly remarked between two compliments, "It would embarrass the theologians if there were men in the moon."

So I ruminated with all the spacious heavens stretched out above me. "O Eternal Lord God, who alone spreadest out the heavens. . . ."

Yes, men have believed some queer things about the sky. We do so still. The curious thing seems to be that what we believe never seems queer till afterwards. We speak currently of the immensity of those spaces, yet man has measured them— an admirable thing that. We believe that it takes some 1000 years for the light of the Pole star to reach the earth; we believe that some of those dim points of light are the light of suns that may have been extinct for millenia. In the field of the telescope we think we can descry the very act of creation, new systems being born, old systems dissolving, to be perhaps reborn, nebulae consolidating and shrinking into suns, dissolving into a puff of flaming gas. There, too, we discern the double stars and those true doubles we call binaries. One of these in the handle of the Plough—Mizar is its name—the telescope has separated for us into two stars of the same system, and we believe that they revolve one around the other once in 20,000 years.

All we see represents one thing—change: spring, summer, autumn, winter.

The Psalmist has sublimely summed it up:

Ipsi peribunt, tu autem permanes: et omnes sicut vestimentum veterascent.

Et sicut opertorium mutabis eos, et mutabuntur: tu autem idem ipse es et anni tui non deficient.

What we believe in regard to the heavens would have seemed as queer to Dante as what Dante believed seems to us. It is true that some few things, some of them of a fundamental character, which he took for facts, seem to us to be false; but ultimately we know no more than he. Indeed, he may have been nearer the truth than we seem to be in regard to fundamentals. Had you asked him, for instance, gazing on the sky and then upon this noble earth—noble in his eyes, for he thought God had created it and separated light from darkness—had you asked him, looking thus, "Whither are we going?" perhaps, had he deigned to reply, he would have quoted S. Augustine in that great passage of "Restless hearts which are restless until they rest in Thee". But if you ask us, gazing on the numbered stars and then upon this blob of mud irradiated in the moonlight, we should answer in some such words as these: "Perhaps towards the constellation of Hercules and away from the constellation of Orion."

But as for me, it is Ptolemy the Astronomer in the Anthology who best expresses what I feel on a starry night:

οἶδ' ὅτι θνατὸς ἐγὼ καὶ ἐφάμερος . . . .

"I know I am mortal, a creature of a day; but when I search into the multitudinous revolving spirals of the stars, my feet no longer rest on the earth, but standing by Zeus himself I take my fill of ambrosia, the food of the gods."

In spite of the moon it was dark in the forest, and Ulisse had taken my hand. Italians do not care to be out in the countryside after dark.

CHAPTER XII

SUMMER ABOUT NORCIA

THE heat was wonderful. It was not heavy, as any great heat in England always is, but vehement and marvellous with all the fierceness and vitality of fire, the pride and beauty of the sun. The hushed fields seemed about to burst into flame. The sun delighted and frightened me, it was wonderful and mysterious. Each day was like a hard, bright precious stone, more dazzling and more heartless than a diamond. Everything was still. And the nights were like sapphires. For three days now, everyone seemed to be in the *pieve* praying for rain. When they uncovered the Crucifix it was as though some strange Presence had come into our midst.

As I lay that evening just without the forest, not far from a little stream that, in spite of the drought, still ran secretly under the trees among the stones out into the parched valley, I heard a clear voice say softly, "Of what is the signore thinking; it is perhaps of his own country?"

Looking round, I saw a pair of eyes staring at me from under a tangle of black hair, and Ulisse came close to me.

I lay back among the broom and answered, "Tell me a story, then, Ulisse—and I shall forget again."

"But the signore has heard all the stories of the Frate Antonio, he has heard all the stories of my mother and my mother's mother—what is there left to tell?"

"Tell me them over again."

"Which of them all will the signore hear? But, indeed, he knows them all by heart! There is that one of the birth of Bambino Gesù—yes? And that of the Madonnina when she was a girl at school, and that of Sampietro who was always hungry, even as myself—which of them all shall I tell, then?"

And I said, "Tell me the *Fuga in Egitto*."

"Signore, why do you always like that best? For my part I prefer those of Sampietro—how he put the devil's head on the *bella ragazza*, but——

"As the signore doubtless knows, Erode had ordered the massacre of the Innocenti, for he wished, ah, how indeed he wished! to kill the Bambino Gesù, who was a greater king than he. So Sangiuseppe and the Madonna had to flee away. Ah, the Madonnina. . . . She carried always in the nest of her arms, wrapped in her apron, Gesù our Saviour. And as she went, sitting on the ass which Sangiuseppe drove before him, as she went, the Pharisees met her and said, 'Beautiful Lady, what do you carry in your apron?'

"And she answered, 'I carry Il Gran' Signore.'

"But the Pharisees mistook her, thinking she said, 'Grano, Signori,' and they answered, 'Carry it, then, to the mill.' So she passed on with Our Lord and Sangiuseppe.

"And again the Pharisees met them and said, 'Beautiful Lady, what do you carry, then, in your apron?'

"And she said, smiling perhaps, 'A mass of flowers.'

"'That is not for us,' they said one to another, and went on their way.

"And indeed, signore, the Madonna spoke but truth, for Il Gesù Cristo is indeed Il Gran' Signore and also a mass of Flowers. Was it a miracle, then, that the Pharisees took one for another?

"And as they went on their way the Madonna had compassion on Sangiuseppe, for he was tired. But everywhere they met companies of Pharisees; and it was necessary to continue their journey, so they left the road for a time and entered into the fields. Signore, it was a field where they were sowing beans— and the bean is the spy of the year. The Madonna blessed the field and immediately the beans sprang into blossom, and she went on her way. Then came the Pharisees at the top of the field and asked the *contadini*, 'Has a woman with a Bambino and an old man passed by?'

"And they answered, 'She has passed by, sissignori.'

"'When?' demanded the Pharisees.

"'When we sowed these beans,' answered the *contadini*.

"And the Pharisees, seeing the beans in flower, turned back and went by another road.

"But the Madonna with Our Lord and Sangiuseppe went still on their way, and as they came to a field of flax the Pharisees came upon them once again, and the Madonna said to the flax, 'Flax, O flax, hide me this Baby.' And the flax hid Him, and the wind passed over the field, so that the waving of the flax dazzled the eyes of the Pharisees and they saw nothing. And when the danger was past the Madonna said, 'Blessed be the flax. May it be so plentiful that the women shall be weary of spinning.'

"Sangiuseppe and the Madonna with Our Lord in her arms had journeyed all night, and Sangiuseppe, for all he walked so strongly, was almost always a long way behind. Suddenly at dawn the Madonna spied not far away even another company of Pharisees, but these, signore, were on horseback, so that she feared more than before that she would fall into their hands. And she cried, 'Run, Giuseppe, run!' And Sangiuseppe, using greatly his staff—that which blossomed, you remember, signore—soon came up to the Madonna, but there were neither houses nor shade, nor even a cave thereabout, only an olive tree. And already the Pharisees cried out, 'Stop, stop.'

"But the Madonna turned to the olive and said, 'Do me the charity, then, to hide us all three.' And the olive opened its trunk as it were a cottage, signore, even as they do still, and the Madonna with the Bambino and Sangiuseppe entered in. Then it closed again. And within there was light, for it was not wanting in oil. But the Pharisees who had seen, a little before, the Madonna and Our Lord and Sangiuseppe, found only the ass grazing hard by; and they could not understand because they were Pharisees. And they sought all night, but found nothing. Then, when they were gone, the olive opened and the Madonna came forth with her little Son and Sangiuseppe. And the Madonna said to the olive, 'May thy fruit be blessed.' And that, signore, is why we say *Olio Santo*, Holy Oil, and that is why this Oil will heal wounds and burns and tumours, is it not so? and the soul also.

"And so, as the signore knows, since the Pharisees themselves could not find the Madonna, they sent for a brigand. Now, signore, nothing may escape the watchfulness of a brigand, and it is part of his business to waylay people in the mountains. This brigand then returned to his companions and said to them, 'If a beautiful lady should pass by, take her for me.'

"And the capo of the band heard him, and said, 'She is yonder in the shadow of the mountain; you may take her easily.' And it was as he said.

"And the Madonna had not time to hide Our Lord or to do anything at all, so they brought her before the capo. 'Beautiful Lady,' said he, 'will you not come and see a *bambino* of mine, who is covered with sores, for we can find no remedy? Ah, if you might give us some help!'

"And the Madonna entered into the cave of the brigands, and there was presented to her the little sick one. And does the signore know what the Madonna did? She took off the swaddling clothes of Gesù Cristo, she unwound the bands round about Him, and placing a trough of water close by her she washed Him very well. Then with that water she washed also the *bambino* of the capo of the robbers. And that baby, signore, in a second of time was healed. The capo of the robbers wished to cover Bambino Gesù with gold, but the Madonna said, 'No.' Then he went with the Madonna a good part of the way, always blessing her. And if the signore will believe me, that one who had wished to take the Madonna was the impenitent thief, the other the good thief. Both of them ended their lives on the cross on Calvary, on either side of Jesus our Saviour. But it was the good thief alone who saw Paradise."

And another day we wandered to the Cappuccini, and were lying on the verge of the woods. The sun had set, the glory that had transfigured the world had departed. Through the immense stillness came faintly the sound of a bell; when that ceased only the call of the night *cecco* broke the silence of the world.

"Does the signore hear that whistling devil?" said Ulisse. He came and touched my hand.

"What does it say then?" I asked.

"I know not!" said Ulisse quickly; "some evil thing, doubtless. How should I know what it says? Has Il Gesù Cristo given me that grace? No, signore, He only gave that gift once, and then it was to the rich Simone in the Gospel."

"What gift?" said I.

"The gift, signore, to understand the speech of the beasts."

"Tell me," said I.

"Signore, I forget, and, besides, I am more hungry than was Sampietro when he stole the ham——"

"What?" said I.

"Signore, it happened thus. Il Santissimo Gesù and the apostles had walked far and far through the wilderness. Signore, they were more weary than I can say, and hungry— but hungry! Presently far away they saw a little village, and when they came there they went into the shop to beg something to eat. Now while Il Gesù Cristo was speaking with the *padrone*, Sampietro spied a ham hanging in a dark corner; so he hid it under his cloak and they went on their way. When they had gone a certain distance and were sat down to eat, Sampietro said, '*Eccolo, Maestro!* see what I have found,' and he brought out the ham.

"But Il Gesù Cristo said, 'Sampietro, one ought not to steal the things of others.'

"'Oh,' said Sampietro, 'I found it, Maestro.'

"'If you found it,' said Our Lord, 'do you know what you must do? You must go back and cry through the village, "Has anyone lost a ham?" If no one claims it you may have it.'

"Signore, Sampietro was very sad as he went alone, hungry too, all the way back to the village—sad, but thoughtful. And when he came to the street he cried at the top of his voice, 'Has anyone lost——' and then in a whisper, 'a ham?' And this he did more than once, but no one answered. Then he returned to Our Lord and the other apostles. 'No,' said he, smiling, 'no one claims it; we can eat it.'

"But Our Lord, who knows everything, said, 'Turn again, Sampietro, along with me.' So they returned together to the village. And when they were come into the street Our Lord said, 'Cry aloud, Sampietro,' and Sampietro cried—what else could he do?—'Has anyone lost a ham?' And immediately the *padrone* ran out and claimed it. But Sampietro for a little did nothing but weep.

"And another day, too, signore, it befell again that Our Lord and the apostles had made a long journey. Signore, it was *Sol in Leone* and hot—but hot! and to reach a certain village by nightfall it was necessary to journey through the day. And that country was full of mountains, difficult to climb without weariness. Also they were hungry, and as the signore may imagine, it was not Sampietro who had most *pazienza*.

"Suddenly Il Gesù Cristo said, 'We will all eat at the top of the hill,' and He bade each of them pick up a stone and carry it to the top. And so, signore, all the apostles took up great stones and carried them on their shoulders, save our Sampietro, who, snorting and grumbling the while, picked up a pebble—but in truth a pebble.

"When they were come to the summit at last, Our Lord said, 'Place the stones on the ground.' And they placed them on the ground. Then Our Lord stretched forth His hand and blessed the stones and the stones became bread. And each satisfied his hunger; but Sampietro remained fasting with only a crumb to eat.

"And not long after the same thing befell—another long journey with hunger and weariness. And again at the foot of a great hill Our Lord bade them each carry a stone to the top. And so they did. But our Sampietro, who remembered his fast, carried, groaning and sweating the while, a great rock—signore, a veritable boulder—on his back. But he said all the while in his heart, 'At least I shall have enough to eat this time.'

"And when they were come to the summit, Our Lord said, 'Place the stones on the ground,' but He did not bless them. After a minute Sampietro said, 'Maestro, why have we brought these stones hither?'

"And Il Gesù Cristo answered, 'To sit on. . . .'"

"Ulisse," said I, after a time, "it is necessary that these tales be written down, since they have the sound of truth, so that they who know them not may hear them."

"It is my opinion also, signore," said Ulisse. "Write them then—you who are always writing."

"That," said I, "is easier to say than to do; and if I do, be sure that not all who read them will understand them, because for some they are too difficult."

"Indeed, yes," said Ulisse; "yet I understand them, and they are good tales concerning Our Lord, the Madonna and the saints whom we love."

"Ulisse," said I, "it occurs to me to write them out tomorrow and to send them to the Inglesi."

"That," said Ulisse, "would be indeed a Christian act, worthy of the signore, because the Inglesi—*scusi*, signore—much more often than not are no Christians at all, and it would be well to turn their hearts."

Now Ulisse had for some time been troubled about my countrymen and their probable fate as heretics, and had evidently been consulting Frate Antonio on the matter, for presently he said:

"*Scusi*, signore! It was not altogether the fault of the Inglesi that they became heretics. It was really the fault of their wicked King Enrico, who wanted to get rid of his good and very pious queen and marry another woman. And when Papa Farnese said No, this wicked king kicked him out of Inghilterra, killed all the *frati* and made himself Anti-Papa in Inghilterra, and so all the Inglesi had to become *Protestanti*. But Frate Antonio has said that even these *Protestanti* may by chance not go to hell."

"What?" I said. "How is that?"

"Signore, *senta*! One day Il Gesù Cristo was walking with Sampietro in Paradiso, as the padrone may walk with the fattore in the podere; and after a while He said—not as complaining exactly, but as stating a fact:

"'Sampietro, I think this place has gone down.'

"Here Sampietro, who is always impetuous and knew very well what He meant, dared to interrupt.

"'Il Santissimo can't blame me,' he said huffily; 'Il Santissimo is not to suppose they all came in by the Gate, *Che! Che!*'

"'Not come in by the Gate, Sampietro? What do you mean?' said Our Lord.

"'If Il Santissimo will but step this way, round these bushes,' said Sampietro, 'He will see.'

"And sure enough He saw. For there was the Madonna drawing the souls up pell-mell, willy-nilly, anyhow, into Paradiso in a great bucket to their eternal gain and undeserved good." O Clemens, O Pia, O Dulcis Virgo Maria.

CHAPTER XIII

OVER THE SOMMA TO NARNI

THROUGH the valleys of oak and ilex I set out from Spoleto, I remember, before the sun was high, on a fair September morning as ever was, for Terni and her falls, which, as it happened, I was never to see; for I had scarcely gone five miles on my way when I was overtaken by rain that meant the end of the summer, for, as they say in Siena, the first rain after the Assumption is the first rain of winter. Was it not of such a tempest that Virgil warned us, so that we might note its coming?

But I was heedless; and, taken with the beauty of the way, I had not observed the signs infallible. Not till the murmur of the woods prevailed against the whisper of the summer day did I understand that nature was awake, her heart tumultuous with some passionate remembrance, and she herself singing upon the mountains.

Saepe etiam immensum coelo venit agmen aquarum
et foedam glomerant tempestatem imbribus atris
collectae ex alto nubes; ruit arduus aether,
et pluvia ingenti sata laeta boumque labores
diluit; implentur fossae et cava flumina crescunt
cum sonitu fervetque fretis spirantibus aequor.
Ipse pater media nimborum in nocte corusca
fulmina molitur dextra. . . .[1]

Ah, but I used to know the whole of that Georgic by heart, hammered into me as it was at school, though even then I came to love Virgil, "so musical, so melancholy", and I remember how at Blundell's one of my form-masters, if we happened on a passage of the *Aeneid* which Virgil had stolen from Homer, never missed the opportunity of sniffing viciously, and "Homer

---

[1] "Often too there appears in the sky a mighty column of water and clouds—mustered from on high roll up a murky tempest of black showers; down falls the lofty heaven and with its deluge of rain washes away the happy crops and the labours of the oxen. The dykes fill: the deep channelled rivers swell and roar and the sea steams in its heaving. The Father himself in the midnight of storm clouds wields his bolts with flashing hand. . . ."

spoiled again" he would say. On one of these occasions I held up my hand and protested, a somewhat unusual thing for a boy to do in those days.

"Yes, sir," I said, "but——"

"Well, boy?"

"Please, sir, I mean, sir, with what a grace he does it."

"That," said my form-master, "is the most immoral remark I have ever heard in this form. And I might add it is all the worse for the small, the very small, measure of truth there is in it."

Happy days! but not so happy as that in the rain on the way to Terni. Through the valley under the storm of rain I went rejoicing; it was one of the great days of my life. I crosssed the Somma alone chanting Virgil's lines. I was drenched to the skin, and the hailstones cut my face like a whip, and the lightning flashed about me. What cared I? The long road hissed before me, and suddenly, as it seemed, under the fury of the storm, was overcome and no longer resisted the invincible rain, but was musical with a million fountains. All nature sighed in the ecstasy of that embrace, and spoke in the song of the storm of the antique tragedies of the gods. And I alone heard it all as I came down into the sacred groves of ilex in the old and beautiful valley, through which a little river ran boisterous before me.

But that was fifty years ago and today it was raining still, when I am ashamed to say, I crossed the Somma in an *autobus* and again I did not see the famous falls of which Childe Harold wrote. Perhaps it was just as well, for they have been hopelessly ruined for commercial purposes, and Terni is now an industrialised town. But I did go into the church of San Francesco to find in the Paradise chapel to the right of the choir the frescoes of the Last Judgment, the Resurrection and Purgatory, by that Foligno master, Bartolommeo di Tommaso.

I came to Narni in the evening.

The inn at Narni is of no great pretensions, but the host is a good host and very rightly he is proud of his picturesque and antique city, but especially is he proud of his view, and the great Roman bridge, so magnificent a ruin, that strives in vain to grapple the shores of Nera: *sulfurea Nar albus aqua.*

NARNI. Ponte d'Augusto.

POGGIO BUSTONE. The convent and Rieti valley.

And well he may be; the Ponte d'Augusto is one of the most beautiful ruins in the world, chiefly perhaps because it has been left alone with age and death. In its youth and prime it carried the Via Flaminia; in its age it warns us of the far from desolate splendours that the Eternal City still guards. An outpost of the Campagna, it knows the gods are dead or dying in that once mysterious desert. What need is there of any splendid road to Rome, since the messengers of Christ, pursued by implacable victory, came, not with beauty and delight in gilded chariots and with horses, but in rags with bleeding feet? Should this so noble bridge of Caesar Augustus bear on its back the brutal and barbaric armies of the Goth, or make the way smooth for the strange bedecked columns, gay with harlots and with silk, of Charles VIII on his way to Naples, there to find no kingdom but an immortal pestilence? The Ponte d'Augusto watches the traveller pass by on another way to Rome unheeding, while it remembers only splendid days. Still one arch is perfect, waiting for the return of the armies of Caesar, which so many ages ago went out to conquer the world. Who can doubt they will return? *Sine auctoritate nulla vita.*

One enters the city by the Porta Ternana, of the end of the fifteenth century, with its portentous towers, to find Narni an almost completely medieval city frowning and picturesque on its olive-clad cliff above the Nera and commanding a wide prospect over the Conca Ternana and from the public garden a magnificent view. Here is surely one of Virgil's Italian cities.

> *Tot congesta manu praeruptis oppida saxis*
> *fluminaque antiquos subterlabentia muros. . . .*[1]

Crowded now with the buildings of the Middle Age: towers, noble palaces, old churches and, over all, the great Rocca built by Cardinal Albornoz and restored by Pius II, before all these its most magnificent possession remains its broken Roman bridge. The only modern thing in the city might seem to be the curious monument *ai caduti*, like a lighthouse.

The Romanesque Duomo of San Giovenale, with its heavy Campanile (1110), has a charming portico which is of the

---

[1] "So many towns his handiwork has piled high on rugged cliffs and the rivers glide beneath their ancient walls."

8

fifteenth century, as is the arch on the right with its chapel, but the portal in the façade is still of the twelfth century, with a classical accent. Within there are four naves upheld by columns and a triumphal arch, but that on the right is of the fifteenth century when the church was restored. On the pilasters at the end of the central nave are two pulpits with reliefs of saints.

The more modern aisle on the right, added in the fifteenth century, has several interesting works of art. To begin with, a fresco in a niche of the Virgin and Child and angels, a work of the early fifteenth century. To the left of the second altar is the tomb of Carlo Boccardi (1498) with effigy. The third chapel is an ornate work of the same time and within is a wooden statue of S. Antony Abbot by Vecchietta, the Sienese master. By the same gifted artist is a fine panel with a figure of S. Giovenale, the church's and the city's patron saint.

One now comes to what is by far the most interesting and once the most beautiful work in the church, the shrine of SS. Giovenale and Cossio by masters of the Cosmati school. The whole shrine or chapel is very classical in form with its vertical design and its square framework, much of which still retains its mosaics. Its two doorways are also decorated with mosaics. On either side above, two statues remain, a Pietà in wood on the left and San Giovenale on the right, but these are later works. Above the central doorway are two sculptured sheep on either side a central cross. All this, and the mosaic pavement beside it, are among the earlier works of the Roman school of marble craftsmen. Mosaic pavements of the same school are in Santa Maria in Pensole and San Domenico. For these works alone Narni is worth a visit. One of the masters of the school, Petrus Romanus, made the pavement in front of the high altar in Westminster Abbey in 1269 and the beautiful tomb of Henry III in the chapel of the Confessor. The marble triptych here within the shrine is of the fifteenth century, and has been restored.

In the chapel in the right transept, of the eighteenth century, is a reliquary containing the body of Beata Lucia da Narni. In the left aisle, opposite the Cosmatesque shrine, is the beautiful tomb of Pietro Cesi by Pellegrino da Como (1477).

In the picturesque Piazza dei Priori, which is surrounded by
fine buildings, such as the Casa Sacripanti with its bas-reliefs,
stand the Palazzo del Podestà, of the fourteenth century, with its
grandiose portico, portale and pulpit, and facing it the Palazzo
Comunale, also of the fourteenth century, with a spacious atrium.
On the floor above is the Pinacoteca with some fine pictures
by Benozzo Gozzoli, Domenico Ghirlandaio and Lo Spagna.

In the Annunciation by Benozzo, the angel stands erect before
the kneeling Virgin, her arms crossed on her breast. Garlanded
columns separate them. The Virgin closely resembles the
Virgin of the panel at Perugia, but has been damaged.

The altarpiece by Ghirlandaio is a Coronation of the Virgin.
It was painted for the monastery of San Girolamo here in
1486. I fear it is largely the work of his assistants, though
painted no doubt under his close supervision. Above, Our
Lord crowns His Mother, who kneels before Him surrounded
by saints and angels. Two angels bear an immense and
extraordinary crown. Below (the picture is divided into two
parts), a crowd of saints kneel in adoration. In the predella we
see S. Francis receiving the Stigmata, the Pietà and S. Jerome
in prayer. On the frame are the figures of six other saints, and
above in the arch eleven cherubim. This is an important work
and must have been designed and supervised by Domenico,
though carried out, for the most part perhaps, by Davide. It
was frequently copied up and down Umbria; for example, by
Lo Spagna at Trevi. The stigmatisation of S. Francis here in
the gallery at Narni by Lo Spagna is a detached fresco.

The church of Sant' Agostino, a fifteenth-century building
with a good if plain portal and frescoes in a niche by some local
master, has little of interest, but over the first altar on the right
is an altarpiece with a Christ in relief and four saints and
predella by Marcantonio Aquili, a son of Antoniazzo Romano,
whose works I was to find in some number later in Rieti.

The church of Santa Maria in Pensole is of greater interest
only for its Cosmatesque pavement. It is a building of the
last quarter of the twelfth century, is divided into three naves
by Romanesque columns, and with its *porticello* seems to be an
intact building of that time.

San Domenico has a portal of the twelfth century decorated

with sculpture, and twelve busts, perhaps of the apostles. Within is a Cosmatesque pavement and frescoes by Mezzastris of S. Cecilia and S. Monica, and on a column to the right a rudely executed painting of the Madonna between two angels, which seems to be coeval with the church. Other works on other columns, two of the Blessed Virgin and some figures of saints, are of the end of the thirteenth century. The figures of S. George and the Dragon, of the fourteenth century, seem to be akin to Sienese work. Here too is a monument to the Condottiere Gattamelata, who was born in Narni.

One comes upon Mezzastris again in San Francesco—a church of the fourteenth century, which is said to have been built on the site of an oratory founded by S. Francis, who was here in 1213, when he wandered all over Umbria preaching pardon and peace. In Narni he worked two miracles recorded by Thomas of Celano. He is said to have sought out the most solitary part of the city and there erected a small house for himself and his brethren. This remained for some two hundred years, when the present church replaced it, now spoiled by having been restored and redecorated in the eighteenth century, so that almost nothing is left of the fourteenth-century building but the façade and its charming portal. The chapel of the saint within, however, remains, and is decorated with frescoes of the life of the Poverello and his miracles here in Narni, by Mezzastris, much spoiled by damp and repaint.

The days pass easily in Narni. I climbed up to Cardinal Albornoz's Rocca, now derelict and deserted, for the sake of the great view it commands, and spent a morning there with a book.[1] Of an afternoon I strolled lazily to San Cassiano, a

---

[1] Thomas, brother of the last Constantine Palaeologus, at the fall of Constantinople in 1453, escaped to the Venetians. He brought with him the head of S. Andrew the Apostle—now a major relic in S. Peter's. The princes of Europe stretched forth eager hands to seize such a treasure, but Thomas, landing in Italy at Ancona in 1460 gave the head to Cardinal Oliva for the Pope who commended him to deposit it in Albornoz's Rocca at Narni. The great festival on the arrival of the head of the brother of S. Peter in Rome is one of the most strange scenes of the Renaissance. Jubilee indulgences were granted to all who attended. The head was brought to Rome in April 1462 by Cardinals Bassarion, Piccolomini and Oliva and was received by the Pope at Ponte Molle on Palm Sunday. Bessarion wept as he placed the casket on the altar before the Pope. Pius II also wept and threw himself on the ground before the head of the Apostle and then addressed Latin welcome to the stranger. Next day the head was brought to S. Peter's. Comment. Pii II, pp. 192 et seq.

foundation of the twelfth century, much rebuilt at various times, but which still possesses a beautiful columned portal, a Romanesque tower and another fine view. I devoted a whole afternoon to visiting Visciano, where the old rude Romanesque church of Santa Pudenziana with its pointed portico, its ancient altar and ciborium and bishop's throne recall the work of the Roman marble craftsmen whose work adorns the Cathedral, San Domenico, and Santa Maria in Pensole, but I always came back to the great Roman bridge over the Nar. From there, and strolling along the stream, one understands the Narnia of old on its lofty hill, precipitous on more than one side and half encircled by those sulphurean waters, which rush through the deep-wooded gorge immediately beneath the city, so well described by Claudian:

> *rarique coloris*
> *non procul amnis abest urbi qui nominis auctor;*
> *ilice sub densa silvis artatus opacis*
> *inter utrumque iugum tortis anfractibus albet.*[1]

---

[1] "Not far away flows the strange-coloured stream which gives the town its name, its sulphurous waters flowing in tortuous course between opposite mountains through dense woods of ilex." *De Sexto Consul. Honorii*, 516 *et seq.*

CHAPTER XIV

THE VALLE SANTA

RIETI

In the first days of October I went to Assisi for the feast of S. Francis (October 4). The little poor man who was pelted with stones and derided in Assisi in the first years of the thirteenth century is now become the patron saint of Italy and, what is more, is probably the most universally revered of all the saints.

After a day or two in the little brown city I returned southward to Terni, for I intended to spend the rest of the month of S. Francis in the Valle Reatina, the Valle Santa, about the city of Rieti.

There were two valleys which S. Francis especially loved: the valley of Spoleto, where he was born and where he died, and the Valle Reatina, to which he made his first pilgrimage and where he spent the last troubled years of his life. This valley is starred, almost in the form of a cross, by the four Franciscan sanctuaries, Greccio, Fonte Colombo, La Foresta, Poggio Bustone, each intimately the scene of an event, even a crisis, in his life. These hermitages, all placed in the loveliest landscapes, are sacred places of the Franciscan religion.

As one climbs up out of Terni past the spoiled cascades of the Velino at Le Marmore and comes into the opening vale at the Lago di Piediluco, it is obvious that the Valle Santa is in fact an upland plateau, though it is as yet hidden by Monte Lungo. Indeed, as soon appears, the valley of Rieti is more properly a *conca* than a valley, a wide upland plateau watered by the Velino and surrounded by mountains, Monte Terminillo, over 6,000 feet, crowned with snow, lording it over all.

Nothing is easier than to go from Terni to Rieti. It is but an hour's journey in the public automobile or by the railway. And though the climb by Stroncone on foot over the mountains by the Colle dei Prati and La Cappelletta (3,500 feet), descending to Greccio, some ten miles from Rieti, is a magnificent journey

with some of the grandest views over mountain and valley to
be found anywhere in Italy, it is an exceedingly long and
tiring day's work, better undertaken with a guide; while
undoubtedly the best, indeed the only, centre from which to
visit the Franciscan sanctuaries of the Valle Santa is the small
and Roman city of Rieti, to which accordingly I made my way.

Rieti lies at the south-east extremity of the green and fertile
Conca Reatina, watered by the Velino, where it is joined by the
Salto. It is the ancient Reate of the Sabines and came into the
power of Rome in 290 B.C. It became a prosperous Municipium
and Cicero compares its vale with that of Tempe; but with the
fall of the Empire its troubles began and the Middle Age filled
it with discord and war.

Besides its great and well-preserved walls there remain
several monuments of that time, though, save for a picture or
two in the Pinacoteca, no picture or fresco of much importance.
The church, however, of Sant' Agostino, with its Romanesque
portal and campanile, is of the end of the thirteenth century.

The Duomo, dedicated in honour of the Assumption, is also
Romanesque, with a portico of the middle of the fifteenth
century, and a great campanile dating from 1252, the work of
Andrea Pietro and Enrico, presumably of Rieti. The central
portal is especially fine, but the only thing within of any great
interest is a statue of S. Barbara by Gianantonio Mari after a
design by Bernini. The beautiful crypt, however, with its
sixteen columns is said to date from the fifth century and is the
original cathedral. It still possesses an inscription of A.D. 375
in honour of the Emperors Valentinianus, Valens and Gratianus.
The rebuilt Episcopal Palace retains its Papal Loggia of the
end of the twelfth century, but this too has recently been
restored. The Arco del Vescovo beside the palace was built by
Boniface VIII in 1298. Besides these buildings the church of
San Pietro in the Via Roma retains its Romanesque portal and
the fine and almost Baroque Palazzo Vecchiarelli is a work by
Carlo Maderna. Out of Via Roma runs the Via San Ruffo
with medieval houses, among which the Casa Zaffarelli and
the Palazzo Chiavellini are the more notable.

The Pinacoteca in the Palazzo Comunale contains, beside
the work of local painters, three works of considerable interest.

The earliest of these is an altarpiece by Luca di Tommé signed and dated 1370. This comes from the church of San Domenico. In the midst Our Lady is enthroned with the Child standing on her knee and at the sides are full-length figures of SS. Peter and Dominic and SS. Paul and Peter Martyr. The influence of Simone Martini is clearly marked in this polyptych.

The second work is a triptych by Antoniazzo Romano, signed and dated 1464, which seems to have been dismembered, with two panels missing, for both the saints, S. Francis receiving the Stigmata and S. Anthony of Padua, on either side the elaborately enthroned Madonna and Child, look to the right. At the feet of the Madonna kneels a small figure of the donor.

Two other works, both by Marcantonio Aquili, the younger son of Antoniazzo Romano, who settled permanently in Rieti, are in this gallery. The finer is an important panel of the Adoration of the Shepherds in a charming landscape. Above the cave, where we see the ox and ass, a group of angels sing *Gloria in excelsis* and above again, in His heaven, God the Father amid the cherubim blesses the world to be redeemed by His Son. The other work is a triptych, signed and dated 1511, of the Resurrection in the central panel and SS. Stephen and Lawrence at the sides. Half-figures of God the Father in benediction between SS. Francis and Anthony are above, and below, in the predella, are five scenes of the Passion.

But where in all this is S. Francis? The answer is, nowhere. Not a vestige of his presence seems to remain in Rieti. He was not used to frequent courts and palaces, and though he lay in the Vescovado for some time, sick and half blind, and was there most barbarously operated on by an Arabian leech, it was at the end of his life, and the Vescovado we see can scarcely be that to which Honorius III escaped in 1225. No; if we seek S. Francis it is not in Rieti we should look for him, but in the little sanctuaries in the hills round about, and first of all at Poggio Bustone. For, according to Wadding,[1] it was there S. Francis dwelt on his first visit to the Valle Reatina in 1209.

---

[1] Wadding, *Annales ad. ann.*, 1209.

POGGIO BUSTONE

Poggio Bustone is the most northern of the four Franciscan sanctuaries in the Valle Santa. It is some sixteen *chilometri* from Rieti and lies on the hills to the east of the Terni high road. One can go most of the way by auto-car, as far as Ponte Crispolti, and thence climb up to the little town some five miles distant in the hills.

The way from Rieti lies first through the fertile vale or Conca Reatina as far as the Fonti di Santa Susanna, past San Nicola and between the lovely Lago di Rieti with its small islands and Lago Lungo, till at the Ponte Crispolti one leaves the highway and, rounding Lago Lungo, begins to climb up to Poggio Bustone, where from the piazza there is a marvellous view over lake and valley and mountain all the way. Poggio has some 2,000 inhabitants and boasts a "Duomo" and a Municipio, and there is a possible inn where one may spend a day or two.

The Franciscan convent of San Giacomo, beyond Poggio, under the rocky slope, sprinkled with oak, of Monte Rosato, is now abandoned and almost in ruin. It is said to have been founded by S. Francis in 1217. He was here, Thomas of Celano records,[1] one Christmas and preached to the people who had come from far and near to hear him.

Once at the hermitage of Poggio about Christmas when a large number of people had been called together to hear him preach, he prefaced his discourse with these words: "You believe me a holy man, and that is why you have come devoutly hither. But I confess to you that during all this fast I have been eating food seasoned with lard." In this way he often ascribed to pleasure what had rather been a concession to infirmity.

The earlier *santuario* of S. Francis is half an hour's climb above San Giacomo by a steep path on which one passes six little chapels, each with a memory of the saint. The sanctuary, really a cavern, now divided into two and fitted with a doorway

[1] II Celano, cap. 94.

and built up, is in the side of a great cliff towering above a precipitous gorge, more or less filled with oaks, where far below a torrent sounds. The first cave is a chapel with an altar and over the altar a painting of the seventeenth century representing the incident that according to the legend took place here in 1209.

This incident, recorded by Thomas of Celano,[1] has been very beautifully and imaginatively paraphrased by Joergensen, whose life of S. Francis is often preferred to that of Sabatier.

A little after his conversion the saint left the Portiuncula and accompanied only by Brother Giles[2] went to preach in the valley of Rieti. . . . After preaching by day he prayed by night. With weary footsteps the saint with the faithful companion climbed up to the solitary cave above Poggio Bustone in the wood under the towering rocks. Giles lay down in some hollow, stretched himself on a bed of dead leaves and composed himself for sleep. Not so the Maestro. In the profound silence broken only by the sound of the torrent and the lugubrious hooting of the owl, Francis bore all the attacks, all the wiles of the demon. In vain did sensual visions tempt him, in vain windy pride assailed him, in vain was showered at his feet riches and gold and all the precious stones of the world. Francis was above all such things. The demons retired beaten, all save one, the most insidious, who came through the lowly door of humility, bending his head as in deep devotion and whispering with a voice of sweetness: "Poor Francesco, how can you believe you will ever be saved? Too wicked you have been in your past life! Do you believe that God will ever pardon you? Never, never, never, Francesco. There is no salvation for you, there is no heaven, there is no paradise. Damned you are, damned, damned . . . !" And the voice of the demon lost itself echoing like the voice of the owl.

But, as the legend tells us, presently an angel came to Francis, an angel of annunciation, and assured him of the forgiveness of all his sins and of the eternal love of God. And, as Celano records:

[1] I Celano, cap. 11.
[2] I doubt if it were Giles. See I Celano, cap. 12. Giles had gone with Bernard to Compostella.

the darkness dispersed, which through fear of sin had gathered in his heart and there was poured into him assurance of the forgiveness of all offences and confidence of restoration of grace was vouchsafed to him. Then he was caught up above himself and wholly absorbed in a certain light; the capacity of his mind was enlarged, and he beheld clearly what was to come to pass. Finally, as that sweetness faded away with the light, renewed in spirit, he already seemed changed into another man.

"*O Francisce*," we read on the picture over the altar, '*hic remissa sunt peccata tua sicut a Deo postulasti.*"

One reaches the second cave up seven steps cut in the rock. This is very narrow, a real grotto. It too has an altar and one reads there: "*In questo sacro speco per molti anni habitò il Padre San Francesco col Beato Egidio ed altri suoi compagni.*" Above is represented Francis sleeping, supporting Giles asleep on his shoulder.

On the feast of S. Francis, on October 4, very early in the morning one of the inhabitants of Poggio Bustone, before the place is awake, goes round the village sounding a drum and stopping before each house, cries out to those within, "*Buon giorno o buona gente*", just as S. Francis had been wont to do. And on the Monday of Easter week the whole village and neighbouring country, in long procession, slowly climb up to the solitary sanctuary, singing as they go, and there assist at Mass.[1]

LA FORESTA

The convent of La Foresta—Santa Maria della Foresta, originally San Fabiano—is much nearer Rieti than is Poggio Bustone; indeed, it cannot be more than three miles from the city. To reach it one leaves Rieti by the Porta Conca, outside which is the railway station. La Foresta lies in the hills in a beautiful situation on the same east side of the Conca. The convent is a very modest, very charming building with a towered chapel or small church, surrounded by woods and pastures. Cypresses and a bosco rise beside it.

If Poggio Bustone is connected with the early life of S. Francis,

[1] See P. Nicola Cavanna, O.F.M., *L'Umbria Francescana* (Perugia, 1910), p. 328.

La Foresta is the scene of an event in his latter days when he was already a sick man and half blind. Very reluctantly, on the advice of Cardinal Ugolino, his friend and the Protector of his Order, and of Frate Elias, then its Minister-General, he set out from the Portiuncula for Rieti, where the Papal court then was, to consult Tebald the Saracen, the Papal surgeon. Francis had only recently received the Stigmata on Monte La Verna, and more and more at this time he was, as Thomas of Celano records, "oppressed with various sicknesses more grievous than before", but in obedience to Ugolino, in the summer of 1225 he consented to set out for Rieti with Frate Masseo and the Companions, who were to be his nurses to the end. On the way, he decided to go to San Damiano to say farewell to S. Clare, whom he feared he would never see again, but on coming to the convent he fell so seriously ill that he could not continue the journey. He lay six weeks at San Damiano, where S. Clare had built for him a hut in the garden, a hut of osiers, and it was there after a dreadful night of pain and misery he composed the poem of *Laudes Creaturarum*—The Canticle of the Sun.

When he could be moved, after some six weeks, he set out with his companions for Rieti, through Terni and by the road or track along the course of the Velino, through the gorges, into the beautiful Conca Reatina under the sombre mass of the Apennine, crowned there with the snows of Monte Terminillo. An immense rumour went before the saint pierced with the Stigmata of Our Lord. And to escape the multitude, he turned out of the way some three miles before reaching the smiling city and asked hospitality of the poor priest of San Fabiano, at La Foresta.

> The city folk coming to know that he was gone to the said church ran together for to see him in such sort that the vineyard of the church was altogether spoiled and the grapes of it were all plucked: whereof the priest was sore grieving in his heart and repented him that he had received S. Francis into the church. The thought of the priest being revealed of God unto S. Francis, he called him and said: Dear Father, how many measures of wine doth this vineyard yield thee, the year it yields the best? Replied the priest: Twelve measures. Quoth S. Francis: I pray thee, Father,

that thou bear patiently with me if I tarry here some days, seeing that I find here much repose; and let those who so will pluck of the grapes of this thy vineyard for the love of God and me his poor little one; and I promise thee in the name of my Lord Jesu Christ, that it shall yield thee twenty measures every year. . . . The priest trusted the promise of S. Francis and freely gave up the garden unto all that came to him. And it was a marvel to see how the vineyard was all spoiled and plucked so that scarce any bunches of grapes were left. The time of the vintage came, and the priest gathered in such bunches as remained and put them in the vat and trod them out, and according to the promise of S. Francis got thereout twenty measures of the best wine.[1]

We may suppose that the *frati* presently took possession of San Fabiano and re-dedicated it in honour of Our Lady, calling it Santa Maria della Foresta, and it was so consecrated in 1231 by Pope Gregory IX that was Cardinal Ugolino. The *cisterna* or vat of the miracle is still pointed out there.

S. Francis presently went on to Rieti and was received by Ugolino in the Episcopal Palace which was the scene of almost uncontrollable demonstrations of devotion by the population which fought for the clothes of the saint, his hairs and even the parings of his nails. Indeed, a shepherd having got hold of the water in which he had washed his stigmatised hands, sprinkled it over a sick sheep, which was immediately well. A canon of the Cathedral, sick as a result of his debaucheries, came to him weeping and asking for his blessing. "How can I bless thee with the sign of the Cross, seeing that thou livest according to the flesh?" asked Francis. "Nevertheless I will bless thee in the name of Christ; but mark well that new evils will come to thee if thou returnest to thy vomit." And so it came to pass, for the canon, once whole, returned to his sins and the roof crashed on his head one day when he was feasting in bad company.[2]

It was, too, while in Rieti, though according to the *Legenda Antiqua* not in the Palace, but in the house of Tebald the Saracen, that an angel played for him on the viol. For, one day in his sickness and pain desiring to hear music, he called a

---

[1] *Fioretti* (Temple Classics), cap. XIX.   [2] II Celano, cap. 41.

brother who had been a troubadour in the world and begged
him to borrow a viol and to play thereon for a little. "That
will comfort my brother the body," he said, "and will distract
him a little from his suffering." But the sometime troubadour
excused himself, thinking it might cause scandal. "Very well,"
said S. Francis, "think no more of it. It is true one ought to
make sacrifices to people's opinions." The following night
there came a mysterious visitor, who played the viol under his
window, and in the morning Francis called the too-scrupulous
brother to him. "God has pity and consoles the afflicted," said
Francis, "for last night He allowed me to listen to music
infinitely lovelier than any here below."[1]

S. Francis did not wish to remain long in Rieti, but asked to
be taken to the hermitage of Fonte Colombo which lies about
an hour's walk to the south of the city, out of Porta Romana.

FONTE COLOMBO

Fonte Colombo stands on a wooded height above a valley
running southward. It is reached by a steep path beside which
are several old shrines, now ruinous, in one of which, the second,
is a half-ruined picture to which one may well return. The
little convent at the far end of the path (it is a long climb), with
the exception perhaps of the cloisters, which may be of the
fourteenth century, is a building, much restored, of the middle
of the fifteenth century when the church was consecrated by
Cardinal Almannus, on July 19, 1450. Over the altar here is a
wooden panel, carved in relief, with the story of the Rule here
dictated to S. Francis by Christ Himself in 1223. To the west
of the church is the Bosco Sacro, over the gate of which we read:
*Solve calceamenta de pedibus tuis, locus enim in quo stas terra sancta
est.*[2]

Close by is the little chapel of S. Mary Magdalen which
traditionally was built by S. Francis. Following the same path,

---

[1] II Celano, cap. 126; Bonaventura V, II. *Legenda Antiqua*, 24.
[2] Exodus iii. 5. The voice of God to Moses out of the burning bush: "Put off
the shoes from thy feet for the place whereon thou standest is holy ground."
When Pope Sixtus IV, a Franciscan, came here as a pilgrim he approached with
bare feet and exclaimed with tears, "This is truly a holy place where religion
blossomed anew and where Almighty God dictated the Rule of the Friars Minor."

which now winds gently downwards under the trees, one comes by a descent of rough stone steps to the grotto or chapel of S. Michael. Within is a rude stone which is said to have served S. Francis as his bed; and close by are the little rock shelters used by Leo and Bonizzo, the saint's companions, in 1223; and beside them the stump of an old ilex which was walled up, as we see it, in 1660.[1]

Another flight of steps leads through a trap-door to a narrow cave, scarcely more than a crack in the solid rock, not three feet wide, but eighteen feet in depth. It was here that S. Francis was inspired to write the Rule of 1223 by Christ Himself.

We call Fonte Colombo the "Franciscan Sinai"; it is called so in the *Actus in Valle Reatina*, and we are used to think of it as though it were a Franciscan sanctuary as ideal and peaceful as Rivotorto. But indeed Fonte Colombo was the scene of the two most tragic passages of his life.

The first of these befell in 1223. The Rule he had written in 1221 was repudiated by the Chapter of that year. The Order was in suspense and confusion. Cardinal Ugolino and Frate Elias persuaded Francis to draw up another Rule and he retired here to Fonte Colombo to do this. He took with him Leo and Bonizzo, who was a jurist, and set to work. We know nothing of this Rule, but in all probability it would have pleased those who had refused the Rule of 1221 as little as that, for when the time came to discuss it, Frate Elias, the Minister-General, to whom it had been given, declared he had lost it.[2]

Francis returned to Fonte Colombo and, again praying and weeping before God, began again in great despondency the task which seemed hopeless. In the midst of this despair he saw one night in a dream some starving brothers who begged him for something to eat. He could find nothing but crumbs, little more than dust. Then he heard a voice: "Francis, from these crumbs make bread so that thy brethren may be nourished." Of course he obeyed. Then he saw some eating greedily of this mysterious bread; others who refused it immediately became lepers. Thus Francis understood that the crumbs were the

[1] The tree was broken by snow in 1645 and was walled up to prevent its being picked to pieces by pilgrims, for it was from this tree the legend has it that Christ confirmed the Rule, as we shall see.
[2] Bonaventura, IV, II.

syllables of the Gospel, that the bread was the Rule and they who refused it were to meet with divine chastisement.[1]

While he therefore continued his work, the Ministers of the Order were asking themselves anxiously what the new Rule would be. What followed is best told in the words of the *Mirror of Perfection*.[2]

After the Rule that the Blessed Francis made was lost he went up into a certain mountain (Fonte Colombo) with Brother Leo of Assisi and Brother Bonizzo of Bologna that he might make another Rule, the which by Christ's teaching he did and made to be written [by Brother Leo]. But the greater part of the Ministers got them together unto Brother Elias that was Vicar of the Blessed Francis and said unto him: "We have heard that this Brother Francis is making a new Rule, but we are fearful lest he should make it too harsh so that we cannot observe it. Wherefore we will that thou go to him and tell him that we will not be bound unto that Rule. Let him make it for himself and not for us." To them Brother Elias made answer that he would not go without them. Whereupon they all of them did go together.

Now when Brother Elias was nigh the place where the Blessed Francis was, Brother Elias called to him. And he making answer and seeing the Ministers, said: "What would these Brethren?" Said Brother Elias: "They be Ministers that have heard how thou makest a new Rule, and being afraid lest thou make it too harsh, do say and protest that they will not be bound by it. Make it, say they, for thyself and not for them."

And the Blessed Francis turning his face toward Heaven spoke unto Christ on this wise: "Lord, said I not well when I told Thee they would not believe me?" Then did all hear the voice of Christ that made answer in the air: "Francis, naught is there of thine own in the Rule, but whatsoever is therein is all Mine and My will it is that thus shall the Rule be observed to the letter, to the letter, to the letter, without gloss, without gloss, without gloss. Let them therefore that are unwilling to keep it depart out of the Order."

Then the Blessed Francis turned towards those Ministers and said, "Ye have heard! Ye have heard! Will ye that I

[1] II Celano, cap. 209.   [2] *Speculum*, I.

LA FORESTA.
Convento di
Santa Maria.

CRECCIO. Convento.

shall make you be spoken to again?" Then the Ministers, rebuking themselves, went away confounded and afraid.[1]

But all was in vain. In May of that year Francis attended the Chapter-General of the Portiuncula where his Rule was considered. A few months later he set out for Rome, where, much retouched, it received a further editing from Cardinal Ugolino. On November 29, Pope Honorius III approved it by his Bull *Solet Annuere* and thenceforth it was the official Rule of the Order.

In the second shrine, on the way up to Fonte Colombo, there is a painting over the altar recording this scene at the Sacro Speco. There we see Christ appearing in the ilex tree and with the open book of the Rule or perhaps of the Gospels, dictating the Rule to S. Francis, who kneels with outstretched hand beneath Him. Behind S. Francis, Bonizzo is kneeling also with uplifted hand, and on the other side of the picture Brother Leo is seated writing down the Rule which Our Lord dictates. In the background are the Ministers, the first of whom, Frate Elias, is about to flee away. Above, on the right hand on the edge of the precipitous rock, is the chapel of S. Mary Magdalen. The picture, at least as we now see it, cannot, I think, be earlier than the sixteenth century; but it may, as has been suggested, explain a fresco in the upper church of San Francesco at Assisi, where S. Francis with uplifted arms is receiving a message from Christ in the clouds, while three friars in fear listen to the words of Our Lord.

The second time, of which we have any definite record, of S. Francis being at Fonte Colombo was even more tragic, for it was thither he was borne, bearing the sacred wounds in his body, and almost blind, when Tebald the Saracen physician to the Papal court was to try his barbarous skill upon him. It was for this purpose, over-persuaded by Ugolino and Elias, he had consented in the year 1225 to come to Rieti. This fearful affair can only be told in the reticent words of Thomas of Celano.[2]

The surgeon came and brought an iron instrument for cauterisation and ordered it to be put into the fire until it

---

[1] *Speculum*, I.   [2] II Celano, cap. 125.

9

should be red-hot. Then the Blessed father to encourage
his body, now shaken by horror, spoke thus to the fire:
"My brother fire, who dost outvie all other things in splendour,
the Most High hath created thee mighty, fair and useful.
Be kind to me at this hour, be courteous for I have loved
thee of old in the Lord. I pray the great Lord who created
thee, to temper thy heat now, so that, burning me gently
I may be able to bear it." Having finished his prayer he
made the sign of the Cross over the fire and thenceforth
remained undismayed. The surgeon took the glowing iron
in his hands: the Brethren yielding to human weakness fled:
the Saint with cheerful readiness exposed himself to the
iron. The iron was plunged hissing into the tender flesh
and the cauterisation was slowly made from the ear to the
eyebrow. What pain that fire inflicted is declared by the
words of the Saint, who knew best what it was; for when the
Brethren who had fled came back the father said with a
smile: "Faint-hearted and poor-spirited ones, wherefore did
ye fly? I tell you of a truth I felt no heat of fire nor any pain
in my flesh." Then turning to the doctor: "If the flesh is
not well burnt," said he, "apply the iron again." The
doctor, whose experience in such cases was very different,
proclaimed this a divine miracle, saying: "I tell you,
Brethren, I have seen wondrous things today." And Thomas
of Celano himself comments: "I believe that the man to
whom at his will cruel things become gentle hath returned to
primal innocence."

Francis experienced a great and supernatural happiness; but
this was his last winter in this world. When spring came
Ugolino and Elias had him taken to Siena where there were
other doctors. He remained there till May, when, a dying man,
he set out on the long journey back to Assisi to die at the
Portiuncula in October.

GRECCIO

Of all these Franciscan sanctuaries in the Valle Santa, the
most charming and the most moving is the Santuario di
Greccio, and I had left it till last. So lovely, so delightful is the
great Conca Reatina that I had spent many weeks in discovering

its beauties, so that it was already late autumn when I set out for Greccio.

The little convent lies in the hills some 600 feet above the valley on the wooded slopes of the western mountains, half an hour's walk from the village of Greccio, which lies slightly higher than and some fourteen *chilometri* from Rieti. It is easy to reach either by road or by the railway, and the views all the way are only less lovely than the magnificent panorama spread out before the sanctuary.

The little convent is of the thirteenth century (1260) and, though a good deal restored and added to, it still retains more than a little of its primitive Franciscan atmosphere and is, I think, of all these Franciscan sanctuaries the nearest to S. Francis. Only the church is disappointing, for it is or appears to be completely modern.

A winding path under the oaks leads up to the convent buildings from the road, and brings you almost at once to the chapel of S. Luke, within which the most famous of all S. Francis's doings took place. Then, entering the convent, one is led to the Dormitorio of S. Francis, now a dark chapel, and the little grottos of his companions. Here and in the bare and humble refectory one finds the primitive *povertà francescana* unspoilt. On the floor above is a chapel in which is a portrait of the saint, an undoubted work of the thirteenth century, though restored much later, and beneath the altar the *ferro da ostie*, the irons for making hosts, which S. Francis himself is said to have used, and certainly of his time. Here too is an enamelled Pax of the fourteenth century and various relics. From the pulpit S. Bernardino is said to have preached, and his chapel is close by, with its small choir, and the Dormitory of S. Bonaventura, the official biographer of the saint. Descending through a trapdoor, one comes into a cave—the Grotto of Blessed John of Parma, who lived here from 1257 to 1289. Such facts, so bare a description, mean little and cannot at all convey the extraordinary atmosphere of the place, its primitive Franciscan peace and evangelical *bona voluntas*.

When S. Francis first came to Greccio he had already built himself a *capanna*, a hut or oratory, high up on Monte San Francesco above the village of Greccio, from which he was

persuaded to descend to preach to the villagers and peasants;
and presently their head man, a certain Giovanni Velita, who
was old and fat, besought him to come down to the village that
he might live and preach there. S. Francis agreed on condition
that he might himself choose the spot for his new hermitage.
And, so the legend goes, he called a small boy to him and,
placing a burning torch in his hand, bade him fling it as far
from him as he was able. The child tossed the torch with all
his might, and it was seen to rush through the air as though
borne by an invisible hand, till it fell on the mountain-side
opposite the village, where it set fire to and consumed the trees
and cleared a space just large enough for a small hermitage.
There the villagers of Greccio dug out in the rocky mountain-
side a number of small cells for S. Francis and his companions.
This is said to have happened in 1217.

Many are the stories about S. Francis at Greccio.

Once when he was staying there, one of the Brethren
brought him a live leveret that had been caught in a snare.
And when the Blessed man saw it he was moved with
compassion and said: "Brother leveret, come to me. Why
didst thou let thyself be so deceived?" And forthwith the
leveret fled to the holy man and without being driven
thither by any one, lay down in his bosom as being the safest
place. When it had rested there a little while, the holy father,
caressing it with maternal affection, let it go, so that it might
freely return to the woodland. At last after the leveret had
been put down many times and had every time returned to
the holy man's bosom, he bade the Brethren carry it into
the wood hard by.[1]

Indeed, as Thomas of Celano tells us, S. Francis was fond of
staying in the hermitage of the brethren at Greccio because he
saw it was "rich in poverty and because in a secluded cell hewn
out of a projecting rock he could more freely devote himself to
heavenly discipline". He delivered the inhabitants from a
multitude of ravening wolves which was devouring not only
their sheep, but often themselves, and this, so he insisted,
because of their own evil habits, which God punished in this

[1] I Celano, XXI, 60.

wise. And when they mended their ways, as the saint foretold, they were delivered from the wolves, and grew rich and fat and fell into worse ways than before and their walled village was destroyed by fire.

And then it was at Greccio this episode described by Thomas of Celano took place:

One Easter day the Brethren at the hermitage of Greccio laid the table more carefully than usual with white table-linen and glass vessels. The father came down from his cell, went to the table and noticed that it was placed on high and decked in vain fashion. But on the smiling table he by no means smiled. Stealthily and gradually he withdrew, put on his head the hat of a poor man who was there and went out of doors, carrying a staff in his hand. He waited outside the door for the Brethren to begin; for they used not to wait for him when he did not come at the signal. When they had begun to eat, that true poor man cried at the door: "For the love of the Lord God give alms to this poor sick pilgrim." The Brethren answered: "Come in, good man, for the love of Him whom thou hast invoked." He came in at once and appeared before them as they were eating. They gave him a dish and sitting alone on the ground he made the ashes his table. What think you was the amazement when he said: "Now I am sitting like a Brother Minor. . . ."

But, of course, the most famous of the scenes at Greccio was that which took place on Christmas Eve, 1223. He had come to Greccio a disappointed man, half in despair about his Order, for the Rule of 1223, edited and emasculated as it had been by Ugolino and Elias, in spite of the vision at Fonte Colombo, had just been sanctioned by Pope Honorius III. He came to Greccio after the long and wearisome business in Rome, and at Greccio he found peace.

About fifteen days before Christmas, S. Francis, being at Greccio, sent for Giovanni, who was devoted to him. To him he said:

"If thou will that we celebrate the festival of the Lord here at Greccio, diligently prepare what I tell thee. For I would make memorial of that Child who was born in Bethlehem and in some sort behold with bodily eyes how He lay in a manger on hay with the ox and the ass standing by."

The day of gladness drew nigh. The Brethren were summoned, the men and women of the place with exulting hearts prepared tapers and torches to illuminate that night which with its radiant star has illuminated all the days and years. At length the saint of God came and finding all things prepared beheld them and rejoiced. The manger had been made ready, the hay was brought, the ox and the ass were led in. Of Greccio there was made as it were a new Bethlehem. The night was lit up as the day, the people came and at this new Mystery rejoiced with new delight. The woodland rang with voices, the rock made answer to the jubilant throng. While the Brethren sang and the night resounded with jubilation, the saint of God stood before the manger overcome with tenderness and filled with wondrous joy. The solemnities of the Mass were celebrated over the manger with new consolation. Vested as a deacon Francis with sonorous voice chanted the Holy Gospel—an earnest, sweet, clear and loud sounding voice. Then he preached to the people who stood around, of the birth of the poor King and the little town of Bethlehem. And often when he would name Christ Jesus aglow with exceeding love, he would call Him the Child of Bethlehem, uttering the word 'Bethlehem' in the manner of a sheep bleating, filling his mouth with the sound but even more himself with sweet affection. Moreover in naming 'Jesus' he would as it were lick his lips savouring the sweetness of that word. And one who stood there saw a wondrous vision, for in the manger he saw a little Child lying asleep to whom the saint of God drew near as though to rouse the Child. . . .

It was hard to drag myself away from Greccio. I lingered on but winter was come, already the great mountains were deep in snow; in that high plateau the wind and the rain often fought furiously and I was scarcely equipped for a winter in such a country. Sometimes the thought came to me to spend Christmas here in the Valle Santa, to assist—too happy thought —at the Midnight Mass in that little Franciscan sanctuary at Greccio with its Christmas ceremony of the *Presepio* which has gone from here all over the Christian world. But as it happened I was destined to spend Christmas in quite another place.

At last I set out. Rome beckoned me to a more accustomed hospitality. Within the walls of the Eternal City winter would lose half its acerbity. So I set out over the rain-drenched Conca Reatina, past the lake of Piediluco, a mirror of azure but a few weeks ago, and now steel-dark and rough with storm. I was glad to see the lights of Terni and happier still when on the following evening I saw the walls of Rome, the broken aqueducts of the Campagna, and Monte Cavo serene and sacred towering over all.

CHAPTER XV

CHRISTMAS IN DOLCEDORME

A H, that Midnight Mass! . . . I am not likely to forget it. I had gone with Ulisse, who guided me through the dark and narrow ways, up to the Collegiata, enthroned above the city, under those enormous and precipitous rocks, like giant's teeth, which distinguish Dolcedorme.

It is a large church, rebuilt after an earthquake, in the seventeenth century; but large and spacious though it was, it was full. And not only of the faithful, not only of the women and the *poveri*. The whole city seemed to be there when the bell sounded for the third time.

In their own place sat the women, young and old, devout enough, and for the most part already on their knees. Behind and about, against the pillars and side-altars, stood the men, a vast crowd. And the noise! The whole church was filled with it, and the air was already stifling.

Over all the rumour came at last the organ. In the *coro* they began to sing *Te Deum*. It was the end of Matins. Mass was about to begin.

Still the people came in under the heavy leather curtains. The church was packed. More candles were lighted: more music poured from the organ. Finally, in procession, behind the great Byzantine cross, came *Sua Eccelenza*—the whole concourse bent like a field of corn under a wind—blessing as he came. He was to sing Mass. Over the Crucifix on the high altar his single candle shone.

Ulisse and I stood before a pillar on the Epistle side, half-way down the great nave. Mass began. *Dominus dixit ad me . . . Kyrie eleison . . . Christe eleison . . . Kyrie eleison.*

Monsignor intoned the *Gloria in excelsis*. The organ burst out into a great peal of music, the bells rang, everyone sang or whistled. . . . Most whistled.

Whistled!

Not with the lips only as one whistles an air, but with the

fingers in the mouth to make a noise, as much noise as possible. Still others had brought whistles with them, and were using them with all their might.

I was astonished. I was scandalised. Surely my ears deceived me. It was so hot and the odour. . . .

But no, the whistling continued. There was Ulisse with both his fists at his mouth, whistling for all he was worth.

Ma come! Was this a theatre or a church? Was this some piece being hooted off the stage or the first Mass of Christmas? I turned to Ulisse:

"*Ma si, signore, di qua e di là si fischia.*"

"They're whistling all over the place!" But why?

There was a little silence; the *Gloria* had finished itself.

Surely Monsignor would not continue? But no, the Mass proceeded as usual. The great Epistle proclaimed Him *qui dedit semetipsum pro nobis, ut nos redimeret ab omni iniquitate.* . . .

The Gospel, known from childhood, unfolded itself from the edict of Caesar Augustus to the peace born on earth to men of good will.

Slowly we came to the Christmas Preface, the Christmas *Sanctus*, sung here to a strange dancing measure as in the picture of Botticelli. I had forgotten the unseemly interruption at the *Gloria*. I had forgotten everything. . . .

There it was again! Suddenly, at the Elevation! But worse than before, more exulting, more joyous, more insolently enthusiastic and rejoicing. It was beyond all possible bounds. In England. . . .

"But what is it, then?" I leant to Ulisse.

"*Ma, signore,* it is the shepherds! *E un pio ricordo dei suoni pastorali quando nacque nostro Signore.*" "A pious remembrance of the shepherds' music when Our Lord was born." But I . . . I, too, would whistle. I . . . I, too, whistled—only the sounds would not come. What could be the matter with my throat?

"*Peccato!*" whispered Ulisse, that one cannot hear also the voice of the ox and the ass.

CHAPTER XVI

FROM NARNI TO ORVIETO

AMELIA AND LUGNANO

I HAD spent most of the winter in Rome, but when April came I returned to Narni, for I wanted to make the journey to Orvieto through Amelia and Lugnano across the uplands which lie between the Nera and the Tiber.

It was a fine spring morning when I set out from Narni, and as I went, there came singing into my mind those lines which open the most beautiful of all the beautiful Odes of Horace:

> *Diffugere nives, redeunt jam gramina oampis,*
> *arboribusque comae;*
> *mutat terra vices et decrescentia ripas*
> *flumina praetereunt;*
> *Gratia cum Nymphis geminisque sororibus audet*
> *ducere nuda choros.*
> *Immortalia ne speres, monet annus et almum*
> *quae rapit hora diem. . . .*[1]

How is it that lines Latin or Greek hammered into one at school, which meant less than nothing to us then, come back to us later with such a rush of emotion, so poignant a meaning as to bring tears to the eyes? Learned mechanically as part of a form "repetition" without a hint of their beauty and forgotten as soon as learned, suddenly they "come home to us", as Newman says, and pierce the heart as almost nothing in our own tongue, familiar and beloved though it be, is able to do. Is this the secret of something we call classical? Does it explain why, when we first see the Parthenon, the great Gothic cathedrals of the Middle Age, all that has been built since antiquity, seem a mistake?

[1] "The snows have fled away, already the grass returns to the fields and the leaves to the trees, the earth is going through her changes and the rivers with declining floods flow past their banks. The Grace ventures nude to lead the choir with the Nymphs and her twin sisters. The Seasons and the hour that robs us of the gracious day warn us not to look for an unending life."

So I went on over the hills, Horace's Ode in my heart and on my lips, often looking back on towered Narni and the broken bridge of Augustus. Yes, the snows were all fled away, already the grass was shining in the fields, the trees were green with the young leaf.

> . . . Thus with the year
> Seasons return . . .

And presently, between the immense horizons, here Monte Soracte rose, there the cone of Monte Cimino, and then before me I saw Amelia towering up on her hill, crowned by her Cathedral and surrounded by her magnificent walls.

Few are they who come to Amelia, which has little but her beautiful self to offer; almost no pictures unless it be the mediocre altarpiece by her son Pier Matteo d'Amelia (*op.* 1467–1508); so sought after in his day and now forgotten. Almost the only picture certainly by his hand is that of a Madonna and Child enthroned between S. John Baptist and S. Francis with a predella containing *tondi* with figures of the Dead Christ and the Virgin and S. John Evangelist, while above in a lunette is God the Father and two angels. This is now here in the Palazzo Comunale. Yet Pier Matteo d'Amelia was a favourite painter of the Popes; he assisted Pintoricchio in his work in the Sistine Chapel and Fra Filippo Lippi in his famous frescoes in the apse of the Cathedral of Spoleto; grew rich and flourished exceedingly. If this work in the Palazzo Comunale is really his it is difficult to understand his reputation, for it is a sentimental mediocre Umbrian picture deriving from Pintoricchio and Antoniazzo Romano. But perhaps the Popes, as our own prelates today, liked mediocrity and sentimentality.

Yes, Amelia is poor in pictures, but in the church of San Francesco there is the tomb of Matteo and Elisabetta Geraldini which might be by Agostino di Duccio so lovely is it, while the church itself, which dates from the thirteenth century, has a fine ruddy façade with a double rose, and a beautiful double cloister of the fifteenth century.

Nor is the Duomo, reconstructed though it has been in the eighteenth century, to be neglected, crowning the little city as it does with its majestic twelve-sided campanile, of the

eleventh century still, as was once the church which it over-
shadows. It is dedicated in honour of S. Fermina, patroness of
the city, who was martyred, bound to a column, which is now
at the right of the entrance. Close by hang two standards taken
from the Turks at the Battle of Lepanto (1527). Here, too,
in the left transept is an altarpiece of the Madonna and Child
with angels, an Umbrian work of the fifteenth century; and
in a chapel here, above the tomb of the Bishop Giovanni
Geraldini, there is a fine bas-relief of the Virgin and Child
with figures of Faith, Hope, Charity and Fortitude. Can they
be by Agostino di Duccio, who was perhaps patronised by the
Geraldini family, one of whose members, Alessandro Geraldini,
was the first Bishop of San Domingo in the Americas in the
beginning of the sixteenth century?

There are several palaces here, the finest of which is the
Palazzo Farrattini, which may well have been built by
Antonio Sangallo the younger, as local tradition has it. In the
Piazza Grande, too, still stands the medieval Tribune from
which the herald of the Commune once proclaimed the official
edicts. Then there is the Palazzo Nacci of the fifteenth century,
with its fine portal and cortile and loggia, and the Palazzo
Petrignani of the sixteenth century, with its frescoes of the
school of Zuccari.

And, of course, Amelia is not without its memories of
S. Francis. Just outside the great walls, without Porta Romana,
is the little church of Santa Maria ad Quinque Fontes, Santa
Maria delle Cinque they call it. Here, local tradition insists,
S. Francis preached to the people of Amelia in 1213. The little
church is scarcely more than a small chapel and within are
votive frescoes which no doubt date from the fourteenth or
fifteenth century.

I went on over the mountains along the same wonderful road,
through a richly cultivated or wooded country, to Lugnano.
I passed the Fosso Grande among the ilexes and wondered if
it was here the *popolo Amerino* grew their osiers of which Virgil
speaks in the Georgics:

Atque Amerina parant lentae retinacula viti.

Today they boast of their plums which I was too early to enjoy

I passed Porchiano quite surrounded by low walls and round towers, and, presently, not Cimino only but Montefiascone I saw, a pale city shining on high; and so I came to Lugnano, Città della Teverina, on its isolated hill, very imposing with its medieval walls, its ancient houses and, as I was soon to know, its magnificent Romanesque church of Santa Maria Assunta.

This church, with its beautiful portico and architrave, upheld by four columns and two mighty piers at the ends, seemed to me the most entirely Roman of all the churches of Umbria. The portico resembles that of San Giorgio in Velabro in Rome; and above, in the façade, a magnificent rose with two windows on either side recalled to me the façade of San Pietro in Toscanella. It is all of the second half of the twelfth century and unspoilt. What is curious is the arches above the architrave. This portico was once adorned with mosaic work of the Cosmati school. Under it are two reliefs of the Visitation and S. Michael.

Within, the church is divided into three naves by columns, and the pavement, now in ruin, was once of Cosmatesque mosaic. Over an altar on the right is a late work by Niccolò da Foligno. It is a triptych of the Madonna and Child enthroned and surrounded by angels and at the sides S. Francis and S. Sebastian. The noble crypt, upheld by ten columns, with its windows, still adorned with the mosaics of the Cosmati school and its wonderfully sculptured screen, contains many remains of its Romanesque sculptures, of high importance, I should suppose, in the history of the art of the twelfth century. To see this church is alone worth the journey from Narni, though the road were dreary instead of one of the most surprising in Umbria.

About a quarter of a mile outside Lugnano to the south is the church of San Francesco. It dates from 1229 with the convent, and stands on the spot where, according to local tradition, S. Francis performed a remarkable miracle very characteristic of him. For, as he stood preaching, a wolf leapt out of the surrounding woodland and seized a small child, standing there listening with its mother. The woman screamed and Francis, seeing what had happened, turned to heaven. At that moment a flock of wild geese passed over and the saint commanded them to descend and liberate the child. And so it was, for they attacked the wolf with so great fury that he dropped his prey and made off into the woodland. *Se non è vero.* . . . I have related this legend very baldly, but if you wish the full details you must consult Gonzaga's *De origine Seraphicae Religionis*, published in Rome in 1587.

I say that the Via Amerina is one of the most surprising in Umbria, but the full splendour of it lies between Lugnano and Orvieto. I only stopped once on the way, at Alviano,[1] to see in the Pieve the altarpiece by Niccolò da Foligno of the Madonna in glory surrounded by musical angels and crowned by cherubim, a work which seems to look back to Benozzo Gozzoli, though signed and dated 1484.

But it was the road that enchanted me. There, as from a lofty terrace over the Tiber valley, I could survey the world from Monte Soracte in the Campagna on the verge of the Patrimony to Mont' Amiata in the Senese. That was what lay before me along the twenty miles or so between Lugnano and Orvieto, till I descended into the Paglia valley and the evening light struck the mosaics of the Cathedral of Orvieto on its isolated pedestal of tufa and I went up to the city by its so long drawn out approach in the twilight.

[1] Here it was that S. Francis bade the swallows to be silent that were building their nests in the Castello, so that he might preach, and they obliged him (I Celano, cap. 21). The Towered fifteenth-century Castello, which is the main feature of the place, belonged to the Doria Pamphili. It contains a seventeenth-century fresco representing the miracle of S. Francis.

CHAPTER XVII

ORVIETO

THE CATHEDRAL AND THE CITY

D'ANNUNZIO has well described Orvieto: "Imagine a rock in the middle of a melancholy valley, and on the top of the rock a city, so deathly silent as to give the impression of being uninhabited—every window closed—grass growing in the dusty grey streets—a Capuchin friar crosses a piazza—a priest descends from a closed carriage in front of a hospital, all in black, and with a decrepit old servant to open the door; here a tower against the white rain-sodden clouds— there a clock slowly striking the hour, and suddenly at the end of a street, a miracle—the Duomo!"

Peace and silence: that is what the traveller will find in Orvieto, for far from the contemporary uproar she still dreams of the miracle of Bolsena which her Cathedral was built to commemorate. It happened thus: a certain German priest had come as far as the little town of Bolsena on his way to Rome, where he hoped, in the capital of his religion, to set at rest his doubts of the Real Presence of Our Lord in the Blessed Sacrament. Resting there for a day on the shores of the beautiful lake, he at the request of the people said Mass for them in the church of Santa Cristina. And although S. Cristina is rejected by all authority, she has her lovers in the sweet Umbrian country, who will never forget her; and perhaps for their love she brought these things to pass, being in heaven at the time. For it happened that when our German doubter elevated the Host, more than ever troubled in his mind concerning the doctrine that none of these simple folk in the church there thought of doubting for a moment, he saw drops of blood upon the Corporal, "each stain severally assuming the form of a human head with features like the Volto Santo—the face of our Saviour". Oh, wonderful! What shame in his heart, what anger at his doubts, what love, what certainty, what gladness! Overcome by fear and reverence, he, sinner that he was, dared

not consume the Holy Species; but with eagerness, with love
reserved the Body of Our Lord, and set out in haste for Orvieto
where the Pope then was, and, not without shame, confessed to
him not only the miracle, but his doubts also. The Bishop o
Orvieto, at the command of the Pope, hastened to Bolsena and
brought from the altar of Santa Cristina the Sacred Host and
the Blessed Corporal. The Pope himself—Urban IV it was—
passed with all his court and clergy, with joy, with music in
procession to meet him, who indeed bore Christ along with him

Thus, according to the legend, was instituted by Pope Urban IV
in 1264 the magnificent feast of Corpus Christi whose office
S. Thomas Aquinas the Angelic Doctor composed. Twenty-six
years later, in 1290, on the highest point of the city of Orvieto
Pope Nicholas IV laid the first stone of the glorious Cathedral
of Santa Maria we see, on the site of two ancient churches, San
Costanzo del Capitolo and Santa Maria del Vescovo, and there
in was erected in the left transept the Cappella del Corporale
where in a marvellous enamelled casquet by Ugolino di Maestro
Vieri was placed the Blessed Corporal stained with the blood
of Our Lord.[1]

The Cathedral, built to commemorate this miracle, is the mos
beautiful in Umbria, and the flaming façade is perhaps the
loveliest in Italy. The church stands on a marble platform in
a wide piazza. Facing it are the Palazzo Faina and the Palazzo
dell' Opera del Duomo, founded in 1359, with a great Baroque
façade of the seventeenth century, then the Ospedale. To the
right of the great church is the Palazzo Papale, or Apostolico
built in 1297 by Boniface VIII and now the Museo dell' Opera
and behind it the Palazzo Vescovile, which was restored in 145·
by Nicholas V, and again in the sixteenth century.

We do not know who the architect of the Cathedral may have
been, but among those who worked upon it were the Cos
matesque marble craftsmen, and Arnolfo di Cambio and Rosse
da Perugia, under the direction of Frate Bevignate.

The glory of the Duomo is of course the façade, which wa
perhaps first imagined by Arnolfo di Cambio with but a single
and central pediment or gable; but in 1310 the Sienese master

---

[1] This reliquary is sometimes called "Tabernaculum DNJC", or "Tabernacol
del Corpo di Xpo".

ORVIETO. San Domenico: Arnolfo di Cambio, Tomb of Cardinal De Braye

ORVIETO. Opera del Duomo: Luca Signorelli, Self-portrait.

Lorenzo Maitani, gave it the three triangular pediments we see, and its marvellous colour and decoration in mosaic and sculpture, between 1327 and 1337; and his work was continued by Andrea Pisano, Orcagna and others till 1388. The uppermost story was added by Antonio Federighi of Siena (1444–90).

The sculptures in bas-relief on the façade were executed between 1310 and 1327, in part by Lorenzo Maitani and in part under his supervision. They belong therefore to the golden age of the art of Siena, the age of Duccio, Simone Martini and the Lorenzetti. They are perhaps the greatest achievement of the Sienese school of sculpture and are among the most lovely things in Italy. They owe something to the influence of Giovanni Pisano, but, as with all Sienese work, we find a satisfaction with mere splendour and grace, and rather a desire for beauty than for life or action.

The whole story of the Creation and the Fall of Man is represented on this façade. A little conventionally, you might say, these Sienese artists deal with their art, and yet what pathos in that figure of Adam whom God approaches so eagerly, so graciously in the garden. The astonished angels wait, with how profound an agitation, for this new thing. And again, when that deep sleep fell upon our father, and God with blessing—for He does bless her—draws woman from his side, and two angels hesitate in the garden among the trees, the one seeming to tell the other of all that had gone before, when Adam lay a marvellous shape of dust waiting the touch of the finger of God; as you look on this sublime scene the picture of Michelangelo comes to you as he painted this very thing on the ceiling of the Sistine Chapel. There Adam, half alive, lies over the world and stretches out his finger—how languidly—to touch the finger of God; he is almost unconscious, still wrapped round by dreams, yet a touch of the finger-tips will suffice to awaken him to life itself, and all that God holds, woman and the future, in the fold of His garment. But here Christ is the chief figure in that act of creation, God the Father being represented by a hand, while the Holy Spirit in the form of a Dove with outspread wings hovers over the waters and the earth amid the stars.

Sienese work though this is, there is energy and realism in that figure of Adam, where he stands with Eve for a moment

10

beneath the Tree of Knowledge, and God, with a kind of severity, forbids them to eat of that fruit. Eve listens with a curious meekness, an easy acquiescence. But Adam stands at his full height and looks God in the eyes as a beloved son, and really understands that this tree which he touches with his fingers bears the forbidden fruit. Here is a poem as noble as Milton's *Paradise Lost*.

And in the relief of the Resurrection, the people crowd, they press forward with passion towards the light, herded almost by their angels in the first dazzling ecstasy of the resurrection. In the lower part again they struggle and thrust aside the stones of their graves. Many have already stepped half out before they have succeeded in thrusting away the lid of the tomb— thrusting it away for ever.

In the relief of the Hell a brutal emotion, half-hideous laughter, half despair and weeping, has swept over these poor people tortured by devils. Their fate has driven them mad; they no longer feel anything but terror, while the Vine that is Christ, loaded with fruit, sweeps upwards, for ever beyond the gaze of their agonised eyes.

But Lorenzo Maitani, that great artist, was not content to design the façade and to cover it with reliefs; he designed the mosaics also. He set up a *fabbrica* of mosaic in Orvieto in 1321, and the early mosaic pictures on the lower part of the façade were executed by him or under his supervision. This work was continued by his son Vitale, by Andrea Orcagna, and by other great artists. But of the early mosaics that adorned the façade not a vestige now remains. It was not until the year 1570, two hundred and sixty years after Maitani had begun the work, that the façade was completed. Only one important alteration was made in the original design, and that was the work of another Sienese, Antonio Federighi, in the middle of the fifteenth century. Already, in 1417, more than thirty years before Federighi took office, proposals had been made for a change in the design. Finally, in the year 1450, Isaia da Pisa had been commissioned to make a new design for the uppermost storey of the façade. The design this artist provided was the cause of great controversy, not settled until after Federighi became *capo-maestro* in the year 1451. Federighi finally decided to raise the

height of the central gable of the façade, by inserting a row of
niches above the circular window similar to those Maitani had
placed on each side of it. He also increased the height of the
pinnacles which flanked the central gable. Thus he gave the
façade a more imposing appearance than it would have presented had Maitani's final design been carried out. For the
rest, the façade today differs in no very important particular
from that designed in the fourteenth century.

Within, the great church is generally found to be a disappointment. Of course, the glorious façade has no co-ordination with
it, but this great bare Romanesque interior, full of light as it is,
spacious too, recommended itself to me, and I have come to love
it for just these two Latin qualities—spaciousness and light. It is
260 feet long and nearly 100 feet wide, divided into three naves
by ten columns and two piers, black and white in colour, with
fine capitals. The ten chapels along the nave are semicircular
and there is a door in both aisles. The choir and sanctuary are
higher than the nave and the two transept chapels are later
additions. The simple coloured roof is unpretentious, even
charming.

Just within the great doors in the central nave we come upon
Antonio Federighi's holy water stoup of the fifteenth century
and the font, originally a sixteenth-century work and surmounted by a pyramid and a statue of the Baptist which
replaces, as it is said, the lost figure by Donatello. Opposite is
a spoiled fresco by Gentile da Fabriano of the Virgin and Child.

The choir is filled with fine stalls of the fourteenth century and
painted in fresco with scenes from the life of the Blessed Virgin
by Ugolino di Prete Ilario of Orvieto (fourteenth century) and
with two scenes of the Annunciation and the Visitation painted
a century later by Antonio da Viterbo.

The great chapel on the left, which with the equally large
chapel on the right forms a sort of transept, is the Cappella del
Corporale. The chapel is covered with frescoes by Ugolino di
Prete Ilario, telling the story of the miracle of Bolsena. In a
magnificent reliquary over the altar is venerated the Corporal
of the miracle stained with Christ's blood, and for this the chapel
was built in 1350. The reliquary, which is not easy to see, is
perhaps the finest example in Italy of medieval goldsmith's

work, covered with enamels by Ugolino di Maestro Vieri. It is of silver-gilt repoussé and chased, architectural in the form of the façade of the Cathedral, with a wealth of translucent enamels which tell the story of the miracle of Bolsena. It was commissioned in 1337 by Bishop Traino Monaldeschi and is dated 1338, when it was finished for the feast of Corpus Christi. Ugolino had assistants, and he and they made the reliquary of copper gilt for the head of S. Savino, now in the Museo dell' Opera.

On the right of the chapel was a great fourteenth-century panel picture of the Madonna della Misericordia, with the full-length figure of the Virgin surrounded by angels and with a great crowd of kneeling suppliants at her feet. It is now in the choir. This is one of the best of Lippo Memmi's works, painted when he was most under the influence of Simone Martini, full of expression and with a suavity of design characteristic of Simone. Mysterious and lovely, the Madonna with hands joined seems to pray for us and to receive our prayers, while companies of angels guard her round about, and at her feet kneel—is it the people of Orvieto or some religious confraternity of which she was the patroness? The beautiful iron gates and screen here are the work of Giovanni di Michele of Orvieto in 1366.

In a subterranean chapel under the Cappella del Corporale there is a fine fresco of the Crucifixion by Cola di Petrucciolo of Orvieto dated 1380.

On the opposite side of the church, forming as it were the right transept, is the large Cappella Nuova, now called the Cappella della Madonna di San Brizio, from the fourteenth-century altarpiece of the Madonna and Child enthroned with angels. It was built in 1409, and in 1447 Fra Angelico was called upon to decorate it in fresco. He was at work in Rome at the time, but agreed to spend the three hottest months of each year—June, July and August—in Orvieto till the work was finished. He took with him his assistants, Benozzo Gozzoli and Giovanni di Antonio. As it turned out, however, he only remained in Orvieto for about three months in all and was unfortunate from the outset. One of his helpers fell from the scaffolding and was killed and then humidity damaged much of his painting. He finished two of the four triangles of the vault, but they have been much repainted and seem even originally to have been as much the work of Benozzo as of Beato Angelico. When the Beato went away never to return, Benozzo continued to work here till 1449. Only in the heads of some of the prophets may we find the hand of Fra Angelico, though no doubt the scheme and design are his.

In the last year but one of the fifteenth century, Luca Signorelli was appointed to decorate the chapel, and he filled it with the greatest and most dramatic works even he was ever to create; indeed, except in the Sistine Chapel, no such work is to be found in Italy for imaginative power and technical excellence. "These masterpieces," wrote Morelli, "appear to me unequalled in the art of the fifteenth century, for to no other contemporary painter was it given to endow the human frame with a like degree of passion, vehemence and strength."

Signorelli filled the vaulting left vacant by Angelico and Benozzo Gozzoli with figures of the Apostles, the symbols of the Passion, the Fathers of the Church, and so forth, but below he has painted in seven frescoes of the end of the world: the Coming of Antichrist, the Crowning of the Elect, the Resurrection, the Judgment, Heaven, Hell and the Destruction of the World.

"For his divine work of the Last Judgment in the Sistine Chapel, Michelangelo," says Vasari, "courteously availed himself to a certain extent of the invention of Signorelli as, for example, in the angels and demons and some other parts where he imitated the mode of treatment adopted by Luca as may be seen by everyone." In looking at this work here in Orvieto it is perhaps a question whether Michael borrowed to advantage.

Nothing more extraordinarily thoughtful and subtle, nothing more masterly than the Antichrist is to be found in Michelangelo's Last Judgment. So like to Christ as indeed always to be mistaken for Him from a distance, Antichrist has all the beauty, all the cynical hatred of mankind, which listens to him in adoration that, after Luca has suggested it to us, we might expect. It is hardly necessary, one might say, for the devil to whisper to him; in his heart all the cruelty and villainy of the universe have been sown and have come to flower. Opposite, the fresco of the Resurrection, with its huge naked angels sounding their death-destroying trumpets, decked with the banner of the Cross, crushes us beneath its tremendous power. Visions as splendid as those of Dante dawn upon him—the Punishment of the Wicked, the Reward of the Blessed, and Paradise, Heaven and Hell. With his overwhelming vision as our companion, we walk the streets of Orvieto, ever finding it necessary to return again to the Cappella della Madonna di S. Brizio, where above the poets of Greece and Rome and Italy we see the tragedy of our world, the drama of the soul of man.

On the right of the Cathedral rises the Palazzo Papale, a magnificent building originally dating from very early times, added to in 1264 and finally built by Boniface VIII in 1297. It was restored in 1896 and is now the Museo dell' Opera. One climbs the great flight of steps and comes into a vast salone crowded with works of art, among which are various drawings for the façade of the Duomo. The most attractive and perhaps the most important things here are a number of panels by Simone Martini and a self-portrait by Signorelli.

The panels are the dismembered parts of a polyptych which is signed and dated 1320. A good deal of discussion has arisen round these panels, and many critics believe them to be rather the work of Lippo Memmi than of his kinsman Simone. At any rate, these panels are less exquisite and more monumental than Simone's other paintings, but there can, I think, be little doubt that the central panel of the Madonna and Child is Simone's. Of the four side-panels of SS. Peter, Paul, Dominic and the Magdalen, three are looking the same way, so that there must be, one would think, two panels missing. Two of these side-panels are not equal in quality to the central panel of the Virgin and Child, but the panels of SS. Peter and Paul seem unquestionably to be from Simone's own hand. Such seems to be the general opinion, though Mr. Berenson, probably more wisely, gives all to Simone, for why should we insist or expect that a master should always be at the top of his form or always paint in exactly the same way? In a corner of the Magdalen panel the Bishop of Soana appears as donor, and this panel therefore must have stood next to the central Madonna.

Signorelli had painted a full-length portrait of himself in sombre black in the fresco of Antichrist in the Cappella della Madonna di S. Brizio. Here in the Museo we have a double portrait of himself, the painter of the chapel and of Niccolò Franceschi, the treasurer of the Cathedral. These portraits are entirely untouched and therefore of high importance. On the back, Signorelli has signed the portraits with a long Latin inscription composed by Niccolò beginning: LUCAS SIGNORELLUS NATIONE YTALVS PATRIA CORTONESIS ARTE PICTURE EXIMIUS MERITO APELLI CONPARADUS . . . ALEXANDRO VI° PON. MAX. SEDENTE ET MAXIMIANO IIII INPERIANTE ANO SALUTIS M°CCCCC° TERTIO KALENDAS IANVARIAS.

The portraits are on tile or brick. Signorelli appears in the prime of life, full of vitality and determination.

The other work here by this great master is a large painting in oil of S. Mary Magdalen, inscribed and dated 1504. This is an altarpiece from the Cathedral. The saint is represented life-size and the picture is broadly painted, indeed even coarse in execution, though powerful enough. The Magdalen wears a resplendent garment wonderfully embroidered in gold, with a brown mantle lined with green.

Among the most lovely objects in this rather heterogeneous collection, the wonderfully beautiful gilded reliquary of S. Savino, with its translucent enamels by Ugolino di Maestro Vieri, the goldsmith of the Reliquiario del Corporale in the Cathedral, should not be missed. This reliquary of S. Savino is said to have been asked of him as a test of his ability before the commission for the great Reliquiario was given him. It is a beautiful work of the goldsmith's art. I found in the lower salone of the Museo the dismembered tomb of the Cardinal De Braye, a master work by Arnolfo di Cambio. But I prefer to write of it as I have always known it in its place in the church of San Domenico whither presumably it will return.

There is here, too, a wealth of magnificent Church vestments and embroideries, among them some after the designs of Botticelli, of the Circumcision, Resurrection and Assumption of the Blessed Virgin.

I came upon another work by Signorelli in the Romanesque

church of San Rocco in the Piazza del Popolo. It is a fresco of S. Mary of Egypt. And wandering from church to church, in San Giovenale, a very ancient foundation on the edge of the city to the north-west, I found a lovely if greatly damaged fresco, perhaps by Cola di Petruccioli, of the Annunciation and the Nativity, exquisite as a wild flower. The church is full of fourteenth-century frescoes, and I spent an hour there among them.

In San Lodovico in Piazza dei Ranieri, also to the west of the city, is a very curious Banner of the Innocents painted in 1410 by Andrea di Giovanni of Orvieto. Above is a bust of Our Lord surrounded by four cherubim. Below in the midst of a mandorla of angels with the Lamb beneath is Christ again, as a boy. About the mandorla are the symbols of the four Evangelists and groups of aureoled saints, and below again two groups of the Holy Innocents, their wounds upon them, adoring the boy Jesus. The picture is signed and dated 1410. It is a curious rather than a beautiful work.

The church of San Lorenzo in Arari, at the south-west corner of the city, in a piazza bearing its name at the end of Via Ippolito Scalza, is a recently restored building full of restored frescoes; that in the semicircular apse, of Our Lord enthroned between Our Lady, S. Laurence, S. John Evangelist and S. Francis, would seem to be originally of the thirteenth century. Here is the most interesting thing in the church, a ciborium of the twelfth century over an Etruscan altar; but it too has been restored.

The church of San Domenico is on the other side of the city in the Piazza Roma. It was built in the first half of the thirteenth century, and is said to be the first dedicated in honour of the founder of the Dominican Order. It has, however, been restored often, and was dismantled in the war of 1939–45. The nave has become part of the Accademia Femminile and the transept and apse which still remain, I suppose, a church, are all upside down. Its fine Gothic portal does not belong to it, but was brought here from Santo Spirito outside the city.

The church, which is in so regrettable a state, ought to be famous, for it was in the convent here S. Thomas Aquinas composed the Office of Corpus Christi by order of Urban IV.

The only treasure left it, and that was dismantled in the war and taken to the Museo dell' Opera, is the masterpiece of Arnolfo di Cambio, the tomb of Cardinal De Braye, who died here in 1282. This magnificent work is signed HOC OPUS FECIT ARNOLFUS, but he did not originate the form. The tomb of Cardinal De Braye is only a development of that built for Pope Clement IV in Viterbo by Petrus Oderisi, who probably built the tomb of Henry III in Westminster Abbey. It is fortunate in that some of its sculptures have been preserved, though it has lost the trefoil tabernacle that was its original framework. When it was perfect it must have been a most beautiful harmony of mosaic and sculpture, surpassing all the known tombs of the Popes. The lower basement supported the two shafts of the canopy, now destroyed. The effigy of the Cardinal lies on a draped sarcophagus; above it is a pointed roof from which hang curtains drawn away to disclose the effigy, by two angels. Over the canopy is, in the centre, an inscription, and above, in a pointed niche, is a group of the Madonna and Child, on one side of which is a figure of the kneeling Cardinal presented by S. Paul, and on the other S. Dominic.

But Orvieto is not only a city of many beautiful things, it is also full of curiosities, such as Etruscan remains and charms, an archaic Greek Aphrodite and the well of S. Patrick, built by Sangallo in 1527 for Clement VII, who after the sack of Rome had come to Orvieto for safety. In order to ensure the supply of water in case of siege on this tufa hill, he had this strange well made. It is 62 metres in depth and is like the Tower of Pisa buried in the earth, save that there are two stairways, the one above the other. Looking down, one sees the water at the bottom like a perfect small jewel.

But, after all, it is not in such mere curiosities as this that the charm of Orvieto lies, but in herself isolated on that barren precipitous rock of volcanic tufa. Reached as she now is from the railway by a funicular lift, the traveller little understands how difficult she is to approach. But he who comes from the valley by the road that winds for miles up her tufa hill, continually asks himself where is the city, where is Orvieto?—completely hidden as she is. And so he may even yet understand that she was a city of refuge. Yet whether under the Monaldeschi or the Popes or the Neapolitan king, always her streets ran with blood—it is as though it were her symbol. And at last there came to her the very Blood of Christ. She remains the city of that miracle and mystery and at Corpus Christi the whole city, led by great prelates, goes out in procession to meet Him, opens her gates to receive Him with joy, and seems to pass into the great Cathedral with Him, and even yet to be hanging on His words and kissing His feet and hands and waiting for His blessing. And Orvieto, with finger on lip, pale and immaculate over her melancholy valley, waits for that Voice as of many waters.

QU'EST-CE QUE C'EST Q'UN MIRACLE?

It happened that one summer morning, long ago, Padre Bernardino and I were standing together in the Cappella del Corporale in the Cathedral looking at that marvellous reliquary of silver-gilt goldsmith's work with its twelve scenes of the miracle of Bolsena in translucent enamels, the work of Ugolino di Maestro Vieri of Siena in 1338. We had been visiting some Franciscan sanctuaries in the neighbourhood and had come to Orvieto because Padre Bernardino, who had a friend in the Cathedral, hoped to be able to show me the great reliquary without my having to pay the very large fee demanded for a sight of it. In this he had been successful.

As we examined this masterpiece of medieval art, repoussé and chased, in the form of the façade of the Cathedral, more than four feet high and two feet wide, shining and glowing with its enamels, we were joined by two of my fellow countrymen, in appearance Dons of some University. They stood there looking at the Reliquary, till one of them, shutting his guide-book, turned to me and asked:

"What is the Miracle of Bolsena?"

When I had told him as briefly as I could, I went on to explain how fortunate we were, owing to Padre Bernardino's kindness, to see this great masterpiece of goldsmithery out of its shrine of marble mosaic.

Presently we all turned away down the nave discussing the story of the miracle; and seeing that Padre Bernardino, in his

brown habit, was my companion, one of the strangers, having
no Italian, I suppose, as we came out into the piazza suddenly
broke into French and half turning to Padre Bernardino
demanded:

"*Qu'est-ce que c'est q'un miracle?*"

Turning to me Padre Bernardino said in his charming English:
"Do you tell him what is a miracle."

"But, Father," said I, "I am no theologian. Still I should say
a miracle is a manifestation of the power of God."

"*Caro figlio,*" he replied, "that is precisely true."

"Your religion," said the other stranger to Padre Bernardino,
when he found he spoke English, "your religion is all compact
of miracles, is it not? For instance its central doctrine, Transubstantiation?"

"That, *caro signore,*" said Padre Bernardino, "is not a miracle."

In passing across the piazza we had come to a caffè and the
strangers suggested we should sit down and take something to
drink. When we were sipping our *espresso:*

"You say," said he who had demanded to know what is a
miracle, "you say that Transubstantiation is not a miracle.
How is that? If this business of Bolsena is a miracle how can
Transubstantiation not be a miracle? Both are surely equally
incredible—as far as reason goes?"

"*Caro signore,*" said Padre Bernardino, nursing his cup of
coffee, "though Transubstantiation is a wonderful work of
Divine grace and above the power of nature and is due to God
alone, it is not a miracle, for miracles are by definition apparent.
The change of the substance of the bread and the wine in
the Eucharist is not apparent. If it becomes apparent as in what
you call, *caro signore*, this 'business of Bolsena', that is a miracle.
A miracle must be manifest, must be apparent to the senses."

"You speak, Father," said the first stranger, "of Transubstantiation as being above the power of nature, but surely all the
world is agreed nowadays that whatever happens is natural,
and that what is not natural does not happen. A miracle, as you
define it, is surely unnatural and therefore does not happen."

Padre Bernardino raised his hand:

"Your views, *caro signore*, rest upon the assumption that the
material universe alone exists. That is not so. Besides there are

many events which your scientists recognise as inexplicable by any known law of nature, but their inability to find a scientific explanation is no reason for denying the existence of an event if it is adequately attested."

The stranger was very patient:

"But, Father, it is certain that the uniformity of nature rules out miracles, which if they happened would be a violation of natural law. Is that not so?"

"And you yourself, *caro signore*," said Padre Bernardino, "are you not accustomed to violating, as you say, the natural law? When you throw a ball into the air you 'violate' the law of gravity, but do not thereby disarrange the order of nature. A new force appears and counteracts the natural forces. The analogy from the act of throwing a ball to the act of God is complete as far as concerns your 'break in the uniformity of nature' or 'a violation of its laws'. "

There was a brief silence. Then the first stranger turned to Padre Bernardino:

"So, Father, you really believe in the miracle of Bolsena?"

"I do not say that. I am not compelled to believe it. It depends on the evidence. But on the other hand, I see no reason which compels me to refuse to believe it."

"You are, I think," said the other, "compelled to believe in the resurrection of the body, Father. Is that a miracle?"

"It will be a miracle when it happens," said Padre Bernardino.

"There," said his interlocutor with a laugh, "there I agree with you."

But Padre Bernardino beamed on him, and then finished his coffee.

"It may surprise you, *caro signore*," he said, "when I tell you that through the infinite power and grace of God, I have myself performed a miracle. Oh, only a little one, a mere bagatelle. Permit, that I tell you how it happened."

"But I thought," said the first stranger, "it was only saints who were supposed to work miracles."

"You are mistaken, *caro signore*. Even the simplest and rudest of the faithful may sometimes, though rarely, by the power of Christ's grace, perform these wonders. But let me tell you of my own experience.

"It befell in one of our smallest and most humble *santuarii*, with but half a dozen *frati* in occupation. I was on a visit there and very uncomfortable I found it, for the place was subject to a diabolical infestation and within the limits permitted by God, was all but uninhabitable. Everything possible had been tried, the whole place had been washed out with holy water, scrubbed with soap, even lime-washed, and it stank of paraffin, but still it swarmed—swarmed with bugs, hundreds, thousands, myriads of bugs. As one lay on one's bed they came over the pillow in mass formation, as one sat at table they were climbing up the table legs and dropping from the ceiling.

"What to do? I conferred with the Padre Guardiano; we considered the house to be diabolically possessed and I decided —the powers having been duly accorded me—to resort to Exorcism.

"I prepared holy water, salt and oil, and very early in the morning after a sleepless night I began the rite

> *Exorciso vos immundissimi . . .*
> *Adjuro vos per judicem vivorum et mortuorum . . .*

At the third *Exorcismus*—

> *Adjuro ergo vos omnes immundissimi . . .*

there was seen to be a long dark line some four or five inches in width, like the *serpens antiquus* of the exorcism, winding and un-dulating and throbbing along the passage-way out of the door into the olive garden. It consisted of thousands, myriads of bugs. Under the olives they went, through the grove and up over the rough wall of stones, out of the convent *podere*. That night we slept, that day we ate, in peace."

But this was too much for our hosts, who suddenly seemed to have had enough of Padre Bernardino. They rose, paid for our refreshment and departed. We both watched them as they went.

Then I turned to that triumphant fountain of irony and remembering past admonishments wickedly said:

"Humility is rare, is it not, among the learned?"

He caught my eye. Then gazing after the strangers now almost out of sight, Padre Bernardino murmured:

"And even rarer among the ignorant."

BOLSENA

As you come over that wonderful road with its great view of mountain and vale from the city of Orvieto to the city of the miracle, to Bolsena among its vineyards, perhaps past Bagnorea, where the author of the *Legenda di San Francesco*, whom we know as S. Bonaventura, was born, something of that ancient mystery seems still to invest the little city, so languid, so fantastic in its beauty, in a silence so profound, a light, a sunshine so subtle. Forlorn upon her lovely lake, with its islands, on one of which Amalasuntha was done to death by her Gothic assassins, over the pale green water there came to her a whisper of that Mystery which has confounded the world; a Presence hidden in such absolute, simple, elementary things as bread and wine, changed into His subtile life, His perfect beauty —a thing too beautiful to be untrue, apprehended as it were, though dimly during countless centuries—the God hidden in the vine, the divine nature of the bread of life. And indeed this country—volcanic, tawny and ardent, strewn with strange rocks of basalt in the mysterious shapes of temples, here a quincunx, there a triangle or circle—seems to have been created for the manifestation of some divine thing beyond our understanding. Doubtless the miracle of the Corpus Christi was not the first that happened here. Cristina, saint and martyr, though without the Roman Calendar, had seen angels hovering over that pallid lake, had talked with them and they had clothed her at last in a wonderful white garment, as she was almost sinking in its waters with a great stone tied about her neck by her murderers. And yet, as ever happens in the lives of the saints, so disappointingly, so dishearteningly, though God Himself intervene, of all not one but in the end died the victim of his foes. It is but for a moment that heaven interposes between the saints and death; in the end martyrdom, only delayed by God's menace, has its way with them. So it was with Cristina. Three times the angels saved her only to let her perish at last by a far more terrible death than drowning.

It is in her church, a building of the eleventh century, we find the Cappella del Miracolo, where the still blood-stained marble of the altar is venerated, on which the doubting priest said the Mass that created the Cathedral of Orvieto and the feast of Corpus Christi, and in allusion to which Raphael painted the sublime fresco of the Disputa in the Vatican.

The finest work of art in the church of Santa Cristina is the altarpiece by Sano di Pietro, a triptych with the Madonna and Child enthroned in the centre and at the sides SS. George, Peter, Paul and Cristina. A figure of S. Dominic in adoration has been added in the seventeenth century. Above we see the Annunciation and a *tondo* of the Saviour. In the predella the half-length figures of the dead Christ, the Virgin and S. John are by Sano, but the other panels with scenes from the legend of S. George are perhaps by Benvenuto di Giovanni.

During the residence of Cardinal Giovanni de' Medici, afterwards Pope Leo X, as Papal Legate in Bolsena in 1512, he commissioned Giovanni della Robbia to make the Tabernacle with the Christ-Child standing on the Sacramental Chalice with hand raised in blessing, which was originated by Desiderio da Settignano in his Tabernacle in San Lorenzo in Florence. Giovanni's assistants or pupils are answerable for the relief of the Madonna and Saints over the entrance to the church, the S. Leonardo and two penitents over the sacristy door and the altarpiece with the Miracle of Bolsena. To Benedetto Buglioni (1446–1521) is due the recumbent figure of S. Cristina.

The frescoes in the Cappella del Rosario in the right nave, and in the Cappella di Santa Lucia, seem to be of the fifteenth century, and Sienese.

One passes from the left nave by a Romanesque doorway of the eleventh century into the Cappella del Miracolo and thence into the Grotta di S. Cristina, and this with the Cappella di S. Michele is the beginning of the Catacombs which have been partially opened here. In the right-hand grotto is the ancient altar with a beautiful ciborium. Here is preserved the stone which failed to drown the virgin saint, but on the contrary saved her.

CHAPTER XVIII

TODI

THE motor run of some thirty miles from Orvieto to Todi is one of the finest in Umbria and far more worth while than the usual approach to the little city through the Tiber valley from Perugia.

The road crosses the Paglia, the torrent that flows below Orvieto to join the Tiber to the south, by the Ponte dell' Adunata and soon begins to climb, zigzagging as it rises into the mountains, giving you wonderful views of Orvieto on its isolated tufa bastion, over the olives and the oaks, till presently the whole of central Italy, from the Monti Sibillini in the Marches to Mont' Amiata in the Senese, is spread out before you, with here Cetona, there the whole of the Cimino range with the beautiful cone of Monte Venere, and Montefiascone on its hill over the Lake of Bolsena south-westward, and due south the lonely, defined form, as of a wave about to break, of Monte Soracte on the verge of the Campagna. Then, as you begin to descend from these lonely and silent heights, the valley of the Tiber opens beneath you and presently you pass the picturesque village of Prodo, and a little later you catch a glimpse of Todi, most beautiful, crowning her hill. You lose her to find her again and soon, crossing the Tiber at Pontecuti with its triangular walls by a mighty great bridge of seven arches and a fine towered gate, over the chestnuts you see the great Renaissance church —or temple is it?—of Santa Maria della Consolazione in its wide piazzale, and climb up from it into the little ancient city where Iacopone da Todi, the author of the *Stabat Mater*, was born.

Todi is one of the most ancient cities in Umbria; it boasts of a foundation older than that of Rome. Its walls are certainly in part Etruscan, patched by the Romans, and again by the Middle Age and Renaissance, that have both left their mark, how splendidly, on this little city built on so precipitous a hill In its day, surely, it was a place of some renown and greatness

Jacopone da Todi's Vision of the Madonna: from his *Laudi* (Florence, 1490).

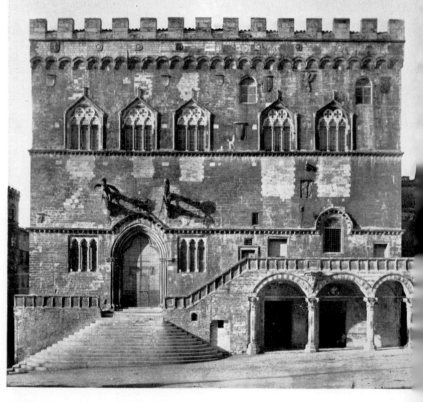

PERUGIA. Palazzo Comunale.

seeing that there is so much beauty even now within its walls. And I for one find it today one of the great surprises in Umbria. Few go there. It is thirty miles from Orvieto, which is itself a neglected city, passed almost always by the traveller, eager for Rome or some famous city of Tuscany. Perugia, with her great hotel, is more than thirty miles to the north of Todi, which on her terrible hill has, after all, but little to offer a hurried tourist. But for those who are not in a hurry Todi holds much—a great and beautiful piazza, more than one very lovely church, and silence.

It is in such silence that we begin to understand those things which the world of today has forgotten, and so disastrously. Here surrounded by the Umbrian hills and valleys, serene and spacious, under the shadow of the laurels and the roses, one watches the giant cypresses, each solitary as a god, count the innumerable hours, and thus one may, perhaps, understand something of that troubadour of God who wept because "love is not loved", who died, as it was believed, not so much conquered by his malady, though that was grave, as from an extraordinary "excess of love", and who beheld as it were in a vision the beauty and tragedy of the world and told it in his rude but immortal verses.

It is as you stand in the piazza before the Palazzo Municipio that you begin to feel how beautiful a city Todi really is. To the north the Cathedral, lovely by reason of its proportion, its colour and its simplicity, brings you a kind of joy. It is a Romanesque church of great beauty, with a façade of later work. A wide flight of steps leads up to the three doors, each surmounted by a rose, which are somewhat elaborate (the great one is of the sixteenth century), but the main part of the church is of the twelfth–thirteenth centuries; and beautiful as it is as seen from the piazza, it is from the east that it appears to best advantage, when all that you can see is twelfth-century work. The apse is especially remarkable. The variety of the ornament, too, is extraordinary; this is noticeable particularly in the windows and the columns which support the arcades on the right flank. The campanile, also, seems to be of the twelfth century, though the octagon is modern. The interior is less lovely, but even there the beauty of the proportion of the

building makes itself felt, and you forget the later additions
and alterations in the severity of the original design. The choir
is of the fourteenth century, and covers a large crypt. You feel
always that the church would have been lovelier with less
ornament. The later centuries have really spoiled a building
that must once have been of far greater beauty than it is today.
The small museum at the end of the nave contains little of
interest, but in the sacristy is a fine Gothic pastoral staff of the
fifteenth century.

The Palazzo Comunale, which consists of the two palaces del
Popolo and del Capitano, and for want of a better name passes
as Gothic architecture, shuts in the east side of the piazza. The
windows are beautiful, and the staircase finer, I think, than the
one at Perugia. The Palazzo dei Priori, on the south side of the
piazza, begun in 1293, was transformed by Leo X in 1514. It
is beautiful too; indeed, the whole piazza is lovely, and never
sufficiently to be praised.

In the Palazzo Comunale there is a small Pinacoteca which
possesses two works of some merit: a triptych by Bicci di
Lorenzo of the Coronation of the Virgin with S. Francis and
S. James and two donors with the Annunciation above; and a
Raphaelesque Coronation of the Virgin by Lo Spagna.

But the finest painting in Todi is not here, but in the church
of San Fortunato. This is a fresco by Masolino (of all masters
the least to be expected here in Todi) of the Madonna and Child
between two adoring angels. It was painted in 1432 and
originally was on the wall to the right of the entrance to the
church, but was transferred to this fourth chapel in the right
aisle. In the lunette to the left of the façade, too, there are
still some traces of a Madonna and the head of an angel.
Unfortunately, in the fresco within the church the halo of the
Madonna has been recently over-gilded. This fresco was
perhaps originally an Adoration of the Magi.

San Fortunato dates from 1292, but was added to in the sixteenth century. The unfinished façade dates from the first half
of that century, but there are many relics there of earlier work,
possibly due to the Cosmati school, which worked at Orvieto
on the façade of the Cathedral. The two statues of the Annunciation on either side the central door recall the style of Jacopo

della Quercia of Siena. The church within is covered with
frescoes of the fourteenth and fifteenth centuries, and the
ornate stalls in the choir by Antonio Mattei da Gubbio are
of the very end of the sixteenth century. The church was
Franciscan, and in the crypt is the tomb of Frate Iacopone da
Todi, the Franciscan poet. The Romanesque cloister which
belonged to the Franciscan convent is worth a glance.

Among the several churches here which have always something or other to recommend them to a lover of art and architecture is Sant' Ilario, which dates from 1249, with its fine
campanile. But the most interesting and perhaps the loveliest
of Todi's churches is Santa Maria della Consolazione, without
and below the city. This is Bramante's dream of a church, a
Greek cross under a dome. It was begun in 1508 and finished
a hundred years later, and all the classical architects of the
time, Peruzzi, Antonio da Sangallo, Vignola, Alessi and Scalza,
seem to have had a hand in its design, though it was actually
begun by Cola di Matteuccio da Caprarola.

Santa Maria della Consolazione is one of the most lovely,
if not the loveliest, of high Renaissance churches in Italy—
that is to say, in the world; energy and identity within formal
limits. No mysterious vistas here, no forest of columns lost in
twilight, nothing but perfect order, space, proportion. Here the
spirit and the mind take flight.

In Santa Maria della Consolazione we have at last a really
fine realisation of the high Renaissance ideal in architecture.
It is not a perfect realisation, but it is the best we possess. In
looking on this church we may discern what S. Peter's in
Rome might have been but for the Reformation. The idea of
Bramante, it will be remembered, was to build S. Peter's
as a Greek cross under a dome. It was an effect of space and
light he aimed at, light and space confined, and so not confined
within a perfectly proportioned building. Well, the Reformation came and spoiled all that. Rome remembered the pilgrims
from the north, and how important it was to impress them, and
so decided to build the long nave which obscures and obstructs
the dome; and the dream of Bramante vanished. Coming into
Santa Maria della Consolazione, we realise, for the first time
perhaps, what we have lost.

It is not a church; it is a magical space in the heavens between
the sun and moon, and the light is level and beautiful. It is
strange this effect of space—absolute space, flight almost, in
what is really so small a building. And it is right that this ideal
should have been achieved, if anywhere then in Umbria, where
the beauty of the whole country is really that sense of serenity,
of light and spacious air. It is the secret that Umbria has striven
to confide to the world through her painters: through Perugino
best of all, and at last through the lucid and tranquil genius
of Raphael. These men composed with space as a musician
composes with sound, and indeed the effect is very like. You
seem suddenly to have stepped out of our world into a pure
and clear sunlight, not terrifying by its infinity, but enfolding
you with security and a kind of perfection. You gaze upwards.
That dome borne on the wings of clouds on clouds of angels,
soars in its beauty and its perfection like a splendid and
irresistible thought in the mind of man. There is no uncer-
tainty, no dimness, no tricks of shadow, no self-accusation, no
deceit, no fear, no shame at all, but the clear light of the sky
that is the most lovely and precious thing in the world. And it
is thus that the men of the Renaissance chose at last to meet their
God. You think there is no mysticism in that, no mystery?
But you do not know the mystical power—strange and more
wonderful than the spirit of the forests of the north, or of the
cathedrals of the Gaul and the Goth—to be found in the
unappeasable sunlight of a still, hot day. That silence is more
profound than the whispering depths of the most ancient forest,
or the echoing intricate splendours, the dim unseen vaultings
of the great Gothic churches of the north. If in the already
worshipped sun there be mystery, or in the unpierced heaven
there be angels, though we may not see; if in silence surrounded
by light and the immense loneliness of space, God dwells so
that I may find Him always near, then Latin genius, which has
taught us all the arts as a mother teaches her children, and to
which we owe everything that is precious in the world, has not
made this unthinkable failure in architecture of which we accuse
her so easily, but has comprehended there too more than she
has ever been able to lead us so much as to apprehend; and we
in our gloomy, miserable lands preferring even now darkness

before light in our trumpery cities, must acknowledge at last with what grace we may the indestructible, untiring genius of Latin blood, that it has become the fashion to scoff at and to despise.

But I was forgetting Iacopone, the Franciscan poet. He never saw that noble church the Consolazione, for he was born about 1230 of the noble family of the Benedetti here in Todi. We know little of his life, and his astonishing legend that a late Franciscan friar gathered in the Chronicle *La Franceschina* is perhaps not to be relied on.

Iacopone studied in Bologna and exercised here in Todi his profession as Procuratore Legale. Towards 1268 he married the beautiful and gentle lady Vanna, daughter of Bernardone, Conte di Collemedio. He loved her; and her tragic death during a festa when the platform on which she was standing collapsed and killed her, brought about his conversion, for when Vanna's body was recovered it was seen that beneath her gala robe she wore a hair-shirt. From the worldly, luxurious and extravagant life he had lived hitherto, the memory of his gentle Vanna turned him away; he became a tertiary of the Franciscan Order and for ten years gave himself up to a life of mortification and penance. He became in fact a nuisance to his family and his friends, appeared in the streets in rags and at family gatherings in fantastic disguises, tarred and feathered or half naked. Whether indeed the loss of his wife had driven him crazy is a question we shall never be able to answer. He became a popular poet, strung verses together which the people and the peasants sang and loved to hear, for they were inspired by a biting wit and spared nobody, yet were full, too, of an ecstasy of devotion in which Our Lord, the Madonna and the saints were dramatised and became humanised with love and sorrow. He would preach till his hearers were in tears or lost in laughter. His religious verses in the vernacular, which seem made for singing, were so unrivalled that many lauds and verses have been spontaneously attributed to him with which he had nothing to do.

About 1279 he entered the Franciscan Order in Todi as a friar and an even more tumultuous period of his tumultuous life began. As might be expected, he opposed the Conventuals

and sided with the Spirituals in the quarrel in the Order over
the strict observance of the Rule of S. Francis. He even,
according to Angelo Clareno, made one of the deputation sent
to Pope Celestine V in 1294 to ask the Pope to order that the
Spirituals should be accorded a certain autonomy in the Order.
The concession was granted by S. Celestine, but was abrogated
by Boniface VIII, against whom Iacopone at Lunghezza in
May 1297 signed the famous manifesto of opposition, together
with the Cardinals Iacopo and Pietro Colonna, the protectors
of the Spirituals. But Palestrina, the fortress of the Colonna,
was occupied by the Papal troops and Iacopone was imprisoned
in the Castel San Pietro above the town. There he composed
some of his most moving, as well as some of his more aggressive,
poems in a horrible dungeon where the Pope would sometimes
come and jeer at him. "When are you coming out, Iacopone?"
the Pope would say. "When you go in," Iacopone would
answer.

Well, he was excommunicated, and it was this dire sentence
which seems to have broken his spirit. All he now begs is for
absolution, not that he might be released or delivered from his
cesspool or that he might no longer be starved and frozen, but
that he might receive absolution and so the Sacraments be
restored to him. But Boniface heeded him not. Even the
Indulgence of the Jubilee in 1300 was denied him. "You have
entered the fold as a fox, you have reigned like a lion, you will
go out like a dog," Iacopone is said to have told him.

And so it befell. In 1303 the Colonnesi, supported by Philip
le Bel of France, seized Boniface by violence at Anagni. The
Pope was released, but the humiliation had driven him mad,
and though he recovered himself he died of a violent fever on
October 11, 1303. This appeared to Iacopone as a divine
judgment (Laude LVIII). As he had prophesied, he came out
of his dungeon the day Boniface went in. He was more than
seventy years old, and he seems to have passed his last years,
not in Todi, but at Pantanelli and at Collazzone between Todi
and Perugia, where he died in the convent of San Lorenzo, a
house of Poor Clares, on Christmas Day 1306. As he lay dying
he sang a song of love and happiness and in "an excess of love"
his spirit passed:

In fuoco l'amor mi mise. . . .

So died, perhaps, the greatest of the Franciscan poets, certainly
the most fruitful in the vernacular and the author of his stately,
sorrowful, immortal Latin Sequence:

> *Stabat Mater dolorosa*
> *Iuxta crucem lacrymosa*
> > *Dum pendebat Filius;*
> *Cuius animam gementem*
> *Contristatam et dolentem,*
> > *Pertransivit gladius.*
>
> *O quam tristis, et afflicta,*
> *Fuit illa benedicta*
> > *Mater Unigeniti.*
> *Quae moerebat et dolebat*
> *Et tremebat cum videbat*
> > *Nati poenas inclyti.*
>
> *Quis est homo, qui non fleret,*
> *Matrem Christi si videret*
> > *In tanto supplicio?*
> *Quis non posset contristari*
> *Piam matrem contemplari*
> > *Dolentem cum Filio?*
> et reliqua.

From Todi I made my way up the valley of the Tiber to
Perugia, passing Collazzone on its lofty hill where Iacopone
died and Cerqueto on the other side of the valley where is a
fresco of S. Sebastian by Perugino, his earliest dated work
(1478). The valley had nothing but its own beauty to detain
me till I came to Deruta, where they have been making
majolica since 1387 and earlier; indeed, they claim priority over
all other centres in the production of this pottery. They certainly seem to have discovered here at a very early date the
secrets of the Moorish potters, for the lustred ware of Deruta
has a perfect similarity of technique with that of Valencia and
Malaga. This lustred ware was the glory of Deruta, but the
man whose talent gave to its very original style of decoration

a definite form is nameless. The light blue pigment with which
the design was outlined and shaded, combined with a metallic
film of yellow-brownish tint, make up his palette. The art of
this master, whoever he was, finds its complete expression in
those large platters bearing a bust of man or woman, saint or
sphinx or strange animal, with an inscribed banderole, while a
border of ornament consisting of oak leaves or the like surrounds
the whole.

There are, too, embossed models which come from Deruta,
shield-shaped inkstands painted in relief, yellow or blue; dishes
with reliefs painted in blue or those lustred vases with two
handles and a large monogram sometimes crowned, as in the
one at South Kensington. The manufacture, which had fallen
into decline after its most glorious moment in the sixteenth
century, was commercially revived in the nineteenth century,
and in 1910 became a *Società anonima* for the production of
household and other wares, some of which are pretty enough
in a more or less mechanical way, but they are no longer works
of art in any sense.

But Deruta can offer the curious traveller something better
than this modern activity. In the Pinacoteca in the Palazzo
Comunale, with its Romanesque fragments still about it, there
are two paintings by Niccolò da Foligno. One of these is the
central panel of an altarpiece with the Virgin enthroned adoring the Child lying on her knees. She is surrounded by fifteen
angels and below kneel S. Bernard and S. Francis and the small
figure of the donor. This picture dates about 1457, when the
painter was about twenty-seven years old and was under the influence of Benozzo Gozzoli. The other painting here by this
master is a processional banner, presumably dating from some
ten years later than the Madonna panel, when Niccolò had come
under the influence of Crivelli. The banner is painted on both
sides: on one side we see S. Antony Abbot venerated by the
members of his confraternity of penitents; a mitre is being
placed on his head by an angel and above is the Crucifixion.
On the other side we see S. Francis and S. Bernardino, behind
whom two angels hold a patterned silken hanging; while above is
a representation of the Flagellation. This last is the best part
of the banner, very much finer in quality than the rest.

In the church of San Francesco, a fourteenth-century building spoiled in the seventeenth century, is a fresco of SS. Roch and Romano, with a bust of God the Father between them in a medallion, by Fiorenzo di Lorenzo, very Umbrian in feeling. Close by in the church of Sant' Antonio Abate is an important work by that charming Umbrian painter, Bartolommeo Caporali (?1420–?1505), a Madonna of Mercy with kneeling worshippers and SS. Francis and Bernardino. Above are four angels, one with drawn sword, and above in the vault, ruined figures of God the Father and the four Evangelists. Another work by this charming little master is in the Fanciullata chapel just outside Deruta; this represents the Virgin with six angels and SS. James and Anthony, beautifully clear in colour.

In the late afternoon I drove on to Ponte San Giovanni, and so up to Perugia.

CHAPTER XIX

PERUGIA

PERUGIA stands on her great isolated hills absolute queen of all this country, of old towered and terrible of aspect for all her beauty, ever at attention and with great angry eyes searching out her enemies.[1]

Of Etruscan origin, being indeed one of the principal cities of that mysterious people, we know nothing of Perugia till she submitted herself to Rome in 309 B.C. That is but the first of numberless surrenders—to the Popes, to many tyrants, to her own terrible sons, to the brutality of the mob, to Italy and the modern world. The hand of the Emperor Augustus has rested on her throat as certainly as that of the later tyrants, Baglioni or Pope. It was Augustus who in 38 B.C. rebuilt the city, which one of the citizens, Caius Macedonicus, in order to save her from the great emperor, burnt to the ground, so that she is now Augusta Perusia, and Perugia Etrusca no longer. Yet in spite of capitulation and outward obedience, she has ever nursed in her soul a fierce spirit of liberty, which has made her story one of the bloodiest in the history of Italy. In the heyday of her power she owned no temporal sovereign and brooked no interference, but treated Pope and Emperor as mere pawns in her game for the Lordship of Umbria.

Though Perugia, Perusia Turrita, has, at least as you approach her today from the south and west, lost her imperial aspect, for not only have her towers vanished, but upon the very forehead of the city rises the huge modern Prefettura and the banal Grand Hotel Brufani, yet she is still the queen of hill cities, is still fiercely beautiful within and without her Etruscan

---

[1] Perugia is said to have possessed no less than seven hundred towers. See Crispolti, *Perugia Augusta*, p. 15, and Siepi, *Descrizione Top.-stor. di Perugia*, Vol. II, p. 828. This is not an exaggeration. Today all have gone save one. Among them was the great campanile of the Cathedral which was destroyed in 1375. It was believed to have stood for 3,600 years and to have held in its foundation the Palladium of Troy. Siena had so many towers that "the city seemed a cane-brake"; cf. Ugurgieri: *Le Pompe Sanesi*, II, 307.

walls on which Rome and the Middle Age and the Renaissance
have not forgotten to leave their marks as beautiful if not as
indestructible. Her streets are even yet named nobly—Via
della Cupa, Via della Conca, Via dei Priori, Via di Sant'
Ercolano, Via dell' Aquila. Her gates, many and splendid,
have, too, in their very names a suggestion of her inviolable
beauty—Porta Eburnea, Porta Augusta, Porta Cornea, Porta
Sole, Porta Marzia, Porta Santa Susanna. Within her palaces
is some of the serenest work of Perugino, and Bonfigli, and
Fiorenzo di Lorenzo; and her prospect is of a thousand hills and
valleys. Far away to the north and west lie the bare mountains
of the Senese, while to the south the hills are crowned with
famous and lovely cities where Monte Subasio looks towards
Rome with the city of S. Francis kneeling on its skirts, a religious, in the homely brown habit, vowed to God. Like a lily
in the vale beneath hovers S. Mary of the Angels, delicate
with the colour of the day—white, or almost rosy, or sombre,
under the sky. And far away to the west rise the mountains
above Todi and Orvieto, and, all between, the sweet Umbrian
plain, the valley of Spoleto. And though in early morning this
exquisite landscape is delicate and fragile and half-hidden in
mist, at sunset it is filled with the "largeness of the evening
earth" and a serenity of silence and repose that is, as it were,
suggested by the gesture of the mountains. It is, above all this
perfection, absolute queen from horizon to horizon that
Perugia stands regnant.

It was in the sixth century that Justinian, desiring to drive
the Goths out of Italy, sent the General Constantine to Umbria,
a vastly larger country then than now. Constantine seems to
have made Perugia his headquarters, and to have been left
unmolested till, in the year 545, Totila appeared, and having
obtained possession of Assisi, prepared to drive Constantine
from Perugia; but he found her, as ever, not easy of conquest;
to be overcome rather by treachery than by fighting. The siege
which followed is said to have lasted for seven years, but at last
Perugia fell before the fury of the Goth, "upheld to the last
by a new power, namely, that of her faith". It was the greatest
of her patron saints, S. Ercolano, who upheld her, and in those
years of terror formed her character there in the midst of

mystical Italy, making her for ever after not unmindful of those
mysterious powers which in all ages men have been anxious
to win to their side. So to the starving city S. Ercolano, its
bishop, comes with wise counsels; and as in ancient Rome, so
in Perugia, in spite of the scarcity, food was thrown from the
walls, and the Goths discouraged. Bonfigli has painted the
story with simplicity and sweetness in the Cappella dei Priori,
now a sala of the Pinacoteca. It would seem that an ox, having
been fed with what corn remained to the city, was thrown over
the walls, when the Goths, finding it, supposed the Perugians
to have so much to eat that they fed even their beasts with corn.
"But by chance," says Ciatti, whose history of the city is full
of an old-world *naïveté*, "but by chance a young priest spoke
from the walls with some Goths and all unknowing revealed
the terror and death reigning in the city." And so the stratagem
of the good bishop failed; yet on that day Perugia fell not
without honour, and in all her future has never forgotten
S. Ercolano, who was martyred in her cause, seeing she chose
him for her patron saint.[1]

In 592, Perugia, on her high hill, became a Lombard duchy,
but was soon restored to the Byzantine Empire. Through all
that mysterious age she grew stronger and more fierce. Her
invaders were many, she suffered many violations. In the year
726 we find her, together with many another Italian city,
siding with the Pope against the Emperor Leo III, the Icono-
clast, when he published his edict against images in churches,
which led to the separation of the Greek and Latin Churches
in 729; to be united again at the Council of Lyons in 1274, only
to be separated finally in 1277. Certainly, during those years
of fierce and brutal energy, Perugia owed much to the Papacy.
Thus, in 744, when King Rachis of the Lombards besieged
Perugia, Pope Zacharias came to plead with him not unsuccessfully, and it is certainly true to the spirit of that age that the
king became a monk after listening to the Pope, retiring to the
Benedictine monastery of Monte Cassino.

In the year 800, however, Charlemagne, having invaded Italy
in 774, overcome the Lombards, and been crowned as Emperor

---

[1] Sacchetti, Nov. 169, says, "The Perugians trust more in Sant' Ercolano than in
Christ, and hold him to be greater than the greatest saint in Paradise."

of the West by Pope Leo III, Perugia came under the dominion of the Pope as a gift from the Emperor.

The earliest documentary evidence we have of the existence of the Commune of Perugia is of the year 1130. During the feudal period the nobles were immune from taxation and it was only in the thirteenth century that the Popolo protested against this privilege. The usual struggle followed and resulted in the triumph of the Arti. The history of the city during these years, during which she was for the most part loyally Guelph, is one of continual warfare with her neighbours—Assisi, Siena, Arezzo, Città di Castello, Gubbio, Foligno, Spoleto. In 1358 Perugia won her greatest victory, over Siena. Having succeeded in defeating almost all her rivals, she laid upon them heavy burdens: thus Foligno was forbidden to rebuild her walls, Città della Pieve was compelled to provide bricks to pave her streets, Arezzo to yield her marble to decorate the Cathedral of San Lorenzo. Yet in spite of her fierceness, her strength and her pride, she was ever unable to master herself, falling always a prey to her own passions, consuming her energy, not in wars with her rivals alone, but also in massacre and havoc among her own citizens. Thus she wasted herself, turning her fierceness against herself at last, till her streets ran with blood, her Cathedral was defiled, her greatest sons assassinated, and she herself a mere beautiful bastion on a bleak hill-side.

To describe the quarrels of the great families of the fifteenth and sixteenth centuries, of the Baglioni and Oddi, would serve no useful purpose. Their names are known for every kind of brutality and murder to every traveller in Italy from the sketch of Perugia which the late J. A. Symonds published in his *Sketches in Italy*. Matarazzo too, to whom, of course, Symonds and every modern historian of Perugia is indebted, in a master-piece of simple narrative—if indeed that naïve chronicle be the work of the distinguished humanist—is full of the dramatic story of their hatred, their glory and their despair. I must refer the reader to those pages. It is, however, worthy of notice that it was during the years of internal revolution, when every sort of crime was rampant, when murder and destruction went barefaced up and down the streets, that Perugino and Fiorenzo

di Lorenzo were painting their quiet and lovely pictures of the
birth and death of Christ, while the young Raphael was at
work in the studio of his master, Perugino. It has been said that
in Raphael's S. George in the Louvre, and perhaps in the horse-
man trampling upon Heliodorus in the *stanze* of the Vatican,
we have a picture of Astorre Baglioni, that terrible and yet
beautiful figure, which Raphael's eyes may once have rested
upon.

It was to Pope Paul III that Perugia owed the experience of
a new, and not altogether unnecessary, despotism. In 1535,
Ridolfo Baglioni having murdered the Papal Legate, Paul III
determined to send troops to drive Ridolfo out of Perugia. In
this he was successful, and became himself ruler of the city.
But in 1538 the Perugians revolted. Paul III promptly defeated
them, and two years later laid the foundation, upon a ruined
palace of the Baglioni, of the Rocca Paolina, which bore the
legend *ad coercendam Perusinorum audaciam*. The Perugians came
to regret even the Baglioni, but thus began a rule in Perugia
strong, steadfast and despotic, which, save for the incident of
Napoleon, was not to pass away till our own time, when, on
September 14, 1860, the city was taken by the troops of Victor
Emmanuel, and became an integral part of United Italy. The
first action of the Perugians was to tear down the Papal fortress
to the last stone: the site is now occupied by the Prefecture and
the Piazza d'Armi.

So the splendour and the terror of the past have sunk into
the mediocrity of today. Beauty such as once belonged to
Florence or Venice or Rome was perhaps never hers. She was
a scarped crag of the mountains, burnt with fire, beaten by the
wind, ringing with cold in the winter, splendid with the sun.
Her Palazzo Comunale was one of the most fierce and majestic
in Italy and even her Cathedral was as relentless as a fortress,
at least in appearance, but the destroying centuries have
perhaps lent it something of their tolerance, giving the clinkered
brick the surface and the colour almost of a precious stone.
It is not beauty but strength and passion that you find in its
brown walls that have been splashed with blood and washed
with wine. A greater than any Baglioni has lain there. "There
is no one," says Thomas of Eccleston, "who dies as solitary and

neglected as a Pope." So it was with the greatest of them,
Innocent III, who died in Perugia in 1216. The coffin still
open, the body of the Pope was carried to the Cathedral, where
the funeral was to take place. "It was then," says Jacques de
Vitry, who had just come to Perugia where the Papal court was
in *villegiatura*, "it was then I really understood the nothingness
of grandeur here below. The night preceding the funeral
robbers broke into the Cathedral, and despoiled the Pope of
everything precious upon him. I saw with my own eyes his
body, half naked, lying in the midst of the church already
stinking."

Indeed, within the Cathedral there is scarcely beauty at all,
only silence and space and a softer and more sombre light than
is usual in an Italian church. And yet in its homely, if bare
aspect it attracts you where a more splendid building might
leave you cold. Its most precious possession, the wedding or
betrothal ring of the Blessed Virgin, is kept under many locks
in many caskets in the chapel to the left of the west door, and
may be seen but four or five times during the year. Made from
some agate stone, it is popularly believed to change colour
according to the hearts of those who look on it. It was brought
to Perugia in 1472 by Fra Vinterio di Magonza, who had
"piously" stolen it from the Franciscans at Chiusi. In this chapel
too, till 1797, when Napoleon took it to France, whence it has
never returned, hung the picture of the Marriage of the Blessed
Virgin, by Perugino. A copy fills the place of the original
picture now in Caen.[1]

On the other side of the church is the chapel of S. Bernardino, which belonged to the merchants' guild. A Deposition
by Baroccio is over the altar; the window, perhaps the best in
the church, is of the sixteenth century.

A very delightful picture of the Madonna, painted by
Giannicola Manni, a pupil of Perugino's, hangs over the little
altar against the third pillar on the right. It is the famous
Madonna delle Grazie, the most lovely miracle-picture in
Umbria. With hands raised she seems to deprecate our prayers
and to bless us. Innumerable silver hearts, and invisible thankfulness surround the altar of a "miracle" picture in which we

[1] See *The Study and Criticism of Italian Art*, Vol. II, by Bernard Berenson.

cannot but find at least a miracle of beauty. It is to this altar that the mother always brings her child, to lay him for a moment at the feet of the Madonna after his christening in the baptistery close by.

In the choir in the apse are some fine wooden stalls with carved and inlaid work. On the wall in the left aisle is a Pietà with God the Father above by Agostino di Duccio, relics of an altar of 1475, in the Chiesa della Maestà delle Volte between the Cathedral and the Vescovado.

One passes into the cloister, thence into the Museo dell' Opera del Duomo, where have been assembled not only some fine pictures from the Cathedral, but the great miniatured choir books of the sixth to the thirteenth century from the Biblioteca Capitolare which have considerable importance, for Perugia was famous all over Italy for her miniaturists. But the finest picture here is the great altarpiece by Luca Signorelli, one of the noblest pictures in Perugia. The Madonna is enthroned with her little Son between S. John Baptist, S. Onofrio, S. Laurence and S. Ercolano, and beneath are two beautiful angels, one of whom tunes his lute (1484). Here, too, are a Pietà by Bartolommeo Caporali of Perugia (1486); an altarpiece by Meo da Siena, a Madonna and Child by Andrea Vanni, and three Processional pictures of the fifteenth century.

In the chapel of Sant' Onofrio, reached from the right transept, the Blessed Egidio, Brother Giles, the third companion of S. Francis who passed much of his life in the hermitage on Monteripido outside Porta Sant' Angelo, and Frate Corrado of Offida, one of those who with Frate Bernardo and Frate Leo, *Pecorello di Dio*, strove for the strict interpretation of the Rule and Testament of S. Francis, are buried. They lie here through the action of Cardinal Pecci, Archbishop of Perugia, afterwards Pope Leo XIII, who removed their neglected relics from the ruin of San Francesco al Prato. Popes Urban IV and Martin IV are buried here. The remains of Innocent III were removed to the Lateran in 1892.

Outside the Cathedral are the Piazza San Lorenzo, or del Municipio, and the Piazza Danti. In the latter, the bronze statue of Pope Julius III, by Vincenzo Danti, used to stand,

PERUGIA. Fontana Maggiore (detail).

PERUGIA. Collegio
del Cambio. Perugino.

but it has now been moved back to the steps of the Cathedral facing the Piazza San Lorenzo, where it originally stood. It was erected by the Perugians in gratitude to the Pope who restored their civic privileges.

Close to the statue of Pope Julius, where it now stands against the Cathedral wall, is the little pulpit from which S. Bernardino of Siena used to preach so passionately. It was while preaching here that it is said he heard his favourite bell, called Viola, which hung in the campanile of the convent of S. Francesco al Prato, now a ruin, fall to the ground, and, stopping his sermon, said to the people, "My children, Viola is fallen, but she is not hurt." But S. Bernardino, with all his eloquence, preached in vain. The people wept to hear him, burnt their books and pictures and finery on the stones beside the beautiful fountain, and then in a few days passionately cut each other's throats in the very place where they had listened to the good saint, and even in the Duomo itself. And was it not here, too, that the dead body of Astorre Baglioni lay in state during two days, together with that of his murderer and cousin, Grifonetto?

The beautiful fountain which stands in the midst of the piazza was built in 1277 from designs, it is said, by a Perugian artist, Fra Bevignate. The lovely statuettes and bas-reliefs which adorn it were designed and sculptured by Giovanni Pisano. On an ample circular base of steps rests a many-sided basin with groups of columns to strengthen it at the corners. Above this rises a second basin, many-sided too, with statues at the corners, and from the midst of this is upreared a bronze bowl from which rises a magnificent group of nymphs and dragons. The linked arms of the nymphs are alternately resting on their hips and raised to support the pedestal of dragons; together they form one of the most exquisite designs ever achieved by the sculptors of the thirteenth century. This superb crown rises from a short pedestal and the writhing dragons rearing up with beating wings and each with one paw uplifted seem to beat time for their fantastic dance. Nowhere else has Giovanni Pisano shown such an ardour of imagination, such a unity of upward leaping rhythm.

The mighty and picturesque palace, the Palazzo Comunale, which closes the piazza opposite the Cathedral, is among the

finest Gothic buildings in Italy, and is the glory of Perugia.
Begun at the end of the twelfth century by Giacomo di Servadio
and Giovannello di Benvenuto of Perugia, it was finished in the
fifteenth century. The great entrance in the Corso is still
guarded by statues of S. Ercolano, S. Costanzo, and S. Louis
of Toulouse, the three patron saints of Perugia. S. Louis of
Toulouse, the Franciscan, was the great-grandson of S. Louis
of France. He was therefore the brother of Robert, King of
Naples, who aided Perugia to beat the Ghibellines at Todi.
It was on this occasion that the Perugians chose S. Louis for
one of their patrons. We find also about the great door of the
Palazzo Comunale the two lions of the Guelphs, together with
the griffins of Perugia. On the north side of the palazzo, towards
the Duomo, the more ancient and tremendous, are two magnificent bronzes, the lean lion of the Guelph cause and the griffin
of Perugia, while beneath is the Scala della Vaccara, a beautiful
flight of steps restored, perhaps to its original design. The
chains hanging from the great bronzes are those of the gallows
of Siena, outside the Porta Nuova, taken in 1358.

It was here in the Piazza San Lorenzo that S. Francis was
preaching in 1223 to a great multitude of people, when he was
interrupted by a company of knights who "after their manner
rode up armed and hindered the word of God with warlike
sports. S. Francis rebuked them and foretold their punishment.
Not many days later discord arose among them, neighbours
took up arms against neighbours, the burghers attacked the
knights, the nobles fell on the plebeians and all fought with such
fury that there was a great slaughter."[1]

At the end of the piazza, on the left is the Vescovado and
on the right, beside the Duomo, rises the ancient Canonica di
San Lorenzo, which in the thirteenth century was a constant
and *villegiatura* of the Popes, called the Vatican of Perugia.
Here in 1294 Peter Murrone the anchorite was elected Pope
Celestine V. A few months later he abdicated and is denounced
by Dante for cowardice and placed in hell. But in 1313 he was
canonised. Pope Honorius III was here with his court in 1216
when S. Francis sought him for confirmation of the Indulgence
of the Portiuncula, a privilege without precedent outside Rome

[1] II Celano, *Legenda*, c. viii.

and the Holy Land. The previous night Christ and His
Mother had appeared to the saint at Santa Maria degli Angeli
and S. Francis had obtained this wonderful privilege for his
beloved Portiuncula, the Blessed Virgin bending before her Son
to show that she approved the request she had heard; and Christ
bade S. Francis to go to Perugia to obtain from the Pope
official ratification of the unique favour.

In the presence of the Holy Father, Francis said to him,
"I have lately restored a church dedicated in honour of the
Blessed Virgin, Mother of God. I am now come to solicit an
Indulgence in favour of those who visit this church on the day
of its dedication, which Indulgence they may gain without
having to make any offering whatsoever."

"It is usual," observed the Pope, "that an offering should be
made . . . and it is an Indulgence for how many years you desire?
Of one year? Of three years?"

"What is three years, Holy Father?"

"Do you want three years? Or seven years?"

"It is not years but souls I desire."

"What is it thou sayest? Souls?"

"It is that whoever shall enter this church, confessed, and
absolved, shall have a remission of all his sins and of their
penalty."

"That is an exorbitant thing and entirely contrary to the
usage of the Roman Court."

"It is not by my own will, but by the will of Our Lord Jesus
Christ that I ask this."

"Very well, I accord it to thee; in the name of Our Lord let
it be done according to thy desire."

The cardinals present protested loudly at these words and
supplicated the Pope to bethink himself that such a favour
would be harmful to the Indulgences of the Holy Land and
of Rome; but the Pope refused to withdraw what he had
said.

"The Indulgence," he said, "is good in perpetuity, but only
once in the year; that is, from the first Vespers of one day to
those of the next."

Anxious to be gone, Francis bowed himself and was already
turning away when the Pope called him back.

"O great simpleton, art thou departing then without a diploma?"[1]

"Your word suffices me, Holy Father. If this is the will of God He will manifest Himself at need. My diploma is the Blessed Virgin; my notary is Christ and the Holy Angels are my witnesses."

There are many memories of S. Francis in Perugia. He was imprisoned for a year in the dungeon beneath the Palazzo del Capitano in Piazza Sopramuro, now Piazza Garibaldi, when in 1202, at the age of twenty, he was taken prisoner in the battle between Assisi and Perugia not far from Ponte San Giovanni.

> Francis with others was taken and was put in chains with the rest and endured the horrors of imprisonment; his fellow captives absorbed in sadness bewailed their wretched plight; Francis exulting in the Lord laughed at his chains and despised them. His companions rebuked him and deemed him mad, but he answered prophetically, "Why think you that I exult? Another thought is with me. I shall yet be worshipped as a saint all the world over." Among his fellow prisoners was a knight, a very proud and unbearable man, but while all the rest shunned him Francis's patience did not fail. He endured the unbearable knight and induced the others to receive him.

One enters the Palazzo Comunale by the great entrance in the Corso; here all the business of Perugia would seem to be conducted. Groups of men stand there talking, and even their uncouth dialect cannot spoil the beauty of their Latin tongue. It is a picturesque sight, these bronzed *contadini* in their sheepskins and their great furred coats, doing their business in the beautiful old portico of their *municipio*. Though all things pass away, in Italy at least there is always left the shadow of former greatness—some suggestion on a fortunate day of all the centuries, in a great ruined gateway or the cold broken limbs of a forgotten god.

The palace is entered by this noble portal in the Corso and

---

[1] *Tres Socii* (Foligno, 1898), pp. 98 *et seq.* It is not really possible to paraphrase these *legendae* without spoiling them. Here is the original Latin: "*Et dominus papa videns eum abire vocavit eum dicens: O simplicione, quomodo vadis? Quid portas tu de hac indulgentia? Beatus Franciscus respondit: tantum sufficit mihi verbum vestrum. . . .*"

ascends by the great stairway to the magnificent Sala dei Notai,
the Sala del Gran Consiglio, more than 100 feet long by 40 feet
wide. The frescoes represent a number of legends and stories,
together with scenes from the Old and New Testament, and are
of the school of Pietro Cavallini. In the Sala del Consiglio
Comunale is a fresco by Pintoricchio of the Madonna and Child
with two angels. Above, on the top floor, is the picture-gallery,
the Pinacoteca Vannucci, which contains the best collection of
Umbrian works of art anywhere brought together.[1]

Beside the great Palazzo Comunale is the Collegio del
Cambio, the money exchange, built in the middle of the fifteenth
century by Bartolommeo di Mattiolo and Ludovico di
Antonio and decorated with frescoes by Perugino, and a statue
of Justice in terra-cotta by Benedetto da Maiano, the Florentine
sculptor of the fifteenth century. Perugino worked here on his
greatest, though not his best, decoration from 1498 till 1507,
when he received 350 gold ducats in payment. Can we say that
what the Stanze of the Vatican are in the work of Raphael,
the Cambio is in the work of Perugino?

The purpose of these frescoes, the ideas they would express
seem to be the way of God with man by means of revelation
and by means of human reason, so that we see the revelation
of God's will to the chosen people, the Jews, on the right, and
the reason of man as an instrument of God's will, as shown in
pagan civilisation, on the left. The two pictures of the Nativity
and the Transfiguration which confront us as we enter suggest,
and would seem to seek to express, the sacramental prayer of
the Missal: *da nobis eius divinitatis esse consortes qui humanitatis
nostrae fieri dignatus est particeps Jesus Christus filius tuus dominus
noster. . . .*

However that may be, what finally interests us in these
frescoes is that they seem to reveal to us the Renaissance vision
of antiquity or, at any rate, Perugino's vision of it. The heroes
and philosophers of the ancient world which haunted the
imaginations of the *signorotti*, the tyrants, the scholars and poets
of the Renaissance, here appear as the fragile ghosts they were.
They are no Greeks or Romans, these too charming warriors
with their sweet boyish or even girlish faces, their round limbs,

---

[1] See *infra* pp. 179 *et seq.*

and delicate hands. They have never heard of Ares or Mars; what have they to do with Apollo or Aphrodite? They have only understood the beauty of the delicate wounded hands of Christ, the sorrowful dream of Mary Madonna, the visions of the saints and mystics. These dainty and pensive figures are no Pagans but Christians, however they masquerade as Greeks and Romans; ghosts of the golden age of the Renaissance, even while we look they seem to fade on the wall, to pass away like some exquisite fantastic dream.

The churches of Perugia are many and for the most part of little interest. But in strolling through the city in search of them, many a picturesque street or marvellous view will disclose itself as, for instance, from the piazzetta of San Severo towards Assisi and Monte Subasio, Spello and the valley of the Clitumnus or from the lofty Porta Sole towards the north over the Palazzo Gallenga, the Palazzo dell' Università, the church of Sant' Agostino, and beyond, the great convent of Monte Ripido; and to the right the church of Monteluce, the tower of Santa Maria Nuova, and beyond, the Apennine from Monte Fossato to Monte Cucco to Monte della Strega, the mountains over Gubbio, and then Monte Tezio round to Subasio. Or, from the small church of Sant' Angelo della Pace, to the right one descends to the Via Bartolo, with a magnificent view of the mighty city wall, Etruscan and Roman.

San Pietro dei Cassinesi, whose octagonal, spired tower can be seen from the Piazza della Prefettura, is really the only church which has not been emptied of its treasures. San Pietro, it is said, enjoys this privilege because the monks befriended the army of Vittorio Emanuele in 1860, but the church and monastery are a national monument. As the traveller walks to San Pietro by the Via Marzia and the Via Fioramenti he will pass down the steps of Sant' Ercolano, and come upon that octagonal Gothic church, built against the Etruscan walls in 1200 in the place where Totila is said to have martyred S. Ercolano, bishop and patron of Perugia. Beyond the beauty of its architecture there is nothing of interest in the church.

Passing down the Via Cavour, one comes on the left to the gaunt unfinished church of San Domenico. The strange broken tower is grandiose from the Piazza della Prefettura, especially at night, when its wounds are hidden. Giovanni Pisano is said to have made designs for the church, which was begun early in the fourteenth century; but in the innumerable wars of that period the church he built was destroyed, and so in the middle of the seventeenth century it was rebuilt from the designs of Carlo Maderno. In the left transept is the fine tomb of Pope Benedict XI, 1303, by Giovanni Pisano or, as later criticism has it, by Lorenzo Maitani of Siena. The Pope, the last before the exile in Avignon, lies on a bed under a canopy and the two spiral columns which support the canopy were inlaid with mosaic—stolen, it is said, by the soldiers of Napoleon; charming figures of youthful angels draw back the curtains and disclose the effigy of the Pope. This Gothic tomb is one of the most lovely things in Perugia. The fourth chapel, too, on the south side, has an altar with some terra-cotta statues and other decorations by Agostino di Duccio. The great window behind the high altar is said to be the largest Gothic window in Italy and dates from the fifteenth century; the glass in the lower panels is by Mariotto di Nardo and Frate Bartolommeo di Pietro of Perugia. The choir stalls are fine. The gaunt tower was lowered by Paul III, since it interrupted his view from the Rocca, and indeed overlooked the fortress.

One passes under the stately Porta Romana, built by Agostino di Duccio in 1476, and comes upon the monastic church of San Pietro dei Cassinesi, the most interesting church left to Perugia. It was built in 963 by Pietro Vincioli, a priest of a noble Perugian house who founded here a monastery. It was then an early basilica which came into the hands of the Benedictines, but it was rebuilt finally in the fifteenth century. The courtyard is spacious and the monastery is now secularised and turned into an agricultural school, but in the quietness and loneliness which seem to have fallen upon it, the place retains much of the spirit of a monastic foundation. You pass between the many columns of marble and stone, taken so long ago from the temple of Venus, where now a temple of Christ stands. The church is a basilica still, but with aisles and small transepts. Benedetto da Montepulciano made the roof, which is gaudy; the pictures, however, have considerable interest.

Over the high altar Perugino's Assumption used to stand, but it is gone together with Raphael's "Ansidei" Madonna, which used to hang in San Fiorenzo, and the Sposalizio by Perugino, which was in the Cappella del S. Anello in the Cathedral. The monks tell you that the choir stalls are decorated from Raphael's designs; it is hard to believe it. In the north aisle is a Pietà by Bonfigli, of a curious beauty; and a lovely altarpiece by Mino da Fiesole, over which is a circular Madonna and Child by Pintoricchio, now ruined. The sacristy holds five panels by Perugino of SS. Scolastica, Ercolano, Pietro Vincioli, the founder of the monastery, Costanzo, and Mauro, which are part of Perugino's huge altarpiece, the central panel of which, the Ascension, is now in Lyons. These lovely panels and the Bonfigli are surely sufficient excuse for a visit to San Pietro, but in reality it is the quiet church itself that attracts one most. The view from the gallery at the end of the choir is very lovely, embracing as it does the whole countryside.

It is in quite another part of the city that you find the only other church of much artistic interest—the Oratory of San Bernardino, and that is but a shell, like Sant' Ercolano. Passing under the Palazzo Comunale, down the picturesque and almost medieval Via dei Priori, one turns back many times to see the roofs piled up into heaven, the walls and back of the great palace and the arches of many a shadowy street. From the Via della Cupa here on the left the Via Deliziosa is reached, where number five was the house of Perugino. At the end of Via della Cupa is the Etruscan Porta della Mandorla. After passing the Torre degli Scirri in Via dei Priori, a thirteenth-century tower left alone of all those belonging to the private families of the city, passing more than one church, too, of little or no interest, one comes out at last into the Piazza di San Francesco, where stands in splendour, near the ruined church of San Francesco al Prato,[1] the façade of the Oratorio di San Bernardino, perhaps the masterpiece of Agostino the Florentine. Built in 1461 by the magistrates of Perugia in gratitude to S. Bernardino for his efforts for peace and brotherly love among a people so disposed the other way, it is certainly one of the most charming of the

---

[1] A fine Gonfalone by Bonfigli and a fresco in the crypt remain. Brothers Giles and Conrad of Offida were buried here, but their relics were removed to the Cathedral in 1880. See *supra*, p. 164.

coloured architectural works of Italy. Above is God the Father in glory, with two kneeling angels and eight cherubim; beneath, two griffins; and there in a flaming *mandorla*, surrounded by angels, is S. Bernardino, together with scenes in relief from the saint's life, one of which represents him preaching at Aquila while a star shines over him at midday. Many angels and virtues and arabesques, exquisite in their perfect style and beauty, finish a work which should be compared with Agostino's reliefs at Rimini.

S. Bernardino of Siena, whom this splendid monument commemorates, is one of the most attractive figures of the fifteenth century. He was a true disciple of S. Francis. Born at Massa Marittima in 1380 of noble family, he was an orphan before he was seven years' old, and was brought up by his Aunt Diana. The usual rather disagreeable stories are told of his childhood—stories common to all the saints, so that you wonder, hearing them, that those who in their earliest years were so commonplace and pious attained to such strength and sweetness in age. At eleven years' old he was sent to Siena to school, where even then he seems to have attracted people by reason of a certain dignity in him. Yet he did not escape from the touch of the brutality of his day, though he shamed that man who would have injured him. At the age of seventeen, after a study of civil and canon law, he enrolled himself in the Confraternity of Our Lady in Siena in the hospital of Santa Maria della Scala to serve the sick. In the year 1400 a frightful pestilence, that had already wasted many another city in Italy, fell on Siena. These pestilences were no uncommon thing in that age of brilliant genius, bloodshed and no hygiene. Together with twelve young men, he served the sick, expecting heaven. During four months he seems to have managed the hospital with great skill, and to have shown a practical ability not rare in the lives of the saints, who were often as great in action as in devotion.

It was after this that he took the habit of the Order of S. Francis at a convent of Observants not far from the city. He made his profession, September 8, 1404, on his birthday, which was the birthday also of Our Lady, whom he served so eagerly. In ragged garments he went through the streets while the crowd laughed at him, and seeing one whom they knew to be of noble family in the same condition with themselves, threw stones at him; while his friends, in shame at the figure he cut, pressed him to return with them. But he had heard the very voice of Christ: "My son, behold Me hanging upon the Cross: if thou lovest Me and art desirous to imitate Me, thou also must be fastened to thy cross; thou also must follow Me, and surely thou shalt find Me." Gradually he came to understand his true vocation as the orator of God. He too practised an art, the art of preaching and affecting the hearts of men, the secret of which he found was just an ardent love. For a single word spoken by love was, he knew, more powerful than any eloquence, the profound longing of the heart speaking to the heart with a kind of irresistible sincerity. And those who heard him loved him.

In all that age of slaughter and pestilence, and the awakening of the destructive if creative intelligence of man, he was really a sort of peacemaker, pleading—at times not unsuccessfully— for love between men. And he used to carry with him and hold aloft in his preaching a disk inscribed with a monogram of the name of Jesus. Pope Martin V sent for him more than once to examine him, but dismissed him with a blessing, offering him also in 1427 the bishopric of Siena, as did Pope Eugenius III that of Ferrara, and later that of Urbino—all of which honours he refused, since his diocese was the world, his parish Italy. Being at Ancona and hearing that Perugia was in arms against herself, he hastened thither and announced that God had sent him "as His angel" to proclaim peace on earth to men of good will. Nor was he unsuccessful; for they "forgave one another, desiring to live in peace and to pass to the Right Hand". Later, from that little pulpit on the wall of the Cathedral, he watched Perugia at his bidding burn her books, the false hair of the women, the beautiful pictures, full of desire and life, of the great lords. His influence for a time can scarcely be exaggerated; he filled Perugia for a moment with puritanical gloom, and his rigid rules even became law. In 1438 he was appointed vicar-general of the Observants in Italy, and during the five years he held that office set about a reformation. He then returned to Siena, and being on the road, ever preaching, came to Aquila in the Abruzzi, where he was taken ill of fever, dying on May 20, 1444. He was buried there in that far-away city, and was canonised by Nicholas V in 1450. Thus ended a life as necessary, as typical of that strange fifteenth century, as that of any artist or tyrant. His art was love, as theirs was beauty or power, nor was he less strict in his service. Perugia at least would be less passionate without him.

Close by is the ruined church of San Francesco, where he lodged on his visits to Perugia, and where hung his favourite bell "Viola", and perhaps this explains why this oratory to his memory was built here.

Not far from San Bernardino, towards the Via dei Priori, is the little church of Sant' Agata, memorable only for its doorway, which is the sole remnant of Lombard work in the city.

The church of San Martino, easily reached from the Piazza di San Francesco by the Via della Siepe, Via del Poggio, Via Francolina, Via Armonica and Via Verzaro, has a beautiful altarpiece by Manni(?) and a Crucifixion of the school of Perugino. Thence to the Via Appia is but a step. This picturesque street is one of the most curious in the city. Passing down it one comes into the Piazza Ansidei on the right, and thus into the Via Vecchia, at the bottom of which is the magnificent Arch of Augustus, inscribed with the title of the city, AUGUSTA PERUSIA, the lower part of which is undoubtedly Etruscan.

Passing thence up the Corso Garibaldi, and turning to the right just before the great Porta Sant' Angelo, is the church of Sant' Angelo, a little round columned building, probably a rebuilding of the fifth century, with a beautiful portal of the thirteenth century. It stands on the supposed site of a Temple of Venus, whence were taken the columns for San Pietro. Behind the high altar is a great stone, itself an altar to Marcus Aurelius, while the curious fresco, La Madonna del Verde, is certainly one of the earliest in Perugia. The lovely gate Porta Sant' Angelo is well worth seeing, with its Ghibelline battlements; it was part of a castle of Fortebraccio, the condottiere and despot of Perugia, who was defeated and killed in 1424 and buried in the Cappella della SS. Concezione in the convent of San Francesco al Prato. It is at Porta Sant' Angelo that S. Francis and S. Dominic are said to have met on their way to Pope Honorius, then in Perugia.

In the church of San Severo, dating from the eleventh century, but rebuilt in the eighteenth on the site, it is said, of a Temple of the Sun, is preserved a much repainted fresco, the upper part of which, with the Trinity and saints, is attributed to Raphael, but the view from here is better than the fresco.

In the convent of Sant' Agnese, till lately only open to women, but now, by special permission of the Pope, open to all, there are three frescoes attributed to Perugino. The delightful garden of the nuns, full of old-world flowers and herbs, is perhaps as charming as the frescoes.

Other churches there are: San Matteo outside Porta Sant' Angelo, with early frescoes; Santa Maria di Monteluce outside Porta Pesa, a thirteenth-century convent church with a Renaissance façade of red and white marble squares, which still retains its thirteenth-century portal and formidable stump of a campanile; Sant' Agostino outside Porta Augusta, with its magnificent loggia and choir stalls carved and inlaid by Baccio d'Agnolo of Florence (1502); San Constanzo outside Porta Romana, beyond the church of San Pietro, a church of the twelfth century entirely rebuilt sixty years ago, but which still retains in some sort its twelfth-century portal with its sculptures of Christ in benediction and the symbols of the four Evangelists; and Santa Giuliana outside Porta Santa Croce, beyond the Piazza d'Armi, a Romanesque building of the thirteenth century with a fourteenth-century façade, a great rose, a beautiful portal and a delightful cloister.

Just below the city, out of Porta Romana, before you come to the village of Ponte San Giovanni, there is the Etruscan Necropolis, the tombs of the Volumnii of the second century B.C. This immense catacomb suggests to the traveller, as perhaps nothing else could do, the depth of antiquity all around him. Here is the dust of men who lived more than 2,000 years ago, of whom we know nothing or next to nothing, whose language we cannot read, whose legend we cannot decipher. Their walls and gates are the foundation of Perugia, where they probably settled in the sixth century B.C., and there is a considerable museum full of their work in the Palazzo dell' Università. They too had their heroes and they are our heroes, and if their gods are not our gods it is only because we have deserted them. Troy they knew, its topless towers, its walls and gates, before which we too have waited for a glimpse of Helen whose beauty shattered the world, where young Troilus died dragged behind his own chariot, and Hector in his despair left his perfect wife and astonished little son, never to return. Iphigeneia is here too, the daughter of Agamemnon; the human sacrifice is made, the victim held down by the hair upon the altar; the priest, as ever the slayer, stands ready with the sacrificial knife; and Charon waits with his crazy boat just touching the sands of life. As now, so of old they appeased the gods, they went forth to battle, they loved, they laughed and were in despair.

And then as you turn back from the beautiful vale, if you are fortunate, suddenly you are involved in the simple splendour of some procession between the fields not too unlike those which the Etruscans and the Romans knew: the Madonna in all her robes is borne before an adoring people, while the fields and the vines, the corn and the olives quicken before her gracious coming, and the chanting of the boys, the flickering tapers, the immortal words of the priest persuade you that, as ever, men go forth until the evening and are subject to the sun and watch the clouds; sowing and reaping since the light is sweet and morning a pleasant thing and time and chance happen to all.

And so without or within the walls through many a medieval way—Via delle Stalle, Via delle Volte, Via Ritorta, Vicolo di Sant' Agata, Via dell' Acquedotto, Via del Verzaro, Via Vecchia, for instance—you may wander in and about Perugia, coming upon Etruscan boulders or Roman brick and stone and search out her most ancient gates with their lovely names: Porta Augusta on the north, Porta Sole on the east, Porta Cornea and Porta Marzia on the south-east, Porta della Man- dorla on the south-west. Out of Porta della Mandorla I like to descend the steps of Via Paradiso and, passing through the gate in the medieval wall, Porta Eburnea, turn to the right under a long stretch of the Etruscan wall, re-entering the city by Porta Sant' Andrea and ascending Via della Sposa to the last of the Etruscan gates, Porta Santa Susanna, at the bottom of the Via dei Priori. But it is well worth while to walk round the outer walls of the whole city, which can easily and even delightfully be done, except between Porta Sant' Angelo and Porta Sant' Antonio.

It is curious that one of the Etruscan gates is called Porta Eburnea and another Porta Cornea, as though Perugia had had Virgil in the close of the Sixth Aeneid in mind. It was, according to Matarazzo, through Porta Eburnea that the magnificent House of Baglioni always passed to do battle with their enemies. But the Porta Augusta is, of course, the Etruscan arch *par excellence*. The lofty Porta Sole is mentioned by Dante in the *Paradiso*, but the so-called "gate" we know is not that known to Dante, which probably stood at the top of the modern Via Alessi and was destroyed in 1543 for the construction of the Papal fortress, unless, indeed, Dante's gate is identical with the so-called Arco de' Tei, still to be seen on the right of Santa Maria Nuova. The Porta Cornea came to be called the Arco di S. Ercolano, for it is close to his church, or the Porta Leonea, from the Guelph lion which may still be seen above the keystone. The Porta Marzia was bricked up in 1542 and was destroyed finally with the Papal fortress and rebuilt but yesterday.

The gates of the medieval *borghi* were very numerous; there were many more than five *borghi*, each of which had its own great gate.

The approaches to Perugia, now graded and zigzagged, were of old direct, steep and difficult, little more than mule tracks. Some idea of what they were like may be had from the Via Colomata outside Porta Sant' Andrea. This was once the principal route out of Perugia for Tuscany. By it the Emperor Sigismund entered Perugia on August 27, 1433, and up its steep ascent the Oddi rode to their ruin in 1495.

CHAPTER XX

THE PINACOTECA VANNUCCI

THE PICTURE-GALLERY OF PERUGIA

THE Pinacoteca Vannucci, the Galleria Nazionale dell' Umbria, on the top floor of the Palazzo Comunale of Perugia, contains the most complete and representative collection of Umbrian pictures that has anywhere been brought together, as well as a number of early Sienese paintings and a few outstanding masterpieces of various schools; a Madonna and Child by Duccio di Buoninsegna, an altarpiece by Fra Angelico, and one by his pupil Benozzo Gozzoli, an altarpiece by Piero della Francesca and another by Luca Signorelli.

Unlike Florence and Siena, Umbria had no Giotto nor Duccio to point out the road she should follow in her art. Umbrian painting, which is not solely centred in Perugia, but which had several centres—Gubbio, Foligno, to name no others —in which it flourished, was really provincial in the true sense of the word. And it was from beginning to end the handmaid of the Church, and remained Christian when almost everywhere else art had become pagan.

And situated as Umbria is between Florence, Siena and the Marches, each the centre of an important school of painting, her art from the beginning was strongly influenced by one or other of these schools and chiefly, perhaps, by Siena. Moreover, there rose in the thirteenth and fourteenth centuries the great Basilica of San Francesco in Assisi, where the chief Tuscan masters, Giunta Pisano, Cimabue, Giotto, Simone Martini and Pietro Lorenzetti were at work, though it would seem these great artists made but little impression on the local Umbrian schools.

In the beginning it was a quite indigenous school of miniaturists which carried the fame of Umbrian art into the great world, so that Dante speaks in the *Purgatorio* of Oderigi or Oderisi of Gubbio as pre-eminent, till he was superseded by a certain Franco of Bologna and he by Cimabue, who in his turn is surpassed by Giotto in public fame. In the early years of the fourteenth century Gubbio produced Guido Palmerucci, who was a close and unmistakable follower of Pietro Lorenzetti, and indeed it is on the whole the art of Siena which is the main influence in early Umbrian painting, and the many early Sienese pictures in the Pinacoteca here in Perugia would seem to bear witness to this.

The influence, too, of certain March painters is evident: Fabriano just across the border produced Allegretto Nuzi, the master of Gentile da Fabriano; and later Carlo Crivelli was to influence very strongly one of the most characteristic of Umbrian masters, Niccolò da Foligno.

Fra Angelico and his pupil and assistant, Benozzo Gozzoli, arrived in Umbria, the latter in the middle years of the fifteenth century, and left his mark, and may be said to be responsible for the most characteristic Perugian painter of that age, Benedetto Bonfigli, and finally for Fiorenzo di Lorenzo. And then the greatest and, as a mystic, the most characteristic of all Umbrian painters, Pietro Vannucci, called Perugino, also and fundamentally experienced the influence of Florence in the person of Verrocchio.

Perugino in his turn is the master of the most beloved name in painting, Raphael Sanzio, who, born on her borders in Urbino, spent the most impressionable years of an impressionable life in Perugia and never loses that spacious and serene perfection he caught from her landscape and from the great landscapist and poet who was his master.

It is with some such background as this, inadequate though it inevitably must be, that one passes through the many rooms of the Pinacoteca Vannucci.

The finest Italo-Byzantine picture in Umbria is to be found here in the first room. It is an altarpiece of the Last Judgment and scenes from the life of S. Felix, signed on the sword of S. Paul, Magister Pescius. It comes from the town of Giano near Montefalco and is in an admirable state of preservation, and very fine in colour. It dates from the last quarter of the thirteenth century.

Of the early works of the Sienese and Umbrian schools, the most important is the panel of the Virgin and Child by Duccio of

Siena. The Virgin is in half-length, the Child sitting on her left arm. Above are six figures of angels. The forefinger of the Virgin's left hand is curiously long, as it is in the triptych in the National Gallery, which this panel very much resembles. The picture comes from the church of San Domenico here in Perugia. It was till recently entirely repainted as to the chief figures, and the cleaning has left it rather flat. It is, however, a fine work by the master, and must have been painted just before Duccio's masterpiece, the great Maestà in Siena.

Of some importance with regard to the Sienese influence in Umbria is an oblong panel signed by Vigoroso da Siena, which is or was dated 1282. The central part is filled with a half-length figure of the Virgin with the Child and at the sides are various saints.

Several rather melancholy works here by Meo da Siena show the strong influence of Duccio. The polyptych with the missing panel is signed at the base of the panel of the Madonna and Child. Another polyptych and a fine panel of the Virgin and Child and some half-ruined pictures by him have been gathered here. Several pictures by his school, too, hang on the walls of this gallery.

The panel here of the Madonna with the Child standing on her knee surrounded by four angels with S. Paul, and is it S. Benedict?—the picture comes from the monastery of S. Paolo di Valdiponte—is by Marino da Perugia, who may have been the son of Oderisi of Gubbio. It is in this picture we find a March influence mixed with the Sienese. The Child standing does not occur in Duccio's pictures, but is found in the art of the Marches.

One of the most delightful pictures here is a small panel very highly decorated in gold of the Madonna with her little Son in her arms while He looks up at her and caresses her chin with His left hand and clutches her wrist with His right. This picture, too, an Umbrian work, shows the influence both of Sienese and March masters.

The most outstanding and the strongest master, possibly Umbrian, of the end of the thirteenth century is the Maestro di San Francesco, a nameless painter who gets his title not only from the panel with a full-length portrait of S. Francis in

13

Santa Maria degli Angeli, but also from those early frescoes of his in the nave of the lower church of San Francesco in Assisi. There are a number of small panels, parts of an altarpiece, and a vast Crucifix by this master here, and another Crucifix by some pupil of his. He was a follower of Giunta Pisano, and the only date of his work we have is that of 1272 on the huge Crucifix in this gallery. It is a very powerful work and it is complete with the Virgin and S. John at the ends of the cross-piece, and, above, the Virgin in an attitude of prayer between two angels, and, above again, in a round, a half-figure of Our Lord. Very noticeable in the grand figure of the crucified Saviour are the eyebrows and the dark line under the eyes which are characteristic of the work of this master and appear again in the beautiful and tragic panels of the Deposition and in the single figures of saints which once made part of an altarpiece.

The influence of this great artist is to be seen in the enormous triptych with the Virgin and Child in the central panel, and in the wings under the Annunciation eight scenes of the life of Christ on either side. The whole design is Byzantine, but the colour and the liveliness of the figures in this huge miniature are Italian. It comes from the convent of Sant' Agnese and on the outside of the wings are damaged figures of S. Francis and S. Clare.

Unquestionably of the Rimini school is the small panel of the Magdalen entirely covered with her hair and supported by angels and surrounded by saints, which must date from the first years of the fourteenth century. This beautiful little picture with its enamel-like paint is rather damaged, but is one of the treasures of the gallery. It was once in a chapel here in Perugia where prisoners condemned to death were allowed to receive the Last Sacraments.

We have thus at the very outset many and excellent examples of the various schools which influence Umbrian painting.

The salone originally the Cappella dei Priori is decorated in fresco by Benedetto Bonfigli, perhaps the most characteristic master of Perugian painting in the fifteenth century, the father of the Perugian school. These frescoes were begun by Bonfigli (whose panel pictures are hung elsewhere) in 1455, but were

not finished for a generation or more. They consist of scenes
from the legend of S. Ercolano, Bishop of Perugia, slain by
Totila, and the life of S. Louis of Toulouse. Some are in a
poor state, but the fresco of the burial of S. Louis is of great
beauty, notably in the architecture, where the church is
rather like San Pietro dei Cassinesi here outside Perugia,
while in the fresco of the siege of Perugia by Totila we recognise
the church of Sant' Ercolano. In the last two frescoes, also in
spite of their damage, one sees other Perugian buildings—the
Palazzo Comunale, the Cathedral and San Domenico.

Three sculptures by or ascribed to Arnolfo di Cambio, and
two beautiful silver-gilt Chalices of the fourteenth century, one
the work of Cataluccio da Todi, and an ivory pastoral staff are
exhibited in this room.

Some fine Sienese pictures of the fourteenth century by Lippo
Vanni, Bartoli di Fredi and Taddeo di Bartolo, and a predella
by the fifteenth-century Sienese, Benvenuto di Giovanni, are to
be found here.

The Lippo Vanni is a delightful panel of the Virgin and
Child, one of this master's most charming achievements. It
comes from San Domenico. Our Lady is seen in half-length,
her little Son sitting on her left arm embracing her and pressing
His face against His mother's. The elaborate patterned work
of the Child's dress is characteristically Sienese.

An important altarpiece is here by the friend and partner of
Vanni, Bartolo di Maestro Fredi (1330–1410). The Madonna
is seated on a wooden throne with the Child. On the left are
the Prophet Elias and S. Catherine of Alexandria. Before them
is an angel with a viol. On the right are S. Mary Magdalen
and S. Antony Abbot, also with a musical angel before them.
Above is the Annunciation, much damaged. This is one of
Bartolo di Fredi's finest works.

Quite as charming are the pictures here by Taddeo di
Bartolo (1362–1422), the follower of Vanni and Bartolo di Fredi.
Chief of these is a magnificent altarpiece in which, in the centre,
is the Madonna with the Child on her knees and, below, two
musical angels. In the side-panels are full-length figures of
S. Mary Magdalen, S. John Baptist, S. John Evangelist and
S. Catherine of Alexandria. The picture is signed and dated

1403. It comes from the convent of San Francesco al Prato. The back of this beautiful altarpiece is that here in five compartments, with S. Francis in the centre and S. Ercolano, S. Anthony of Padua, S. Louis of Toulouse and S. Costanzo. The predella and pinnacles, if they ever existed, are missing; otherwise this altarpiece is complete.

Two other panels by the master come from the same church of San Francesco: a S. Peter and a S. Paul.

Another work by Taddeo, not so fine, comes from Sant' Agostino. There we see the Virgin in the midst of the Apostles at the Pentecost with tongues of fire descending upon them. In spite of the inferior quality of this rather coarse and awkward work, it was signed by the painter and dated 1403, the same year as the magnificent altarpiece from San Francesco.

The panel picture by Benvenuto di Giovanni (1436–1518) of various saints is one of the last works of the Sienese school proper. It is notable for the admirable portrait of the donor, which fills one of its compartments.

The two major single treasures of the gallery are the altarpiece by Fra Angelico and the altarpiece by Piero della Francesca.

The altarpiece by Fra Angelico is a masterpiece, indeed he never surpassed in feeling and quality some of the smaller figures. The Madonna and Child are enthroned under a baldacchino. On either side are two angels, the foremost two offering baskets of roses. On panels at the sides are various full-length figures of saints: on the left S. Dominic and S. Nicholas, and these are the most exquisite; on the right S. John Baptist and S. Catherine of Alexandria, perhaps the work of an assistant. The frame is adorned with twelve small figures of saints, viz. the Magdalen, S. Benedict, S. Thomas Aquinas, S. Laurence, S. Catherine of Siena, S. Peter Martyr, S. Louis of Toulouse, S. Jerome, S. Peter, S. Paul, S. Stephen and S. John Evangelist. In two small rounds are the angel and Virgin Annunciate. The frame itself is modern, but all these figures are original works of the master, except possibly the Annunciation figures, which may be the work of the assistant who painted the figures in the right-hand panels, S. John Baptist and S. Catherine of Alexandria. Of the four scenes in the predella that of S. Nicholas staying the executioner who is about to behead three persons, with its beautiful landscape, is by Angelico; the other two are by the assistant, as is the panel missing here, now in the Vatican.

This most lovely altarpiece comes from the church of San Domenico, where it stood over the altar in the Guidalotti chapel of S. Niccolò, and it dates from about 1437. It was restored and put together, for it had been dismantled, in 1918. Unfortunately, the face of the Virgin has been damaged; otherwise it seems to be in an excellent state, surprisingly bright in colour, and some of the figures of saints are of such beauty that I do not think Angelico ever surpassed them.

The large polyptych by Piero della Francesca is the other great single treasure of the gallery. It is a puzzling work. In the midst is a late Gothic altarpiece, the Madonna and Child enthroned in the centre with four full-length saints, SS. Anthony, John Baptist, Francis and Elizabeth at the sides, much in the form of Fra Angelico's altarpiece here. Above, in a seven-sided pediment, is the Annunciation; below are two rounds with figures of S. Clare and S. Agatha, and below in the predella three scenes: a miracle of S. Anthony, S. Francis receiving the Stigmata and a miracle of S. Elizabeth of Hungary.

This strange work was painted for the Franciscan nuns of Sant' Antonio, and perhaps there we may find its explanation. The altarpiece as we see it is most incongruous—an unhappy conglomeration of Gothic in the main part with Renaissance above. Moreover, the main part is on a gold ground within a heavy Gothic framework, while above we have a very simple sevenfold frame which might well once have been an ordinary, if elaborate, Gothic pediment not uncommon in Sienese altarpieces of the fourteenth and fifteenth centuries. Either the Annunciation never originally formed part of the polyptych, or can it be that Piero in his old age, passing through Perugia on his way to Rome from Borgo San Sepolcro, was called upon by the little Franciscan nuns of Sant' Antonio to repaint an old Gothic altarpiece not unlike that which Fra Angelico had painted for the Guidalotti in the Dominican church of San Domenico? Can it be that he found the main part of this altarpiece already gilded and possibly painted, or at least with relics of an old composition, and in humility, that chief Franciscan virtue, he repainted the main part of the altarpiece on its gold ground and within its old framework with the Virgin and Child we see and the four full-length figures of the Baptist and three Franciscan saints?

Above, the old altarpiece was perhaps more completely damaged, so that here Piero felt himself more free. So that he painted there, after the precepts of Alberti, a marvellous study of architecture, the corridor of some Florentine or Urbinate Renaissance cloister in the manner of Brunelleschi or Laurana, reviving therein the ghosts of an older Annunciation, resurrecting them after his own manner, giving them that monumental solidity so characteristic of him, lending them his own colours and magically transforming there the old scene on its gold background into a mysterious moonlight.

However this may be, and my explanation is as awkward as the picture, I find the main part of the altarpiece disappointing, as indeed are the predella scenes. But the Annunciation I find one of the most enchanting of Piero's works. I can never leave it without returning again and again. And then how characteristic it is of the artistic moment dominated by perspective and the theories of Alberti and the practice of Brunelleschi, Laurana, Uccello and Masaccio! What that gracious and formidable angel is announcing to the Madonna, so classical in her monumentality and repose, is not the birth of Christ, but the rebirth, the renaissance, of Antiquity. It may well be that this is a work of Piero's old age, but if so, your old men shall see visions.

There are some other interesting pictures of this time, the most rare and perhaps the most charming of which is the Madonna and Child by Gentile da Fabriano. The panel is considerably damaged, but is still unrestored. The Virgin is seated on a Gothic throne about which grows a wood of small trees. The Child sits naked on her knee. Below, a number of little angels are singing, a scroll of music before them. The Madonna is lovely and typical of Gentile's art, the Child is less pleasing. This picture, too, comes from San Domenico.

The panel of Benozzo Gozzoli, the pupil and assistant of Fra Angelico, shows us the Virgin and Child seated on a cushion between SS. Peter, John Baptist, Jerome and Paul, with a predella in which are half-figures of Christ standing under the Cross with the Madonna, and S. John on either side between SS. Thomas, Laurence, Sebastian and Bernardino, and in the pilasters of the frame SS. Dominic, Francis, Peter Martyr, Catherine of Alexandria, Elizabeth of Hungary and Lucy. It was painted for the Collegio della Sapienza here in Perugia, and is signed and dated 1456. The coat of arms is that of Benedetto Guidalotto, who founded the Sapienza. It is one of Benozzo's most delightful and independent works, though lacking in emotion.

The large Sienese polyptych by Domenico di Bartolo is nearly twenty years earlier than the Gozzoli panel and is signed and dated 1438. It comes from Santa Giuliana. In the midst is the Madonna and Child enthroned, with a donor, the abbess Antonia, kneeling in adoration, whom the Madonna embraces with her hand. In the side-panels are the Baptist, SS. Benedict, Giuliana and Bernard. In the predella are scenes from the life of the Baptist: his setting out for the desert, his preaching, the dance of Salome in the midst, he is arraigned before Herod, his Baptism of Christ. Above, in the gables, are Christ in the midst with the angel and Virgin Annunciate on either side and SS. Peter and Paul over the outside panels. This altarpiece on its wonderful gold ground, though the frame has been repainted, is in a very fine state, is complete and still very charming, and though the larger figures are rather ungainly, the scenes in the predella are like miniatures and delightfully imagined and executed.

Another large altarpiece, but by a Florentine master, is that by Bicci di Lorenzo. It is a late work, and though the general decorative effect is beautiful, it has not the technical excellence of the altarpiece by Domenico di Bartolo. It is an elaborate affair: in the midst is the Marriage of S. Catherine who stands on one side, while the Child places the ring on her finger as His Mother, who is borne on clouds supported by cherubim and adored by two angels, holds Him. On the other side is S. Agnes, and S. Dorothy, a much smaller figure, kneels in the centre. In the side-panels are SS. Anthony of Padua, Louis of Toulouse, John Evangelist, Ercolano, Constantius and

Laurence. The presence of S. Ercolano would seem to prove that the picture was painted for some Perugian church and the Franciscan saints that it was for a Franciscan convent. In the predella are the Noli Me Tangere, and the Maries at the Sepulchre, the Martyrdom of S. Agnes, S. Elizabeth giving alms and the Baptism of Christ. Above, over the central panel, is the Annunciation, and over the lateral panels, S. Francis receiving the Stigmata, S. Jerome and other saints praying.

The large altarpiece of the Virgin and Child with saints in glory, here attributed to Luca Signorelli, is unfortunately a schoolpiece. The Pietà by Piero di Cosimo is, on the other hand, an important work. It shows the strong influence of Leonardo da Vinci. The Blessed Virgin, who is represented here as of considerable age, unlike Michelangelo's vision of her in his Pietà in S. Peter's in Rome, is seated with the dead Christ on her knees, His head and feet supported by S. John and the Magdalen. The Virgin Mother's hands are raised in deepest sorrow and prayer. In the beautiful landscape the three crosses are seen on a lofty hill and above, in the sky, three angels bear the instruments of the Passion. To the right, in the background, S. Martin shares his cloak with the beggar—a strange incident to introduce into a Pietà, but then Piero di Cosimo was ever full of fantasy and no doubt must have had some mystical meaning here—if, indeed, we are right in thinking this is S. Martin and not some Roman soldier with the divided garments of Christ.

We come to the Umbrian school, with the pictures of Giovanni di Piermatteo called Boccatis (1435?–1480?). It is true Boccatis was born in Camerino in the Marches, but it is impossible to make a definite division between the March painters and the Umbrian, for there is a strong likeness between them, and this is especially true of Boccatis, who came to live in Perugia in 1445 and even wanted to become a citizen. The most delightful of his pictures here, the Madonna del Pergolato, was painted soon after his arrival in Perugia for the Confraternity of San Domenico. In this fascinating altarpiece, which, alas, has been varnished so that it is hard and bright in colour, the Madonna with the Child on her lap is enthroned under a flowered pergola in the midst of a choir of child angels singing in chorus and playing instruments of music. On the right kneels S. Gregory, and S. Augustine stands beside him. In front kneel S. Francis and S. Dominic, who present four members of the Confraternity. The two saints on the left have been repainted by Giannicola Manni; they are S. Ambrose and S. Jerome.

Delightful in composition as this main part of the altarpiece is, it is surpassed by the predella, which is unquestionably one of the most exquisite works in the gallery. It consists of five panels: S. Thomas Aquinas presents a model of the church of San Domenico, and at the other extremity is S. Peter Martyr. Between these two glories of the Dominican Order are three scenes of the Passion of Our Lord: the Kiss of Judas, the Via Crucis and the Crucifixion. These small panels are of the very highest quality, exquisite in colour and technique. One does not know which to linger with longest—the capture of Christ in the shadow of a mysterious cypress wood or the Via Crucis, outside the towered walls of a city by the sea where Christ bears His Cross amid a cavalcade of knights and standards.

This still delightful and once most lovely work is signed OPUS IOHIS BOCHATIS DE CHAMERENO F. and dated 1447. It is in some ways surpassed in beauty by the polyptych at Belforte near Tolentino, and then here in this gallery the Madonna dell' Orchestra is lovely enough. There we see the Madonna in a magnificent robe of patterned velvet with the naked Child lying in her lap, enthroned under a Renaissance baldacchino sculptured—is it by Luca della Robbia or Agostino di Duccio?—with a frieze of naked *putti* and surrounded by an orchestra of musical angels, while at her feet are four little winged cherubs, two of which play upon instruments of music and two are plucking a nosegay for her.

Two other pictures by this enchanting little master are in this room: a Madonna della Misericordia and a Madonna and Child with four angels; the former has been ruined by coarse repaint, and delightful though the latter is it cannot compare with his two masterpieces. The triptych here of the Madonna and Child between S. Francis and S. Jerome, by Giovanni Francesco da Rimini, a pleasing master at his best, is unfortunately a mediocre work.

The works of Benedetto Bonfigli (*op.* 1445–96) and Bartolommeo Caporali (*ca.* 1430–*ca.* 1505), both definitely Perugian
masters, both pupils of Benozzo Gozzoli and both influenced by
Boccatis are what more especially belong to Perugia. They were
partners, and sometimes their work is so much alike that it is
doubtful to which to ascribe some unsigned picture.

It was in 1454 that Bonfigli undertook to paint the Priori
chapel here in the Palazzo Comunale, now a Sala of the
Pinacoteca, a work which was not finished when he died in
1496. But, as may be imagined, this important work was not
his first. Among his earlier pictures is that of the Adoration of
the Magi, here in this room, in which he seems to have remembered Gentile da Fabriano's altarpiece of the same subject, now
in the Uffizi; and if this be so, then Bonfigli as a young man
must have visited Florence, for Gentile's picture was painted for
Santa Trinità in that city. The Madonna is seated beside a
broken wall outside a shed, over which three small angels hover
and under which S. Joseph stands. The Child is seated on her
knee and the oldest king is kneeling and kissing the Child's
foot while the other two kings stand behind him with their gifts.
Their retinue is in the background. On either side the Madonna
stand the Baptist and perhaps S. Ercolano. The landscape of
bare hills stretches away past a walled city to the horizon. The
picture comes from San Domenico. This is a gracious though
rather feeble work.

The Gonfalone with the Madonna della Misericordia, in this
room, dates from 1464, and the Gonfalone of S. Bernardino from
the following year. In the background of the latter is the façade
of the Oratorio di S. Bernardino. But a far better work is the
panel of 1467 here in this room, in which we see the Madonna
adoring her little Son, who is seated on her knees, while four
angels crowned with Bonfigli's wreaths of roses kneel at her feet.
This is, perhaps, his loveliest work, both in sentiment and
colour. Yet the picture here of the Annunciation, which might
well be an earlier work, is full of Bonfigli's peculiar *naïveté*
There, before a Renaissance portico, Our Lady kneels to
receive the salutation of Gabriel Archangel, a figure like
some paradisal bird crowned, too, with celestial roses. Between
them sits S. Luke on his ox, writing the first chapter of his Gospel:

In mense autem sexto missus est angelus Gabriel a Deo in civitatem Galilaeae ad virginem et nomen virginis Maria. Above, God the Father in the midst of His child angels sends forth the Dove of the Holy Spirit to Mary's breast.

But Bonfigli is not always as attractive a poet as this, the injured panel of the Madonna enthroned with four saints has little of the almost Botticellesque elegance of the Annunciation, fine though the four wings of some lost altarpiece are, each with two angels crowned with roses and bearing baskets of flowers and the instruments of the Passion.

Perhaps Benedetto Bonfigli is the most delightful artist Perugia was to produce. His contemporary and partner, Bartolommeo Caporali, however, has also great charm, and not least in his remarkable Madonna della Misericordia at Montone, but the works we have from his hand are fewer than those of Bonfigli. In 1467 both painters worked together on a triptych, of which we have here in this room the two panels of the Annunciation and the two panels of SS. Paul and Peter Martyr, SS. Peter and Catherine by Caporali.

The fresco from Santa Giuliana of the Coronation or Assumption of the Virgin, with four rose-crowned angels and, below, half-figures of SS. Bernard, Benedict and Giuliana, is dated 1469, and seems to recall Boccatis. Nothing here, however, can compare with his masterpiece at Montone.

The processional banner here is by Niccolò da Foligno, painted in 1466, the subject of which is the Annunciation. It was painted when he was about thirty-six years' old and has something of the style of his altarpiece in the Cathedral of Assisi.

In the pictures by Fiorenzo di Lorenzo (1440–1522) is to be found the first direct influence not only of Florentine art, but of Florence, in Perugian and even in Umbrian painting. That influence was the art of Verrocchio and at least of one considerable sojourn in Florence.

His earliest work here seems to be the triptych with the Madonna and Child enthroned in a very Florentine shell niche, with two angels kneeling beside her and two adoring members of the Confraternity of Justice, for which this altarpiece was painted, at her feet. In the side-panels are SS. Mustiola, Andrew, Peter and Francis, and in the predella, a Pietà in the midst and half-figures of S. Bernardino, the Baptist, two members of the Confraternity, S. Jerome and S. Sebastian. It is not only the niche which is Florentine, the Madonna is, both in her face and her draperies, almost a copy of Verrocchio's sculpturesque painting, though the harsh colour is all Fiorenzo's own.

The picture of the Martyrdom of S. Sebastian is also very Verrocchiesque in its effect almost of a sculpture, and the architecture, completely Renaissance, can only have come from Florence. This is one of Fiorenzo's best works. The profile head, at the foot of the picture on the right, might be a bust by Verrocchio.

The beautiful Adoration of the Shepherds, with a choir of angels, above the *Gloria in excelsis*, in the background, the lovely distant landscape all point to Florence; indeed, the exquisite Virgin is the sister of Vanna Tornabuoni or Simonetta Vespucci. This delightful altarpiece comes from Santa Maria di Monteluce.

These are among his earlier works; by 1487, when he painted the curious altarpiece with a niche for a statue with SS. Peter and Paul at the sides and the Virgin and Child in a wreath of cherubim with two angels above, he has become much more Umbrian and has already lost the exquisite and fastidious desire for beauty that he learnt in Florence. The great polyptych is later still, where Our Lady with hands pointed in prayer sits enthroned with the naked Child on her knee, neck-laced with a coral horn against the the Evil Eye, and two adoring angels at her feet in a landscape in which we seem to discern the city of Perugia itself, while four full-length saints in the panels on either side—S. Benedict, S. Peter (arrogant and sneering), S. John and S. Francis—rather hard and affected figures which seem to suggest what the art of Niccolò da Foligno could do to one who was no mystic, or what the art of Pintoricchio seemed to be to one who was no longer capable of understanding it.

Fiorenzo seems to have recovered something of his early love of beauty in the frescoes now here in this room, which he painted in 1498 for the church of San Giorgio. The best of these is a Marriage of S. Catherine with a bishop standing beside

the Madonna opposite to S. Catherine. Some sweetness long
forgot has returned to his spirit, if only for a moment, for though
he was still painting fifteen years later, he never recovered the
same serenity and charm, things native to Umbria.

The series of small panels painted with the acts or miracles
of S. Bernardino of Siena have for long been given to Fiorenzo
di Lorenzo, and it is only in fairly recent years that they have
been wholly denied to him,[1] without, however, any success in
securely attributing them to any other known master. They do,
in fact, differ in quality and seem to be by different hands.
Some of them are, however, among the most delightful and
technically perfect little masterpieces of fifteenth-century
Italian art. There are eight panels in all and they decorated a
press or cupboard for the processional banners in the Oratorio
di San Bernardino here in Perugia.

The best panels are unquestionably the two in which
S. Bernardino restores to life a dead child (No. 222) and resurrects
a young girl, Polissena, in a miracle at Rieti (No. 223) where,
on a slab of marble over the arch, is to be seen the date, 1473,
and a Latin inscription.

The first is a wonderful study of the finest Renaissance architecture in which every detail as well as the beautiful whole is
considered and represented. Under the portico of a marble
palace of pure Alberti architecture is a room in which a mother
has just given birth to a dead child which, by the intervention
of S. Bernardino, is restored to life. Women kneel about the
child who is sitting up on the pavement, while a man, possibly
the father, lifts his hands in wonder. Without, on the magnificent patterned pavement of various marbles, a group of most
fashionably dressed young men in doublet and hose discuss
some other matter with the indifference to what is passing of
the two figures in the foreground of Piero della Francesca's
Flagellation in Urbino. One figure in a great cloak and biretta
is talking to a priest or bishop, to judge by the gold cord round
his priest's hat. In the background is a landscape with mountains under a wonderful sunset, where delicate clouds float in
the sky.

---

[1] I think it was Jean Carlyle Graham (*The Problem of Fiorenzo di Lorenzo*,
Perugia, 1903), who first denied that these panels were the work of Fiorenzo.

The other picture, of the resurrection of a young girl, is also a study of architecture. The miracle takes place before a great arch supported by square pillars, all of marble and decorated with nude figures in the spandrels and the keystone, and festooned above with ribboned wreaths. In the foreground a group of figures, three friars and three others, perhaps the father, mother and grandfather of the young girl, kneel about her as, risen from the dead, she sits up on the ground. An elegant youth, in the latest Renaissance fashion of hose and tabarded blouse and long staff elegantly held in his left hand, looks indifferently out of the picture; on the other side an elaborately gowned personage gazes with wonder on the restored maiden. It is here on the arch we find the date 1473, which, as it happens, was that of the visit to Perugia of Vespasiano Strozzi, the ambassador of the magnificent court of Ferrara and the best Latin poet of his time. It is to him, apparently, these works are dedicated, for the inscription over the date runs:

S. P. Q. R. DIVO TITO DIVI VESPASIANI
FILIO DIVO VESPASIANO AUGUSTO
A. D. MCCCCLXXIII
FINIS

We are reminded of this in one of the other panels (No. 229) in which S. Bernardino heals a youth gored by a bull. For there in the left-hand corner is a personage who seems to be, as to head-dress and countenance, a reproduction of Pisanello's medal of John Palaeologus, Emperor of Byzantium, and in honour of Pisanello's art Vespasiano Strozzi had written an elegant Latin poem in the style of Guarini.

In another of these panels (No. 226), a better work than the preceding (No. 229), we again have a study of architecture. In the court of a windowed palace, under a great round-arched portico, S. Bernardino cures a deaf and dumb paralytic, who is seen kneeling and gazing upward at the vision of the saint, who appears like a Jack-in-the-box under the central half-domed arch, which is adorned within, wreathed round with the busts of a man and woman. Below, in the courtyard, surrounding him who was paralysed are two groups of eight figures in all, sumptuously and fashionably attired and treading lightly the marble pavement similar to that in the miracle of the resurrected baby (No. 222).

The other four panels, inferior in quality and no doubt different in execution from the first three (Nos. 222, 223, 226), are nevertheless very striking works, each with its wonderful architecture and its landscape which is sometimes fantastic, as in the healing of a sick man outside a church, where the rocks tower up as in some extravagant dream, while amid the elegant youths there, with their hound and the little child with his terrier, a figure as of the Magdalen kneels in anxiety and wonder, the long golden curls of her hair streaming to her waist.

I said, with regard to the panel of the deaf and dumb paralytic, that the saint "appears like a Jack-in-the-box", and perhaps the most curious and surprising thing about these panels is that they seem to have been painted in a sort of derision of the saint and his miracles. If we look at them closely we shall see that caricature follows caricature, as for instance in the figure of the priest or bishop in the panel of the child restored to life, as well as in the absurd and sudden appearances of the saint himself—one of the most universally revered figures of that time—and the disdainful indifference of the so elegantly attired world present on these interesting, even holy, occasions bears witness to a spirit not, I think, to be found anywhere else in Italian art. This is not the idealised pagan spirit of the court of Lorenzo il Magnifico, it is something that is rather impishly sceptical than poetical. When Bernardino died in 1444 Eugenius IV wanted to canonise him but there was considerable opposition, not least in Perugia which he had filled with Puritan gloom. His preaching had excited the ridicule of the Humanists as Gregorovius (VII, I, 99) records. Can this be the explanation of these pictures?

Who was the author of these panels and who were his assistants? May we find the hand of Perugino here in these wonderful sunsets and these "trees of heaven" delicately towering into the soft sky? Or do we see here the work of several painters, as now seems to be the more general opinion; and, if so, where does Fiorenzo, if at all, come in? These are unanswerable questions, unanswerable certainly by me. Whoever it was or whoever they were who painted these eight panels, they are one of the great treasures of Perugia and a major delight to all who look upon them.

We now come to the works of Perugino (?1455–1523), but most of the pictures here belong to the years of his decadence and only three or four to his great period. In truth, this Pinacoteca, which bears his name, has little of his art that is worthy of him.

The date of Perugino's birth is usually said to be 1445, but may well have been nearer 1450. He came of a family that had lived in Castello della Pieve since the thirteenth century. Vasari says he was actually born in Perugia and that his parents were poor. In 1470 he went to Florence and, again according to Vasari, became the pupil of Botticelli, but this, if we consider the style of his pictures, seems improbable; his master in Florence was rather, perhaps, Verrocchio, who had also been the master of Fiorenzo di Lorenzo, who was perhaps eight or ten years Perugino's senior, and who in his turn was to become his master or at any rate to influence him profoundly. His earliest authentic work is the S. Sebastian at Cerqueto, near Perugia, which is signed and dated 1478. This is a fresco and very Verrocchiesque, indeed the beautiful nude figure of the saint is like a statue. Three or four years later Perugino was painting in the Sistine Chapel one of his most beautiful works, the Christ giving the keys to S. Peter. In 1493 he painted the lovely picture of the Madonna between S. John Baptist and S. Sebastian, now in the Uffizi. In 1495 he was painting the great dispersed altarpiece for San Pietro in Cassinese at Perugia, and in the following year he began his only fresco sequence in the Cambio, and then painted his magnificent fresco in S. Maria Maddalena dei Pazzi in Florence. In 1502 Raphael became his pupil in Perugia. He was then at the height of his fame.

Here in the Pinacoteca Vannucci, it may be we have a work of his which is earlier than the signed S. Sebastian at Cerqueto in the Adoration of the Magi (Sala XII, No. 180),[1] so long attributed to Fiorenzo di Lorenzo. It must have been painted, if it be by Perugino, after his return from Florence and, perhaps,

---

[1] The Pinacoteca is in course of rearrangement (1953). When it is reopened the position of pictures may not be as here stated.

PERUGIA. Pinacoteca: Bonfigli, Annunciation.

PERUGIA. Pinacoteca: Master of 1473, Miracle of S. Bernardino.

after his connection with Fiorenzo, for it shows the influence both of that master and of Verrocchio. The Virgin is seated under a stable shed, with the Child seated on her knee. S. Joseph stands behind her leaning on his staff. Cattle are stalled beside them. The oldest king kneels offering his gift, the other two, one a proud youth like a condottiere, the other, who is looking at him, of middle age with forked beard, stand behind, before their numerous retinue. A "tree of heaven" towers into the lucid air and far away an exquisite landscape lies with fantastic rocks, conical hills and faint, distant mountains. This picture was painted for Santa Maria dei Servi in Porta Eburnea.

Perhaps the next picture we have here from his hand is the now "restored" and ruined Pietà (Sala XII, No. 248), which was painted for the Cappella dei Priori in 1493. The half-figure of the dead Christ is seen against a black background. Forty years ago it was still untouched and was then attributed by Adolfo Venturi to Raphael.

About the same time, it seems, Perugino painted the exquisite picture of the Madonna and Child (Sala XII, No. 220), seated in a landscape with two angels hovering above them, and kneeling behind them the habited members of the Confraternità della Consolazione. This wonderfully serene masterpiece, one of Perugino's most beautiful works, should be compared with the Certosa triptych, now in the National Gallery, for they were painted about the same time.

About the same time, too, Perugino painted the little gonfalon of S. Francis with two brethren of the Confraternità di S. Francesco (Sala XIV, No. 349), which has been entirely ruined and repainted.

Later, perhaps in or about the turn of the century, the master painted the not very attractive Madonna and Child, borne in mid-air by three cherubim and surrounded by S. Niccolò da Tolentino, S. Bernardino, S. Jerome and S. Sebastian (Sala XII, No. 279). The landscape, however, as always with Perugino, is delightful. The predella of this picture is in Berlin.

In 1502 Perugino undertook to paint for the friars of San Francesco al Monte four figures about a Crucifix of wood; the Virgin and S. John and the Magdalen and S. Francis, and

14

on the other side of the panel a Coronation of the Virgin, with
angels above and the Apostles below, but he seems to have left
his pupils to carry out the work, for what we have here is a
very indifferent picture (Sala XIV, No. 263).

Perhaps the finest work by Perugino in the gallery is the
Adoration of the Shepherds (No. 258), a transferred fresco
dating 1505. It comes from the cloister of San Francesco al
Monte. It is still a lovely and most notable picture, showing in
its composition and design all the greatest qualities of the
master's style.

We now come to the works of his decadence, when he seems
to have been content to leave nearly everything to his assistants.
Between 1512 and 1516 these pupils and assistants produced
for the church of Sant' Agostino in Perugia a large retable of
many panels, of which those representing the Baptism of Christ
and the Virgin adoring the Child under a lofty canopy, with
the shepherds kneeling in the distance, are here in this gallery
(Sala XIV, Nos. 249 and 258). Carefully though they have
been painted, these panels are feeble and without inspiration;
even the landscapes are banal. The Beato Giacomo della
Marca (Sala XII, No. 241) was painted even later for San
Francesco al Prato in Perugia, and has as little interest for the
lover of Perugino as the poor composition of the Baptist preaching from a low hummock, surrounded by SS. Francis, Jerome,
Michael Archangel and S. Anthony of Padua (Sala XIV, No.
280), or the even more feeble Martyrdom of S. Sebastian (Sala
XIV, No. 239), painted in 1518 for San Francesco al Prato.

It was now he finished the large retable for Sant' Agostino, of
which I have already noted two panels, and there are many
later panels in the gallery; tondi of the Evangelists, half-
length figures of saints, two full-length figures of the Magdalen
and S. Jerome, and predella panels (all in Sala XIV). Finally,
there is a picture on canvas of S. Jerome in his cardinal's
mantle, kneeling with his lion before the Cross, his cardinal's
hat beside him (Sala XII, No. 242).

The works of Perugino's follower and imitator, Bernardino
di Mariotto, of Giannicola Manni and Pintoricchio whose
works are to be found in Rome, Siena, San Severino and
London, follow.

Bernardino di Betto, called Il Pintoricchio, was born, according to Vasari, in Perugia in 1454, and died in Siena in 1513.
He was, perhaps, the pupil of Fiorenzo di Lorenzo, a follower
of Perugino, and he had a very brilliant career. As a young
man, in 1481-2 he was painting in the Sistine Chapel in the
Vatican as Perugino's assistant. Three years later he painted
the Baglioni chapel in Santa Maria in Aracoeli; then he was
commissioned to paint in Orvieto Cathedral, and in 1492 he
was at work on his most important paintings, the frescoes of the
Borgia Apartment in the Vatican. Later, for the Piccolomini
Pope Pius III, he painted the series of frescoes of the life of
Aeneas Sylvius, Pope Pius II, in the library of the Cathedral of
Siena. But here in the Perugia gallery there are but three works
of his own hand, the earliest of which is the altarpiece he
painted for the church of Santa Maria dei Fossi, here in
Perugia (Sala XVII, No. 274), immediately after painting in
the Sistine Chapel in the Vatican. It is a very architectural
affair, with a charming panel of the Madonna and Child
enthroned with the little Baptist in a landscape, the Annunciation above on either side, and beneath it two full-length
figures of SS. Augustine and Jerome. Above in the pediment
is a Pietà with two angels, and the Dove of the Holy Spirit
over all. In the predella are two scenes from the lives of
S. Augustine and S. Jerome and four rounds with busts of the
four Evangelists. This is the best work by the master in
Perugia.

Another work is the Standard of S. Augustine (Sala XVII,
No. 276), in which S. Augustine is seated with mitre and crozier,
holding an open book on his knee and adored by two members
of some confraternity. It has a patterned background almost
like a miniature and dates from 1500.

The third work represents the Madonna in half-figure with
the Child standing on a balustrade and in the background,
silhouetted against the sky, are two trees, one on either side of
the group (Sala XVII, No. 293). A detached fresco of the
Virgin standing and holding the Child (Sala XVII, No. 277)
is also given to Pintoricchio. It is dated 1520.

A fine picture of the Adoration of the Magi (Sala XVII, No.
187) by Eusebio di San Giorgio, at the time he painted this

picture a devoted follower of Perugino, is worth more than a glance.

Wandering through the later rooms one is rather overwhelmed by the works of Orazio Alfani, but there are a few later pictures, a Madonna by Sassoferrato, pictures by Federigo Barocci, others by Lelio Orsi, which attract one's notice. And then no one should leave these rooms without penetrating as far as where a number of, alas, broken sculptures by Agostino di Duccio have been collected. They come from the façade of the Maestà delle Volte, other fragments of which are in the cloister of the Cathedral.

CHAPTER XXI

MONTERIPIDO, BEATO EGIDIO AND BEATO PAOLUCCIO TRINCI

JUST beyond the great walls of Perugia, on the summit of a cypress-lined hill, overlooking the city and the valley of Spoleto, stands the Franciscan convent of Monteripido, San Francesco al Monte, outside Porta Sant' Angelo. This was for many years the site of the hermitage of Beato Egidio, Brother Giles, the third companion of S. Francis, one of his most famous, devoted and loyal followers. It was, too, later the scene of the activities of the *Zelanti*, those indomitable friars who upheld the strict observance of the Rule and Testament of S. Francis, and the scene of the activity of the man who, in the fourteenth century, re-established them as members of the Order, Beato Paoluccio Trinci of Foligno.[1]

The site of the great convent we see was presented to the Franciscan Order in 1276,[2] by a pious Perugian gentleman, Giacomo Buonconte dei Coppoli, of an illustrious Perugian family, for the repose of his soul and that of his wife Vita.[3] Brother Giles had a hermitage there where he passed much of his life. He was of that little band which "was with the Blessed Francis from the time he began to have companions", and joined S. Francis after Bernard of Quintavalle and Peter Catanii. Giles's biographer was Frate Leo, the beloved secretary and confessor of S. Francis, and the *Fioretti*, too, have a whole section devoted to him. He joined the Order on S. George's day in 1208 or 1209, meeting S. Francis in a wood near Assisi, and was received into the Order probably at the Portiuncula, where he always desired to be buried. He accompanied S. Francis on a journey into the valley of Rieti, the Valle Santa,[4] and on his first journey to Rome (?1210) when the earliest Rule was

---

[1] Cf. *Miscellanea Francescana* (Foligno, 1895), VI, pp. 96–108.
[2] Cf. Bartholi, *Tractatus*, LII, n. i.
[3] Cf. *Miscellanea Francescana* (Foligno, 1889), IV, p. 157.
[4] See *supra*, p. 110.

confirmed *viva voce* by Innocent III. He was the most independent of S. Francis's companions, but would not accept all
the liberty S. Francis gave him. Nevertheless, he went on pilgrimages to S. James of Compostella, to Jerusalem, where he
was the first Franciscan to set foot, to S. Michael on Monte
Gargano, to S. Nicholas at Bari, and to Tunis where, however,
he could not remain. On these journeys he lived by the labour
of his hands, helping with the vintage, gathering faggots, glean-
ing in the fields and giving his grain away. And, having followed
S. Francis to the end, he was present during the last hours of
the saint at S. Mary of the Angels.

When the controversies in the Order broke out uncontrolled,
after S. Francis's death, about the observance of the Rule and
the discipline of the Order, in which Bernard and Leo and
others of the early companions opposed the majority which
would relax the Rule and abolish the authority of the Testament, Giles kept aloof, but his sarcasms when he came to visit
the great church and convent which Frate Elias had built on
the Collis Inferni at Assisi were biting and became famous.
Seeing the grandiose monument so little like his master:

"Ah," he remarked to the friars, "now you only want wives."

"What is this you have dared to say, Brother Giles?"

"I wish to say that since you have abandoned Holy Poverty
it only remains for you to abandon Chastity, to which you were
also vowed."

Nor did he approve of the Order becoming a learned body
like the Benedictine or Dominican. "O Paris, Paris, thou hast
undone Assisi."

To a friar who told him that he had had a vision of hell and
had not seen a single friar there: "I believe thee," said Giles,
"thou didst not go down deep enough."

And one day at Monteripido, when Bonaventura, then
Minister-General, visited the place, Giles greeted him, adding
that God had blessed the minister with many graces in giving
him knowledge and learning, "but we poor ignorant creatures,
how can we love God as you do?" The saint replied that
this was not so. "What," exclaimed Giles, "can an ignorant
man love God as well as a learned one?" Replied the Seraphic
Doctor, "A poor little old woman can love God as much

or more than a Master in Theology." Giles rushed to the
garden wall and cried out to a poor woman who was passing.
"Old woman, old woman, foolish and ignorant as thou art,
thou canst love God better than Brother Bonaventura."

But Cardinal Bonaventura was not a saint for nothing. He
had much veneration for Giles and thanked God for having
allowed him to live at a time when he could converse with such
a man. "I have often seen him with my own eyes," he writes
in the *Legenda Major*, "so rapt in God that he might be said
rather to live amongst men the life of an angel than of a man."

For Giles was an ecstatic and was frequently rapt out of
himself, "his soul would slip out of his body", and at times he
would remain in ecstasy for many days. Here at Monteripido
Pope Gregory IX, who had been the protector of the Order
and the friend of S. Francis, was witness of a long ecstasy, and
exclaimed, "If he die before me I shall require no other miracle
in order to canonise him."

Then there is the beautiful story in the *Fioretti* of how
S. Louis, King of France, came to visit him.

S. Louis, King of France, went on a pilgrimage to visit
the holy places throughout the world; and hearing the
exceeding great fame of the sanctity of Brother Giles, the
which had been among the first companions of S. Francis,
he set it in his heart and was fully prepared to visit him in
person, for the which cause he came to Perugia where in
those days Brother Giles dwelt. And like a poor pilgrim and
unknown, with few companions, he asked with great earnest-
ness for Brother Giles without telling the porter who it was
that asked. So the porter went to Brother Giles and told
him that at the door was a pilgrim that asked for him; and
being inspired of God, it was revealed to him that it was the
King of France; so straightway with great fervour he left
his cell and ran to the door; and without further questioning
albeit they ne'er before had seen one another, kneeling down
with great devotion they embraced and kissed each other
with such signs of tender love as though for long time they
had been close familiar friends: but for all that they spoke
not, nor the one nor the other, but continued this embrace
with these signs of love and tenderness, in silence. And
whereas they had a long time continued together in the

manner set forth above without having spoken together they parted the one from the other and S. Louis went his way on his journey and Brother Giles returned unto his cell.

When the King was gone a certain brother asked one of his companions who it was that had embraced Brother Giles for so long time; and he replied that it was Louis, King of France. When this was told to the other brothers they were exceeding sorrowful and murmuring they said: "O Brother Giles, why hast thou shown thee so discourteous as to say naught to so holy a King that had come from France to see thee and hear from thy lips good words?" Replied Brother Giles: "Dear brothers, marvel not thereat, for neither I to him nor he to me could speak a word; for so soon as we embraced one another the light of heavenly wisdom revealed to me his heart and mine to him, and thus he knew what I would say to him and he to me far better than if we had spoken with our mouths the feelings of our hearts. Wherefore know ye that the King departed from me with marvellous content and consolation in his soul."[1]

On this exquisite story Ruskin remarks, "Not a word, of course, is credible to any rational person," but adds:

The spirit which created the story is an entirely indisputable fact in the history of Italy and mankind. Whether S. Louis and Brother Giles ever knelt together in Perugia matters not a whit. That a King and a poor monk could be conceived to have thoughts of each other which no words could speak, and that the King's tenderness and humility made such a tale credible—this is what you have to meditate on here.[2]

When Brother Giles came to die, his body lay in state for a month in the convent here before it was carried to the church of San Francesco al Prato, near the Oratory of San Bernardino, down in Perugia. This church, built in 1230, fell to ruin in 1737 and Giles's remains were removed first to the Vescovado and then, in 1880, to the chapel of Sant' Onofrio in the

---

[1] *Fioretti*, XXXV (Temple Classics).

[2] *Mornings in Florence*, p. 84. The story is a legend. King Louis of France was never in Perugia. Fra Salimbene records that he was "spare and slender, of a proper height, having the face of an angel and a mien full of grace. He came to our church, not in regal pomp, but on foot in pilgrim's habit with staff and scrip hanging at his neck."

Cathedral. It seems a pity they were not taken to the church here in the convent of Monteripido.

When he was dying in 1262 the Perugians, who knew he wished to be buried in the Portiuncula, placed soldiers about the convent of Monteripido. They were determined to retain at any cost the relics of so great a saint. "Even if he should not be canonised," they said, "we will keep him."

His cell, now a chapel, and his garden are within the precincts of the convent, and there are many relics of Blessed Giles pre-served there. He is the only early companion of S. Francis who has been beatified.[1] He survived S. Francis by more than thirty-five years and was the principal link between the second generation of the Order and the earliest times.

But the convent of Monteripido, San Francesco al Monte, was to have another Franciscan saint beside the Blessed Giles. In the late fourteenth century, when the Franciscan Order was divided between those who lived under the relaxed Rule— the Conventuals—and those who claimed to keep the Rule strictly and were known as Observants, the convent of Monteri-pido was in the hands of the Conventuals of San Francesco al Prato, and in the confusion of the time and of the Order, Perugia, and indeed much of Umbria, were infested with a sect of heretics called *I fraticelli dell' opinione*, who claimed to be the only true followers of S. Francis.

In those times [writes Fra Mariano da Firenze][2] the sect of the *fraticelli dell' opinione* was very strong in the territory of Perugia and held in no small esteem by many; the which sect among other errors did not obey the Apostolic See, held and affirmed that, since Celestine V, there had been no true Supreme Pontiff. And seeing themselves held in high devotion by the people they declared that they were the true Brothers Minor and observers of the Rule of S. Francis; and they drew the people when they could into their heretical errors. They waged a great persecution against the Frati Conventuali, preaching throughout the

[1] By Pope Pius VI.
[2] Cf. Faloci Pulignani, *Il Beato Paoluccio Trinci da Foligno: Documenti e Discussioni* (Foligno, 1926), pp. 24 *et seq.*, 39-40.

quarters of the city, the houses and shops, that these were not Frati Minori at all but prevaricators, because transgressors of the Rule and they had so much temerity and presumption that in the Piazza of Perugia they would confront them and snatch away their *cappuccio* and strip them to their shirts saying S. Francis 'did not teach you to wear these'. And these sayings and actions moved the people so that the friars of San Francesco al Prato dared scarcely leave the convent lest the people turn upon and attack them; and this caused much scandal and unrest among them.

At this time there came to Perugia Fra Leonardo, twenty-fourth Minister General of the Order, with whom the friars took counsel saying: these rogues are persecuting us and we can do nothing because they are defended by the favour of the people. A council was held and many friars said many things: one suggested one thing, one another, but all their opinions were diverse or useless. Finally one of the least among them inspired by God said: "*Padri miei*, none of this is of any use, but if you will consent to follow my counsel I will shew you how to get rid of these heretics." And they answered him, "*Per lo amore di Dio*, to tell them what was to be done." The friar replied: "There is no other way under heaven to get rid of these evil *frati* but to bring into this city the *frati* of S. Francesco, so that it may be manifest that there are in the Order the pure observers of the Rule." To him it was answered: "You say the truth, but where are these pure observers?" And the friar answered; "In the house of Brugliano," and added: "We have the Chapel of San Francesco al Monte [Monteripido] where they could live according to their desire and these evil heretics would be driven away." The counsel of the simple friar pleased everyone as a counsel inspired by God, and immediately the Minister General sent to Brugliano for Fra Paolo Trinci under obedience that he should come to his presence.

Now at Brugliano already in the year 1334, after John XXII in 1322 had finally overthrown even the seeming poverty of the Order by his Bull *Ad conditorem canonum*, which handed to the Order the ownership of its possessions, till then held by the Holy See, a certain Giovanni della Valle was living in exact accordance with the Rule and by permission was yet within the Order. Among his followers was a certain Paoluccio de'

Trinci, born in 1309 of the noble house of Foligno. His mother was an Orsini. This man, the real founder of the Observance, was established in Brugliano in 1368. Brugliano is a high, solitary place in the hills between Foligno and Camerino. Snakes abounded there and as a protection the friars, who by rule and custom went barefoot, wore wooden sandals (*zoccoli*), and it was from these sandals the Observants came to be called in Italy *Zoccolanti*.

Fra Paoluccio was successful in maintaining his reform, the Observance. Within five years his friars were in possession of not less than ten small houses in Umbria and the Marches, and to these was presently added the capital and sacred house of San Damiano at Assisi. It was Fra Paoluccio who was sent for to Perugia.

Fra Paolo arrived immediately with a simple lay brother as companion and a solemn dispute was arranged with the *fraticelli* in the Piazza of Perugia before the University— the *fraticelli* proposing certain articles, to the effect that they were the true friars minor who observed the Rule of S. Francis and not the Frati Conventuali or any of those who came under the obedience of the Minister General. Fra Paolo was present with his companion who, inspired by God like another youthful Daniel, arose in the midst and before all the learned masters said: These affirm that they are the true observers of the Rule of S. Francis, but what does the Rule say in its first chapter? And he began to read the said Rule in that part which says: Frate Francesco promises obedience and reverence to Messer Papa Honorio and to his successors. And he continued in the twelfth chapter, which says that the *frati* shall ever be subject to the Holy Roman Church and that they will be constant in the Catholic Faith. But consider Fathers, Masters, Doctors and you others of the people: these deceived heretics say that they are the true observers of the Rule, but how can this be true since they do not obey the Pope and render no due subjection and reverence to the Holy Roman Church, but on the contrary presume to say that Pope Gregory is not the true and Catholic Pope, nor do they obey the Holy Roman Church? They are then not only transgressors of the Rule, but the worst kind of heretics.

When these men heard they were not Catholics but filled with error and falsity they were astonished and almost beside themselves and could reply nothing. The people whom they had deceived turned upon them and began to stone them....

But the Conventual Friars of San Francesco al Prato were filled with joy, delivered as they were from infamy, and all agreed that they must give the convent of Monteripido to Fra Paolo for his Observants, and this gift was confirmed by the Minister-General, Frate Leonardo.

It might seem, therefore, that it was at Monteripido the Observance was finally and officially established as part of the Franciscan Order and Frate Paoluccio Trinci appears, as Faloci Pulignani calls him, "*Fondatore, Principe, Capo, Duca e Padre dell' Osservanza*", that is, of the Frati Minori Osservanti or, as we know them now after the Bull of Leo XIII, *the* Friars Minor, in distinction from the Conventuals and the much later Capuchins.

CHAPTER XXII

CITTÀ DELLA PIEVE AND THE
LANDSCAPE OF PERUGINO

I WENT from Perugia to Città della Pieve—it is but twenty-six miles—for the sake of Perugino, who was born there. I stayed there for its own sake. It is a little towered city, some miles from the railway, set on a hill 1,600 feet above sea-level.

The Peruginos which remain there are not the best works of the master. It would seem that for the most part they are the work of his pupils, or of his old age. But the city itself, with its views of the lakes of Trasimeno and Chiusi and the valley southward towards Rome, the quiet peace of the place, the magnificent woods beneath it, are in themselves more valuable than the faint and fading beauty of the mediocre work of the great painter who was born there; for they remain for ever in the memory and seem worth everything else in the world because of the sun—the sun which is the smile of God.

And so it is perhaps to the sun, which robes this little city, too, in a mantle of splendid colour all through the day, and at evening adorns her with bright fire and radiant glory, that we owe the curious fascination of this towered place, so small, so poor, so desolate, so forlorn.

The Oratory of Santa Maria de' Bianchi holds the most considerable work attributed to Perugino that the little city can boast. It is a vast fresco of the Adoration of the Magi in the well-known manner of the great Umbrian. Under a lofty shed, uplifted by four graceful pillars, the Madonna sits with the divine Child in her lap, while the three Kings stand or kneel before Him. An immense number of figures move across the picture. And the spacious background, full of light and air, is just one of the painter's exquisite Umbrian landscapes with delicate hill and faint mountain range in the distance. Fantastic trees, through whose branches filters that limpid air, spring here and there from the nearer hills. A few delicate, wing-shaped clouds float lightly, magically, in the soft sky, from which an angel plunges, hinting, as it were, at benediction. And over all lies the profound peace of yesterday, the immaculate morning of the old world. Many and many a time has Perugino painted a scene like this, and almost always with the same secret understanding of space. He seems to say to us, "Lift up your hearts", and to have already anticipated the answer.

There are other pictures by Perugino in the city; in the Cathedral there are two, a Madonna and Child in glory and four saints, painted in 1513, and a Baptism of Our Lord, of about the same time. In San Pietro there is a fresco of S. Antony Abbot between two saints and God the Father above. In Santa Maria dei Servi there is a Deposition painted in 1517. All these are the works of his old age, largely carried out by pupils.

But it was not for these I stayed on day after day in Città della Pieve. This was the little city in which Perugino received his first impressions of the world. Here he spent his childhood. This was the landscape he first looked on. It was to this, it might seem, if we are to believe Vasari and the pictures he left here—it was to this he returned in his age and these hills and valleys were what his eyes last rested on. The impressions one receives as a child, are they ever lost? Might one not hope then, among these hills and valleys, to discover the secret of his landscapes, so full of golden air and serene light and space, where the hills are almost transparent—the trees, those "trees of heaven", so delicate and ethereal? Might one not hope here to surprise the secret of the first realistic landscape painter in Italian art?

The first realistic landscape painter in Italian art: but others before him had put landscapes in their pictures even in the fourteenth century, but there was nothing realistic about them. Even in the fifteenth century the landscape of Fra Angelico, of Benozzo Gozzoli, of Fra Filippo Lippi in such a picture, for instance, as Lippi's Adoration, in the Uffizi, is a wholly fantastic affair, a stage scene. It is true that Piero della Francesca, a whole generation younger than Perugino, in his Baptism of Christ, in the National Gallery, and in his portraits of the Duke and Duchess of Urbino in the Uffizi, was a master of landscape; but beautiful though these landscapes are, they are "distance" landscapes like the landscapes in Pollaiuolo's pictures, the Martyrdom of S. Sebastian, for example, or the Rape of Dejanira, in the National Gallery and at Yale University; they have no middle distance, they are all background and are really experiments, beautiful experiments, in perspective.

The greatest gift of the true landscape painter is an "emotional response to light". This response to light is to be found, perhaps for the first time, in the pictures of Giovanni Bellini, a greater master than Perugino. In an early work of his, the Agony in the Garden, in the National Gallery, the landscape is marvellously beautiful, most moving and tragically lovely in the light of dawn, but it is dramatic rather than realistic. Who has ever seen such a landscape, even in the Veneto? The painter has conceived it, not for its own sake, but for the sake of the subject of his picture. And it is the same in his picture of the Resurrection, in Berlin, and in the S. Francis in New York. In these great masterpieces the landscape has been conceived for the sake of, and to minister to, the subject of the picture with which it is in each case in complete and inspired harmony.[1]

With Perugino it seems the exact opposite is true. The landscape is the subject of his pictures, it is an end in itself, and the figures are there to emphasise or express the emotion of the landscape. Not only is his landscape inspired with light and full of spacious air, it is realistic, as we say, just what his eyes had seen first as a child, what had most filled them with delight all his life long and what he last looked upon as he lay dying, not, it seems, in this little city of Città della Pieve, his birthplace, but at Fontignano, half-way between it and Perugia.

The figures that go to make up his "subjects", his Nativities, his Adorations, his Crucifixions, how pious they are, but it is the landscape that is *santo*. It is as though these figures were not really the subjects of his pictures at all; were there to set off, to present, as a bass accompaniment may do in music, the melody, to help to express the emotion which the landscape, the real subject of his pictures, gives us. Rarely, indeed, have these figures any real existence apart from the landscape: they are ghosts, apparitions and in a moment will be gone.

[1] Perhaps the lovely autumnal Virgin of the Meadow, in London, is an exception in Giovanni Bellini's work; perhaps we have here a genuine visual impression of nature for its own sake.

Perhaps the Madonna and Child enthroned with the Baptist
and S. Sebastian, in the Uffizi, or the triptych of the National
Gallery, or the great fresco of the Keys, in the Sistine Chapel,
and a few others are the exceptions.

Perugino has been called an insincere painter, and accused
of atheism and hypocrisy by Vasari. However that may be,
in an age when all the arts were becoming more and more
pagan, his art, at any rate, remains wholly and unmistakably
Christian, but it is our business to discover what it is that moves
us in his pictures, what they really mean to us. The artist who
painted the marvellous portraits in the Uffizi was certainly not
without ability to represent life, but his large achievement had
little to do with life, contenting itself, as it did, with a sort of
music; the effect of music, at any rate, composed with space;
so that what we see in his pictures, that exquisite grave and
serene landscape of Umbria, quite apart from the figures there,
moves us as the plain-song does, quite apart from the words
which accompany it, to a real religious emotion in which we
become partakers of that universal life whose rhythm we seem
to have overheard for a moment during an interval of particular
silence, when our souls suddenly seem attuned to the movement
of eternity. What in fact we see, what in fact he paints, is
Umbria Santa.

Was this after all just an escape from his time and place, the
Perugia of the Baglioni and Oddi, from the violence too of his
own heart?

In any case it is this extraordinary clairvoyance to something that is perhaps always present in the world, but present
in no satisfying quantity, that makes Perugino's work beyond
that of almost any other painter so religious in its effect. He
makes us one with the eternal firmament and confounds us
with its Creator. And thus he becomes valuable to us as the
first real painter of landscape; of this landscape, no ideal
world of woods and water and mountain and little city, but
the real country about his home, the valleys and hills of Umbria,
so that without extravagance we might call many of his pictures
"A view from Montefalco", "Evening beside the Tiber", or
"Noontide in the Valley of Spoleto", or "Dawn among the
hills". And all this world he has seen as it really is, filled with a

ONTONE. San Francesco: Bartolommeo Caporali, Madonna di Soccorso.

GUBBIO. Palazzo dei Consoli.

sort of beatitude that seems to betray the presence of some
deity. It is there the real "subject", as we say, of his pictures
lies.

Thus, it is as a landscape painter and as a poet, even a
mystic, practical too as the mystics so often are, that Perugino
appears to us; as one who with love has watched the evening
in the valley, the trees by the river, the dawn upon the mountains, and has heard the voice of the Lord God walking in the
garden in the cool of the day; and in the valley at noon he has
whispered to us *Numen inest.*

CHAPTER XXIII

UMBERTIDE, MONTONE AND
CITTÀ DI CASTELLO

IT was for the sake of Luca Signorelli that one early summer day I set out from Perugia in the morning by train for Umbertide. The way is fair enough, as all ways are in Umbria, and before long I came into the characteristic upper valley of the Tiber, and passing up-stream to Umbertide, I found there a majestic octagonal-domed church of the sixteenth century, Santa Maria della Reggia, of lovely proportion and full of light, which was rebuilt in the middle of the seventeenth century by Bernardino Sermigni, architect and painter of this place. Such a church is typically Italian. Nearly all the important churches in Italy belong to the Middle Age. Except for San Pietro in Rome, the Renaissance ideal, more than half spoiled there, has to be found in smaller buildings, generally outside the city, such as the best of these Bramantesque churches at Todi, or Santa Maria del Belvedere, which I was to find at Città di Castello, or San Biagio outside Montepulciano.

It was in Santa Croce, near the bridge over the Tiber, however, that I found the picture of Signorelli, the Descent from the Cross, which I had set out to see. The great old painter was seventy-five when he painted this picture, yet his vigour was not abated. He seems, indeed, to have painted this fine work himself and to have left little or nothing to assistants. The church is small and dark and the picture has been half spoiled by restoration, but it is still a beautiful and noble work, and if some of the figures are perhaps life-studies, especially the figure in the foregound on the left, the composition is wonderful, and there can be no doubt about the sincerity of the emotion. They have just loosed the divine body from the Cross, a rainbow-coloured scarf of Umbria supports it and is caught round the crutch and held by one of the Apostles. The others are mounted on ladders, and gently, slowly, they are trying to lower the body of the Son of God that it may rest for three days in the tomb.

Others of the Apostles hold the ladders, and at the foot of the Cross itself the Virgin Mother has swooned away. Two of the women look upon her, while the Magdalen, half mad with tears, places her hand under the wounded feet of her Lord and, grasping the Cross to save herself from falling, seems about to gather her Saviour into her arms almost as one might a child. In the foreground, on the right, S. John seems to be praying. And then suddenly into this picture, so solemn and tragic, steals the beautiful and only half-sorrowful figure of a girl splendidly dressed, her hands clasped before her. She seems just to have halted for a moment at the sight, and to have lowered her eyes as Madonna, swaying like a lily, has fallen softly to the ground. Who is this figure that passes by?

Not far away in the landscape they bury Christ in the new tomb of Joseph. And, indeed, though the whole picture is full of tragedy, the world, that spacious world of Umbria, is at spring; all the trees have budded, and the fields are golden in the sun, the sky is full of glory and very pure.

But it is in the predella scenes we have the best of this great master. They represent the March of Heraclius, the Discovery of the Holy Cross and the Entry of Heraclius into Jerusalem. One recalls that Signorelli had been Piero della Francesca's assistant when he painted the legend of the Holy Cross in San Francesco in Arezzo, and something of the spaciousness of those wonderful frescoes appears here, too, in the spacious movement of the first of these three scenes. In the second several scenes of the legend are combined: the Queen of Sheba kneels before the bridge of sacred wood, the Empress S. Helena finds the three crosses and tests them. In the third panel, the Entry of Heraclius into Jerusalem, there is a wonderful effect of the movement of a body of men. The Emperor has got off his horse to enter the Holy City and, barefoot, bears the recaptured Cross within the gates. Originally, according to Crowe and Cavalcaselle, there was a lunette above containing a Pietà.

When at Umbertide I proposed to myself to go to Montone, a little lofty town some eight miles away in the mountains to the north. It was for the sake of Bonfigli I set out, for, as I was told, he had painted a gonfalon for that very place, a thing so splendid and lovely that to see it was worth all the weariness of the way, for the road is steep and long. It was not, however, any work of Bonfigli I saw, when just after Mass on Sunday morning I entered the church of San Francesco.

Montone has many traditions, and was the birthplace of one of the greatest of the condottieri, the founder of the Bracceschi clan, to which Niccolò Piccinino belonged—Braccio Fortebraccio. The magnificent Standard, which a place once so famous was able to command, was painted in 1482, and, if we may judge from its style, by Bartolommeo Caporali; certainly Bonfigli can have had no hand in it. In the midst the Madonna rises like a flower, her arms spread a little wearily, supporting her cloak over the people of Montone and their city, above which she stands. Her hands, which S. Francis and S. Bernardino seem about to kiss, are more delicate and fair than the petals of the lilies, and her body, clothed in a marvellous patterned cloak, as delicate as the calix of a flower, rises like the hope of the world from the midst of the people. Around her kneel, beside S. Francis and S. Bernardino, six other saints, among them S. Sebastian and S. Clare, S. John Baptist and S. Brazio, with two other bishops. Above, in heaven, Christ blesses her, and two angels seem to sing *Magnificat*. In truth this gonfalon is worth all the trouble of the way, since it is without doubt the most beautiful Standard in the world. That at Deruta by the same master is almost a replica of it, but without its exquisite quality.

From Montone to Città di Castello is near twenty miles by road, but by train from Umbertide an easy way enough.

Città di Castello is set on the ruins of the Roman Tifernum, which Pliny knew so well, but all its Roman memories seem to have been destroyed by Totila, who sacked it in 542, and it seems to have remained a desolate village, a mere huddle of ruins, till a few years later its bishop, S. Floridus, rebuilt it. Was it for this that, through all the hurly-burly of the great quarrel, it remained true Guelph, and that Gubbio was so often Ghibelline? However that may be, by 1440, in the midst of the useless wars that at that time ravaged Lombardy, the Marche and the Kingdom, Città di Castello placed herself, at the suggestion of the Pope, under the protection of Florence, while Cosimo de' Medici bought the neighbouring town of

Borgo San Sepolcro from him for twenty-five thousand ducats. It is about this time that we first hear of the family of Vitelli, who made themselves lords. Thirty-four years later, in 1474, we find the Papacy, by means of Cardinal Giuliano della Rovere, attempting to reduce these too-powerful vassals of the Holy See. He laid siege to Città di Castello, which alarmed the Florentines, who sent forces to Borgo. Federigo of Urbino then appeared on the scene, and whether by persuasion or terror induced the Vitelli to make terms, none too favourable however, with the Pope. Sixtus IV complained bitterly to Lorenzo il Magnifico that Florence had helped the insurgents. The Papacy had, however, not yet done with the Vitelli. In 1502 Vitellozzo Vitelli was invited by Cesare Borgia to a conference at Sinigaglia, where he was strangled. Thus, Città di Castello came again directly into the power of the Papacy, which it was not able to shake off till, in 1860, Italy was united, and the Papacy as a temporal power for the time being was disposed of.

Città di Castello produced no great painter, her best being that Francesco who was of the school of Raphael. Under the Vitelli, however, she was the patron both of Raphael and Signorelli.

Raphael painted his first signed picture, the first picture really his own, after his arrival in Perugia, for the Gavani chapel in the Dominican church here, at the order of Vitellozzo Vitelli. It must have been executed in 1501 or early in 1502, before the Vitelli were driven out by Cesare Borgia. The picture is now in the National Gallery in the Ludwig Mond bequest and, but for the signature, as Vasari says, "it would certainly be taken for Perugino's work". The composition is exactly similar to the Crucifixion which Perugino had just finished for the friars of San Francesco al Monte at Perugia. It was here in Città di Castello, too, that Raphael in 1504 painted his Sposalizio, now in the Brera. A Banner by him may still be seen in the Pinacoteca, but her glory lies in the work of her guest, Luca Signorelli. Though his picture of S. Sebastian was painted for the church of San Domenico, where it hung beside Raphael's Crucifixion, it is today in the Palazzo Vitelli, now the Pinacoteca. It was painted in 1490, about the same time as the Standard of Urbino, and in spite of its bad condition it is a work of surpassing beauty. One feels, however, a real disappointment in the figure of the saint, as though for once Signorelli had been touched by a certain sentimentalism, to be found, I think, nowhere else in his work. Above the saint, God the Father leans from heaven, and below five soldiers with superb and splendid gestures string their bows. Two of them are nude but for the striped loin-cloth Signorelli loved so well; the others are dressed in Renaissance fashion. Not far away certain burgesses and women look on at the tragedy, while in the distance one sees a street leading steeply up a height to a Roman amphitheatre, filled with a bustle of soldiers.

There are several other works of a high interest in this gallery. First among them is the large ancona from the church of San Domenico, of the Madonna and Child enthroned, surrounded by six angels and a Dominican friar as donor, a Maestà of the same sort as the Rucellai Madonna. It is by the Maestro di Città di Castello, a painter whose name is unknown, who was of the school of Duccio of Siena. Originally a magnificent work, it has been too much restored, nevertheless it remains a beautiful thing.

Then there is a panel of the Madonna and Child enthroned, by Spinello Aretino, as Florentine in character as the Maestà is Sienese. Here, too, is a very impressive bust of Our Lord, shown full face and very severe, with one hand raised in benediction against a background of brocade. This is a work by Piero della Francesca himself, according to Mr. Berenson, though Professor Longhi thinks it by some Flemish artist, but that seems fantastic. Finally, among other works of less importance, I noted a picture of the Madonna and Child enthroned, by Antonio Vivarini of Venice.

In the church of Santa Maria delle Grazie I was delighted to find a fresco by Ottaviano Nelli. It has been detached from the wall and unhappily lacks the charm of his earlier work. And again in the church of San Domenico there is a fresco of the Crucifixion, which is possibly by Antonio da Ferrara (op. 1400–49), who was long at Urbino.

Perhaps the churches of Città di Castello are a little disappointing, but some three miles outside the city, beyond the station, is a most noble and lovely porticoed Renaissance church, a Greek cross under a dome—Santa Maria del Belvedere, built by Niccolò Barbioni, architect of this city in the second half of the seventeenth century. This is worth some trouble to see, and the traveller, in addition, has a magnificent view of Città di Castello against Monte Arnato and, far to the left, Monte Acuto and Monte Tezio, with the valley of the Tiber to the right and Borgo San Sepolcro under Monte La Verna and the Pratomagno in the distance.

And then Città di Castello itself is one of the most charming towns in the upper valley of the Tiber. Its old walls, dating from the early years of the sixteenth century, still hem it in, and it still possesses interesting buildings of the fourteenth, fifteenth and sixteenth centuries; the palaces of the Vitelli, for instance, the Palazzo del Governo, the Palazzo Comunale and the Duomo. Not one of these, however, is half so beautiful as the view of the valley and the hills from the *giardino pubblico* to the west of the Duomo. Through the valley the Tiber flows towards Rome and the sea, and above and beyond rise the mountains, those majestic and indestructible peaks which were before the foundation of any city, and have looked with the same indifference upon Etruscan, Umbrian and Italian; that saw Totila pass by with his Goths, and the Borgia with his Spaniards, and have yielded themselves only to the youth Raphael and Perugino his master, and to that great old man, Luca Signorelli, who loved them.

CHAPTER XXIV

GUBBIO

IT was on another early summer day that I set out from Perugia by the Porta Pesa for Gubbio, across the mountains. The way was musical with streams, for there had been rain in the night, and the world was refreshed and beautiful. Downhill into the valley of the Tiber I went, past the olives and the willows, whose leaves were dancing gravely in the wind, watching their own beauty in the shallows of the great river. Then, when I had crossed the Tiber and had begun to climb, after about five miles I came on the left to the Franciscan convent of Farneto. It must have been about here S. Francis met and blessed the Abbot of San Giustino, as related by Thomas of Celano.[1] The oldest of the convent buildings does not go back to the fourteenth century and the vast Collegio Serafico dates from the end of the nineteenth century. A few steps away is a chapel, the Oratorio di San Francesco, entirely remade only the other day, but it was here, so it is said, that the angel visitor came to consult S. Francis and was sent away by Frate Elias, who could not be bothered to see him, all as related in the *Fioretti*, Chapter IV.

I now came, as I climbed, into a desolate land of mountains and bare hill-sides, utterly forlorn and without the fellowship of trees or flowers. The wind was dismal and lonely, wandering over the moorland as though in search of companions. Now and again a shepherd clad in goatskins towered in silhouette against the farthest sky—a magnificent figure, simple and antique, keeping the world sweet; and sometimes a little group of trees, scarcely sufficient for a copse, whispered together as though in fear of the indestructible silence. Far away, the beautiful valleys of Umbria led me down innumerable vistas towards Subasio and many a little city, full even yet of lovely things—the dreams made material of the great artists, or the lives of the saints. And all day the uplifted Apennine towered

---

[1] II Celano, cap. 67.

in the sunlight, with brows even yet white with snow that the
sun dazzled with glory.

Just before I crossed the watershed I came on the hill-top to
a mass of building with tower and bell-turret which proved to
be the Badia di Vallingegno, but of old was the monastery of
San Verecondo, where it is said S. Francis was employed as a
scullion after he had been thrown into a ditch full of snow by
brigands on his first wandering to Gubbio. He was thus
employed, according to Thomas of Celano, for several days,
"wearing nothing but a wretched shirt and desiring to be filled
at least with broth. But when, meeting with no pity there, he
could not even get any old clothing, he left the place (not moved
by anger but by need) and came to the city of Gubbio, where he
got him a small tunic from a former friend of his. But afterwards," says Thomas, "when the fame of the man of God was
spreading everywhere and his name was noised abroad among
the people, the prior of the aforesaid monastery, remembering
and realising how the man of God had been treated, came to
him and humbly begged forgiveness for himself and his monks."

I continued on my way. Presently, as I topped the ascent, a
stupendous panorama rose before me over Gubbio and its
valley, dominated by the five mountain peaks, the most formidable of which are Monte Catria, Monte Ingino and Monte
Calvo. After another climb, the road began its descent into the
Eugubian plain and, crossing it in magical evening light, so
tender and grave and serene, I entered Gubbio.

Gubbio is the dream of some medieval miniaturist; it must
be, I thought, the only extant work of that most famous artist,
Oderisi. Built on the lower slopes of Monte Calvo, the little
city, now too small for its great old walls, rises in terraces one
above another, where cypresses behind and among the palaces
and churches point their joined hands ever upwards in that
long life which is an everlasting prayer. Behind the city
Monte Calvo, arid and gaunt, lifts its head into the soft sky
and seems to cry to innumerable hills and valleys, and to those
great, indifferent mountains, Repent! Repent! Repent! Over
the city, crowning it so perfectly that it surely cannot have been
placed there by chance, the forlorn Gothic Palazzo dei Consoli
rises as in some dream of the Middle Age.

So old that it is impossible to decide the date of its foundation, or to account for its curious religions, Gubbio still possesses the remains of a Roman theatre in the immensity of that plain which has consumed so great a part of the old city. Utterly destroyed by Totila, it was again besieged in 1155 by Barbarossa, when he had done with Spoleto. And it was then that its famous bishop, S. Ubaldo, saved it from the hands of that barbarian, who indeed was threatening even the Papacy in his insatiable desire for empire.

Then, in 1364, the people of Gubbio invited in the Counts of Montefeltro, who had established their lordship over the town of Urbino, which ever after gave them their title, to expel from their city the tyrants Gabrielli. It was Antonio, Count of Montefeltro and of Urbino, who was called upon, not only by the people of Gubbio, but by those of Cagli also, from which city he expelled the Ceccardi. Less than a hundred years later we read of the magnificent welcome the city gave to Borso, Marquis of Ferrara, who in March 1471, on his way to Rome, spent four days at Gubbio and Urbino, as the guest of the count, with an escort of 500 horsemen, 100 foot and 150 mules.

"He was met at the frontier by the count," says Dennistoun, "accompanied by the Lords of Faenza, Rimini and Pesaro, with a noble following, and conducted to the new palace of Gubbio, by Federigo and his nephew, Ottaviano della Carda, leading the palfrey of this proud parvenu."

That palace of Gubbio, the Palazzo Ducale, is now, alas, a ruin. It stands close to the Cathedral, splendid even in its decay—only the courtyard remains to remind us how beautiful it once was. Built perhaps by Francesco di Giorgio, perhaps by Baccio Pontelli, or again by Luciano Laurana, the architect of the palace at Urbino, it is described by Sanzi as "facing south-east and flanked by mountains on the north, overlooking fertile valleys and smiling champaigns, and excelling the attractions of Urbino in charming prospects and pleasant pathways". The initials of the two Montefeltran dukes, Federigo and Guidobaldo, appear in the decoration, and the oak of the Rovere family, which might seem to suggest restoration, at the least, at a later date.

Differing much [says Signor Luigi Bonfatti (1843)] from the architecture at Urbino, its courtyard is very fine, of the mixed or composite style usual in that age. The windows, doors, and chimneys have stone lintels, exquisitely chiselled in low relief with masterly arabesque designs, those in the interior being touched with gold. The ceilings, now partially decayed, are all of wood in half-relief compartments with heavy cornices, and roses coloured and gilded. The palace was completed by Duke Guidobaldo, who commissioned the cabinet or closet of superb intarsia, thirteen by six and a half feet. This tiny room is nineteen feet high, but the inlaid work goes only half-way up. It is of the finest patterns and workmanship, including several emblematic representations of music, literature, physical science, geography, and war. On the cornice is an inscription now in part illegible.

When, in 1518, the dukedom of Urbino passed to Catherine de' Medici, then a child, and the Pope unceremoniously seized, almost like a highwayman, the territory of the Rovere, Gubbio, "which had shown itself less devoted" to the interests of that family than Urbino *fedelissimo*, was made the capital of the duchy. The Rovere, however, got back their own; Francesco Maria was restored, and Urbino once more became one of the most glorious cities of the Renaissance. But the Papacy still desired to possess a province so near to Rome, so splendid and so famous. And at length the last of the Rovere, frightened by disease, priests and mountebanks, bequeathed to the Popes what they had so often tried to obtain by force. It is a tragical history, that story of a strong and powerful race falling thus into the hands of schemers, and yielding willingly at last, and almost with a sigh of relief, what its ancestors had lived and died to save. Thus Gubbio in 1631 came under the rule of the Papacy.

Gubbio, however, whose life would seem to have been so eventful in worldly affairs, is not altogether insignificant in the history of Umbrian art. Oderisi or Oderigi da Gubbio, that contemporary of Giotto to whom Dante speaks in Purgatory, was the forerunner, it may well be, of the Umbrian schools of painting. "*O, diss' io lui, non se' tu Oderisi,*" says Dante:

"Oh," I exclaimed,
"Art thou not Oderigi, art not thou
Agobbio's glory, glory of that art
Which they of Paris call the limner's skill?"

This legendary painter—for no work of his is actually known
to exist—was placed in Purgatory by Dante, it would seem, on
account of his pride and zeal in his art. The son of a certain
Guido of Gubbio, in 1268 he went to Bologna, and Vasari says
that he met Giotto in Rome. There follows a pupil of Meo,
Guido Palmerucci, born about 1280, whose work may be found
up and down Gubbio, more or less ruined—in Santa Maria dei
Laici, in the Palazzo dei Consoli. He was the master of Martino
Nelli, whose son Ottaviano was the best of the Gubbian
painters. Ottaviano Nelli's works are not rare in Umbria, nor
are they without that decorative value which, after all, is the
chief delight of all primitive painting.

Martino Nelli, the father of Ottaviano, has left certain fragments of frescoes in Gubbio, which are his rather by tradition
than by any direct evidence we possess. But Ottaviano may be
seen in all his country splendour in Santa Maria Nuova, where
he has painted his best picture over the first altar in the south
aisle, the Madonna with the divine Child in her lap, the
Madonna del Belvedere.

But the first building the traveller seeks in Gubbio is not a
church, not even the Duomo, but the gaunt and magnificent
Palazzo dei Consoli, which, if it is magnificent as seen from its
great piazza, is even more overwhelmingly picturesque when seen
from the lower level of the Via Baldassini which lies beside it.
From the base to the summit of the tower it is 300 feet, a ruddy
brown in colour; it is approached by a splendid flight of steps
and was built by Matteo di Giovannello of Gubbio, called
Gattapone, in the fourteenth century, between 1332 and 1348.

At the top of the great flight of steps is a round-arched,
sculptured doorway, the work of Angelo d'Orvieto. The two
arched windows of the lower storey are divided by columns,
the six above under an arched cornice crowned with Guelph
battlements are simpler, and have no columns. High up, on a
level with the upper windows, still hangs one of those cages in

which the communes and the *signorotti* used to exhibit their
enemies to the rage and delight of the populace. To the left,
beside the façade, is the chapel with a fine window. Above is a
beautiful open loggia.

On entering the palace one finds oneself in an enormous and
immensely lofty vaulted salone, among the largest halls in
Italy. Only the Sala del Cinquecento in Florence and the Sala
del Gran Consiglo in Perugia rival it, at any rate, in Central
Italy. It was for popular assemblies; the room over it was the
meeting-place of the Consiglio, reached by a long and steep
flight of stone steps at the opposite end of the great hall. The
fresco of the Madonna and Child between S. Ubaldo and
S. John the Baptist is attributed to Guido Palmerucci, the
Gubbian painter who succeeded Oderisi and was inspired by
Pietro Lorenzetti. His most important work is the fresco in the
chapel here. There we see the Virgin and Child enthroned and
adored by three Apostles and S. Ubaldo, while the Podestà of
Gubbio kneels at her feet. Both these frescoes have been
tampered with.

Climbing the stone steps and passing through the three
doorways which guard it, one comes into two large apartments,
the larger of which was the meeting-place of the Consiglio.
Here have been gathered a collection of works of art and other
objects, the most important of which are the Tavole Eugubine,
found in 1444 under the Roman theatre. They consist of
seven bronze leaves of two sizes, the larger about 30 by 12
inches, and these are inscribed on both faces. Two of them
would seem to be in Etruscan charatcers, the others in Latin,
but the language is Umbrian and dates from about 200 B.C.
They contain possibly the rules of a college of priests—the
Fratres Attidii.[1]

The collection of pictures contains no work of the first
importance, but is interesting for its Gubbian pictures. It does,
however, possess a reliquary from the church of San Francesco,
with six small miniatures of the school of Simone Martini of
Siena. These fourteenth-century paintings represent, on the
one side, SS. Francis, Mary Magdalen and Anthony of Padua,

---

[1] See an interesting study of these Tables by Michel Bréal, *Les Tables Eugubines*
(Paris, 1875).

and on the other, SS. Clare, John the Divine and Louis of Toulouse. Above is a figure of Our Lord. Another Sienese work of some interest is the polyptych of the Madonna and saints, of the school of Meo da Siena, but it is not very attractive. The thirteenth-century diptych by some Sienese master is more interesting. This also comes from San Francesco. Here, too, are a Giottesque Crucifix, two wings of a triptych of the school of Cola di Petruccioli, a Pietà by Vittore Crivelli and a Banner by Guido Palmerucci.

But, when all is said, the works which should most interest one in Gubbio are the paintings of Guido Palmerucci and Ottaviano Nelli. By the former is a very charming *tondo* of the Virgin and Child in which we easily discern the influence and something of the sweetness of Simone Martini, as we do in the predella panel here of the Annunciation by the same master. Other works ascribed to him here are two frescoes of the Virgin and Child and another of S. John Baptist, which come from the church of Santa Maria Nuova. These frescoes have probably suffered from their detachment and restoration and have no longer the charm that once may have belonged to them.

The same must be said of the two detached frescoes by Ottaviano Nelli, though it is difficult to believe they could ever have given us a similar pleasure to that we receive from the Madonna del Belvedere, in Santa Maria Nuova. Perhaps the most pleasing work here is the Noli Me Tangere by Timoteo Viti, a pupil of Giovanni Santi, who has given us at least a very charming landscape. An example of the famous Gubbio ware of the sixteenth century glows like a great ruby in a cabinet of the gallery.

Opposite the Palazzo dei Consoli, on the other side of Gattapone's very formidably supported piazza, is the Palazzo del Pretorio, begun in 1349 and never finished. The sixteenth-century addition, too, hides the north-west corner, but in any case, even if Gattapone had been able to finish it, he never intended it to rival in majesty the Palazzo dei Consoli, though no doubt he had conceived of the piazza as a whole. Unhappily the money ran short. Within the palace are conserved the communal archives and a fine library with eleven choir books, with miniatures of the thirteenth century, once belonging to the

church of San Domenico of the Friars Preachers. Possibly
some of the miniatures may be the work of the almost fabulous
Oderisi.

Following the picturesque Via dei Consoli to the right of the
great palazzo, one comes to the Largo del Bargello with its
charming fountain, the restored church of San Giuliano and the
thirteenth-century Palazzo del Bargello, and so to the Palazzo
Beni in Piazza Giordano Bruno. In the latter palace is a fresco
on the stairway of S. Cristoforo by Ottaviano Nelli, with the
arms of Pope Martin V.

Just beyond the piazza in Via Cavour is the church of San
Domenico, a building of the fourteenth century, but altered
in the sixteenth century and later. There are many nameless
frescoes here recently uncovered. Among them are some fragments by Nelli and his school and a female saint of the school
of Ambrogio Lorenzetti. The frescoes by Nelli, scenes from the
life of S. Vincent Ferrer and S. Peter Martyr, are in the second
chapel on the left. Over the fifth altar on the left is a figure of
S. Antonio Abate, a piece of majolica of the Gubbio school of
Maestro Giorgio Andreoli (ca. 1465–1553).

The majolica of Maestro Giorgio is famous for a metallic
lustre ruby or mother o' pearl, blue, copper, green and
golden, a fine example of which is in the Palazzo dei Consoli.[1]
Maestro Giorgio Andreoli was born in Lombardy and left his
native place for political reasons. He was of noble stock and
came to Gubbio, where he settled under the patronage of Duke
Guidobaldo della Rovere as a master of glazed majolica pottery,
with his brothers Salimbene and Giovanni, presently receiving
citizenship with exemption from taxes on condition that a
permanent industry should be established to the benefit of the
inhabitants. This befell in 1498. The figure of S. Antony
Abbot here in San Domenico is all that remains of an altarpiece in the manner of the Robbia made in 1511 for this chapel
of the Bentivoglio family. But, as I have said, the great achievement and secret of Maestro Giorgio, for which Gubbian ware
of the sixteenth century is famous, are his metallic lustres which,
though the Deruta ware may precede them in this, stand quite

---

[1] See *supra*, p. 226. There are magnificent examples in the Wallace Collection
and the Victoria and Albert Museum in London.

alone and inimitable for their beauty. The bottega was already in full decadence in 1548, and the factory was extinct when Maestro Cencio, the eldest son of Maestro Giorgio, died in 1576.

Continuing along Via Cavour into the Piazza Vittorio Emanuele, one finds the church of San Francesco. Though the church dates from the thirteenth century, it was built after the death of S. Francis by Fra Bevignate of Perugia and has never been finished. It is a beautiful building, with a fine double portal and rose octagonal tower and a triple apse. Other works of interest here will be found in the cloister: a repainted fresco, perhaps by Palmerucci, of the Crucifixion, and others of the translation of the Santa Casa of Loreto and the Assumption by some predecessor of Nelli.

The most important of Ottaviano Nelli's extant works, a vast series of frescoes of the life of S. Francis, has recently been freed from the whitewash of two or more centuries in the choir.

Close by, in the old market-place, is the fourteenth-century church of the Bianchi, Santa Maria dei Laici, where among the old frescoes we may see a picture of the Annunciation, the last work of a painter I am very fond of—Federigo Baroccio of Urbino (1528–1612).

From San Francesco one may return quite through the city and make one's way up to the Cathedral opposite the Palazzo Ducale. The steep and narrow way of the Via Ducale between the Cathedral and the palace is one of the most medieval in Gubbio.

A church has stood here since the fifth century, but the building we see dates from the twelfth century, and was probably built by Giovanni da Gubbio, who is said to have been the architect of the Cathedral of San Rufino at Assisi. This twelfth-century church has, however, been fundamentally tampered with in the sixteenth century. The single vast nave is full of obscurity, the wide arches are still of the twelfth century, but the height of the nave has been much reduced by raising the pavement in the sixteenth century on account of damp. Nelli is said to have covered the walls with frescoes, but unhappily nothing of these remains. We must content ourselves with the picture by Sinibaldo Ibi (1507) of the Virgin and Child with SS. Ubaldo and Sebastian, in the first chapel on the left, with a picture of S. Mary Magdalen attributed to Timoteo Viti, over the third altar, and a Presepio attributed to Pintoricchio, but perhaps by Eusebio di S. Giorgio, over the tenth altar, both on the left of the church. But the best things the Cathedral still preserves are in the Tesoro, a magnificent cope embroidered in gold with seven scenes of the Passion—this is a Flemish work of the sixteenth century—and a beautiful chasuble. The former was a gift of the Bishop Marcello Cervini when he became Pope in 1555 as Marcellus II. It was he to whom Pierluigi da Palestrina dedicated his famous Mass, *Missa Papae Marcelli.*

Leaving the Cathedral and descending to the Via Venti Settembre or the Via Savelli della Porta, which runs parallel to it, and following either eastward towards the Porta Romana, at the end of Via Savelli stands the church of Santa Maria Nuova, which contains Ottaviano Nelli's masterpiece, the Madonna del Belvedere. This is a mural painting, executed in tempera, not in fresco, and is one of the loveliest pieces of colour in all Umbrian painting, astonishingly fresh, and for the most part intact. The Virgin is seated in the centre, the Divine Child on her lap; she is looking at the spectator while the Child is blessing the donor, a woman, presented by an angel. About the Virgin, as though part of her court, are two musical angels, and two other angels hold aside a flowered curtain. Above, God the Father, among the cherubim and angels, crowns her. Two full-length figures of saints, SS. John Evangelist and Antony Abbot, who presents a kneeling donor, perhaps the husband of the woman on the other side, frame the idyllic scene within two spiral columns ornamented with Renaissance, even pagan, figures. The painting is signed OTTAVIANUS MARTES EUGUBINUS PINXIT AÑO DÑI MC . . . III. This exquisite work is the best and most charming painting left us in Gubbio.

Just outside the Porta Romana is the thirteenth-century church of Sant' Agostino which, with the exception of the choir, has been entirely transformed and is now a national monument. The chief interest here lies in the frescoes in the apse, which are the work of Nelli and his pupils, of scenes from the life of S. Augustine. These frescoes on the vaults and walls, twenty scenes in all, are in a remarkably fine state and are not repainted, but the unequal quality of the work assures us that

16

they are not all from Nelli's own hand, but in part the work of
his pupils. A detached fresco of the Madonna and Child on an
altar to the right is one of the best designs Nelli ever made.
Behind the Virgin are two angels with viols, while two others
present little naked figures, souls of the departed. On one side
is a nun. Figures of angels and cherubim have been added to
this fine work in the seventeenth century when it was detached
from the wall.

Another work by Ottaviano Nelli will be found in Santa
Maria della Paggiola, outside Porta San Pietro. The fresco over
the high altar is possibly by the father of Ottaviano, while in a
chapel on the right there is a Pietà by his pupil Domenico
di Cecco di Baldi. In the apse we find Ottaviano himself in a
fresco of the Madonna and Child with angels.

One comes to Gubbio not only for its own sake or to see the
festa held here on the fifteenth of May in honour of Sant'
Ubaldo, a festa of renown, the Procession of the Ceri, when the
towering great figures of S. Ubaldo, S. Giorgio and S. Antonio,
borne on great platforms, each supported by some ten men, are
rushed through the little city in a race up to the monastery of
San Ubaldo on Monte Ingino, which all Umbria goes to see,
or even for the sake of Ottaviano Nelli, her painter son, but
also because of one of the most famous of Franciscan legends,
the story of the Wolf of Gubbio which S. Francis tamed and
reconciled with mankind.

In the Via Savelli della Porta, at number 19, is a little church
dedicated in honour of S. Francis and the peace he made
between the wolf and the people of Gubbio—San Francesco
della Pace. The tradition in Gubbio is that this church, erected
in 1503, stands on the site of the cave or grotto where the wolf
lived after its conversion by S. Francis. The inscription on the
façade is as follows:

MCCXX SENDO S. FRANCESCO CON LA S + HUMI
LIATA FUOR DI GUBBIO QUELLA LUPA CHE HO
MINE ET BETIE DIVORAVA CON
STUPOR DEL POPOLO LA MENO QUA ET
SULLA PRESENTE PIETRA PREDICANDO
SI FECE DAR LA FEDE CON LA ZAPA
DI NON FAR PIÙ DANNO ALCUNO CON
PATTO D'ESSER DALLA CITTÀ NUTRITA
SI CHE ET TUTT POI OBIDIENTE NELLA
VICINA GROTTA ABITAVA.

Within the church, in the wall, is the stone referred to in the inscription, standing on which S. Francis used to preach after he had reconciled the wolf. Beneath is a small pillar sculptured with a cross and the figure of a wolf, which is said to have stood over the grave of the wolf close by, where not long ago the skull of a wolf was found buried in the earth.

The legend is best told in the words of the *Fioretti*:[1]

What time S. Francis abode in the city of Gubbio, there appeared in the country of Gubbio an exceeding great wolf, terrible and fierce, the which not only devoured animals, but also men, in so much that all the city folk stood in great fear, for oft-times he came near to the city, and all men when they went out arrayed them in arms as it were for the battle, and yet withal they might not avail to defend them against him whensoe'er any chanced on him alone. For fear of this wolf they were come to such a pass that none durst go forth of that place. For the which matter, S. Francis, having compassion on the people of that land, wished to go forth unto that wolf, albeit the townsfolk all gave counsel against it: and making the sign of the most holy cross he went forth from that place with his companions, putting all his trust in God. And the others misdoubting to go further, S. Francis took the road to the place where the wolf lay.[2] And lo, in the sight of many of the townsfolk that had come out to see this miracle, the said wolf made at S. Francis with open mouth: and coming up to him, S. Francis made over him the sign of the most holy cross, and called him to him, and bespake him ,thus: "Come hither, brother wolf: I command thee in the name of Christ that thou do no harm, nor to me nor to any one." O wondrous thing! Whenas S. Francis had made the sign of the cross, right so the terrible wolf shut his jaws and stayed his running: and when he was bid, came gently as a lamb and lay him down at the feet of S. Francis. Thereat S. Francis thus bespake him: "Brother wolf, much harm hast thou wrought in these parts and done grievous ill, spoiling and slaying the creatures of God, without His leave: and not alone hast thou slain and devoured the brute beasts, but hast dared to slay men, made in the image of God; for the which

[1] *Fioretti*, cap. XXI (Temple Classics).
[2] The encounter is said to have taken place where the chapel—Chiesa della Vittorina stands—ten minutes' walk to the south of the city.

16*

cause thou art deserving of the gibbet as a thief and a most
base murderer; and all men cry out and murmur against
thee and all this land is thine enemy. But I would fain,
brother wolf, make peace between thee and these; so that
thou mayest no more offend them, and they may forgive thee
all thy past offences, and nor men nor dogs pursue thee any
more." At these words the wolf with movements of body, tail,
and eyes, and by the bending of his head, gave sign of his
assent to what S. Francis said, and of his will to abide thereby.
Then spake S. Francis again: "Brother wolf, if it pleaseth
thee to make and hold this peace, I promise thee that I will
see to it that the folk of this place give thee food alway so
long as thou shalt live, so that thou suffer not hunger any
more; for that I wot well that through hunger hast thou
wrought all this ill. But if I win for thee this grace, I will,
brother wolf, that thou promise me to do none hurt to any
more, be he man or beast; dost promise me this?" And the
wolf gave clear token by the bowing of his head that he
promised. Then quoth S. Francis: "Brother wolf, I will that
thou plight me troth for this promise, that I may trust thee
full well." And S. Francis stretching forth his hand to take
pledge of his troth, the wolf lifted up his right paw before him
and laid it gently on the hand of S. Francis, giving thereby such sign of good faith as he was able. Then quoth
S. Francis: "Brother wolf, I bid thee in the name of Jesu Christ
come now with me, nothing doubting, and let us go stablish
this peace in God's name." And the wolf obedient set forth
with him, in fashion as a gentle lamb; whereat the townsfolk
made mighty marvel, beholding. And straightway the bruit
of it was spread through all the city, so that all the people,
men-folk and women-folk, great and small, young and
old, gat them to the market place for to see the wolf with
S. Francis. And the people being gathered all together,
S. Francis rose up to preach, telling them among other matters
how for their sins God suffered such things to be, and
pestilences also: and how far more perilous is the flame of
hell, the which must vex the damned eternally, than is the
fury of the wolf that can but slay the body; how much then
should men fear the jaws of hell, when such a multitude
stands sore adread of the jaws of one so small a beast? "Then
turn ye, beloved, unto God, and work out a fit repentance
for your sins; and God will set you free from the wolf in this

present time, and in time to come from out the fires of hell."
And done the preaching, S. Francis said: "Give ear, my
brothers: brother wolf, who standeth here before ye, hath
promised me and plighted troth to make his peace with you,
and to offend no more in any thing; and do ye promise him
to give him every day whate'er he needs: and I am made his
surety unto you that he will keep this pact of peace right
steadfastly." Then promised all the folk with one accord to
give him food abidingly. Then quoth S. Francis to the wolf
before them all: "And thou, brother wolf, dost thou make
promise to keep firm this pact of peace, that thou offend not
man nor beast nor any creature?" And the wolf knelt him
down and bowed his head; and with gentle movements of
his body, tail, and eyes, gave sign as best he could that he
would keep their pact entire. Quoth S. Francis: "Brother
wolf, I wish that as thou hast pledged me thy faith to this
promise without the gate, even so shouldest thou pledge me
thy faith to thy promise before all the people, and that thou
play me not false for my promise, and the surety that I have
given for thee." Then the wolf lifting up his right paw, laid
it in the hand of S. Francis. Therewith, this act, and the
others set forth above, wrought such great joy and marvel
in all the people, both through devotion to the saint, and
through the newness of the miracle, and through the peace
with the wolf, that all began to lift up their voices unto
heaven praising and blessing God, that had sent S. Francis
unto them, who by his merits had set them free from the jaws
of the cruel beast. And thereafter this same wolf lived two
years in Gubbio; and went like a tame beast in and out of
the houses, from door to door, without doing hurt to any or
any doing hurt to him, and was courteously nourished by
the people; and as he passed through the country and the
houses, never did any dog bark behind him. At length, after
a two years' space, brother wolf died of old age: whereat the
townsfolk sorely grieved, and seeing him pass so gently
through the city, they minded them the better of the virtue
and the sanctity of S. Francis.

It is said of S. Francis that death, which is to all men so
terrible and hateful, he praised, calling her by name: "Death,
my sister, welcome be thou"; and that one of those best-loved
brothers saw his soul pass to heaven in the manner of a star,

"like to the moon in quantity and to the sun in clearness". And however we may think of him, whether he is to us the most beloved saint in all the calendar, or whether he is merely a delightful figure, a little ailing, a little mad from the Middle Age, he went honourably upon the stones, as Voragine reminds us. "He gadryd the wormes out of the wayes, by cause they should not be troden with the feete of them that passyd by." He called the beasts his brethren; and in all that age of passion and war, of immense ambition and brutal hate, he loved us as Christ has done, and was content if he might be an imitation of Him. "He beheld the Sonne, the Mone, and the Starres, and somoned them to the Love of their Maker."

As we pass up and down the Umbrian ways, it is his figure which goes ever before us.

quo pacis crescit oliva
regnat amor, concors, gratia, vera fides.

APPENDIX

THE SAINT FRANCIS FRESCOES IN THE UPPER CHURCH OF SAN FRANCESCO AT ASSISI

THESE twenty-eight frescoes raise perhaps the most puzzling problem in Italian art of the fourteenth century. That Giotto painted at Assisi in the church of San Francesco seems first to have been recorded by Riccobaldo da Ferrara, who, in one of his chronicles, among other items dated *circa* 1305, states that Giotto painted *"in Ecclesiis Minorum Assisii"*. Later Lorenzo Ghiberti at the end of his life in the middle of the fifteenth century affirms that Giotto *"dipinse nella chiesa d'Ascesi dell' ordine de' frati minori quasi tutta la parte di sotto"*.[1] But whether this refers to the S. Francis series in the Upper Church or to frescoes in the Lower Church seems uncertain. Vasari in the sixteenth century, in the second edition of the *Vite*, attributes definitely the S. Francis frescoes in the Upper Church to Giotto:

> He proceeded to Assisi, a city of Umbria, being invited thither by Fra Giovanni di Muro della Marca who was then General of the *Frati* of S. Francis. Here in the Upper Church and under the corridor which traverses the windows he painted a series of thirty-two frescoes [*sic*] of the Life and Acts of S. Francis, that is sixteen [*sic*] on each side; a work which he executed so perfectly as to acquire great fame from it. And of a truth there is a great variety in these frescoes not only in the gestures and attitudes of each figure but also in the composition . . .

Since Vasari Giotto was universally accepted as the author of the S. Francis series of frescoes till comparatively recently when this tradition has been questioned.

Crowe and Cavalcaselle seem to have been the first to examine these frescoes critically. They admit the co-operation of Giotto in execution as in design more especially in the later frescoes, but they name Rusuti and Gaddo Gaddi among the probable authors of the earlier frescoes all of which they attribute to Florentine artists.[2]

Italian critics, however, for the most part continued to accept Giotto's authorship and speaking generally this view has received the very important support of Mr. Berenson.

[1] *Commentari*, II, 3.
[2] *History of Painting in Italy* (1864), Vol. I, pp. 219 *et seq.*

In the 1900 and subsequent editions of his *Florentine Painters*, Mr. Berenson attributes to Giotto most of the frescoes in the series and in his *Italian Pictures of the Renaissance* (Oxford, 1932) he confirms his previous opinion, attributing the following frescoes in this series to Giotto himself: frescoes II to XIX; while he considers frescoes I and XX–XXV to be in part by Giotto. Frescoes XXVI–XXVIII he attributes to Giotto's followers. The frescoes above the scenes of the life of S. Francis on the west wall, that is the Descent of the Holy Spirit, the Ascension and the Madonna, he considers also to be by Giotto and contemporary with the S. Francis series. While the frescoes of Isaac and Jacob, and Isaac and Esau, of Joseph in the Well, and Joseph and his brethren on the north wall, of the four Church Fathers on the ceiling, and the Deposition, Baptism, Christ among the Doctors and the Resurrection on the south wall he considers to be Giotto's earliest known works. And now in 1953 Mr. Berenson tells me he is still of the same opinion.

I do not know who was the first critic to question Giotto's authorship. Perhaps it was Rumohr, perhaps Wickhoff,[1] who denies any part to Giotto in the series.

In 1907 Venturi published the fifth volume of his *Storia dell' Arte Italiana*,[2] dealing with the painters of the Trecento. He gives to Giotto himself Nos. I, XVI, XIX, XX–XXIII and the remainder he considers to be by companions and followers of the master.

Other foreign critics beside Wickhoff now began to refuse Giotto any participation in these frescoes.

Friedrich Rintelen denies all the frescoes of the S. Francis cycle to Giotto.[3]

Richard Offner is convinced "that the gap between Giotto and the S. Francis series is unspannable". While refusing any of these frescoes to Giotto himself, he assumes "disparity of style within the series due to different executants" who, however, "all adhere to the terms of a general plan—including the colour—laid down by a guiding mind."[4]

Mr. F. Mason Perkins, on the appearance of Dr. Offner's first article, wrote to the *Burlington Magazine* stating that he had long been of a similar opinion.[5] This is fully borne out by the fact that in 1910–1912, Mr. Perkins and the present writer were engaged on a critical edition of the *Lives* of Vasari. The new English translation of the

---

[1] In *Kunstgeschichtliche Anzeigen* (1904), No. 3.
[2] Vol. V, pp. 242 *et seq.*
[3] *Giotto und die Giotto-Apokryphen* (Munich, 1912), pp. 177–210.
[4] *Giotto, non Giotto* in *Burlington Magazine* (1939), Vol. LXXIV, pp. 259–268 and Vol. LXXV, pp. 96–113.
[5] *Burlington Magazine* (1939), Vol. LXXV, pp. 84–85.

text was made by Mr. De Vere and was published by the Medici
Society. It was to be followed by three or four volumes of critical
notes by Mr. Perkins, but though the first volume of these notes was
set up and printed, the war of 1914 prevented publication and the
type was distributed.

I possess, however, what is now probably a unique copy of the
proofs of Mr. Perkins's comments and among them his notes on the
Life of Giotto. In what amounts to a critical treatise covering
seventy-seven quarto pages of small type, in the course of which
he deals with these frescoes of the legend of S. Francis in Assisi,
Mr. Perkins says:

There can be no doubt that the opening fresco [of the S.
Francis cycle] is not only totally different in style but also posterior
in date to those which immediately follow. Stylistically the cycle
begins with fresco No. II. There can be no question of the
youthful Giotto in connexion with these works. They are purely
pre-Giottesque productions belonging to that same Roman tradition to which we owe the earlier decorations of the Upper Church.
The following seventeen frescoes (Nos. III–XIX) reveal the same
characteristics and appear to have been executed by the same
painter, either alone or in company with others. Frescoes III,
IV and V, like II, are evidently almost entirely by his own hand.
From VI onwards signs of co-operation are apparent. In No. XVI
we find a further change of style; the affinities with the preceding
frescoes are however apparent and imply an evident continuation
of the work under the same directing spirit. The same hand is
visible in No. XVII. So far—or at least up to No. XVIII—we
have recognised a certain general similarity in the style and spirit
of these frescoes despite their evident differences of workmanship.
The transition from No. XIX to No. XX marks, however, a
distinct break. In No. XX and in the frescoes which follow we
find a far more advanced and developed manner, together with a
correspondingly increased facility in technical expression. Everything here denotes, in fact, if not a change in the presiding spirit
of the series, at least a lapse of time between the completion of the
foregoing frescoes and the continuation of the series and in any
case a fresh change in the painters themselves. Nos. XX–XXIV
all appear to be by the same artist whose style cannot be traced in
any of the preceeding works save possibly in the fresco of the
Stigmatization (XIX) . . . Nos. XXV–XXVIII are evidently
again by a different artist—in this case no other than the so-called
Master of the S. Cecilia altarpiece. No. I has been ascribed by

several critics to the same author, but here to our mind we find once more another hand. In appearance at least this is the latest fresco of the series and may quite possibly have been painted over a pre-existing work. . . .

That Giotto was the original designer and the guiding spirit of this famous cycle of paintings we do not for a moment believe. There is absolutely nothing in the opening frescoes of the series (II–XI) to encourage the theory that they are by Giotto and every indication on the contrary to support the opinion that they are by matured and practised painters of the Roman school. . . . It is in the later numbers of the series, if at all, that Giotto's contribution must be looked for. . . . The complicated and crowded compositions, the peculiar refinement of the draughtsmanship and the proportions of the figures themselves have actually, however, little in common with the master's work at Padua and it is difficult to believe that his style in the course of a few years could have undergone such a complete evolution as to have made it possible for him to have been the author of both cycles. There remains therefore but a single fresco in which we may look for a closer resemblance to Giotto's manner—the initial composition—No. I. Here without doubt we come closer to his personal style than in any of the preceding paintings and if Giotto's independent handiwork is to be sought for anywhere in this great series, it is to be sought for here.

But so far as its real authors are concerned this famous series has so far formed, and is probably destined to remain, one of the most intricate problems in the history of Italian painting. Apart from this question of authorship, however, and looked at from a broader standpoint, it marks at once the last survival of the classic traditions of the old Roman school and the beginnings of modern Florentine art as exemplified soon after in Giotto and his followers.

So Mr. Mason Perkins wrote in 1912. I have quoted him at some length not only in justice to him, but because he was then, as he still is, living in Assisi and has had a longer opportunity than other critics of living with and studying these famous frescoes of the legend of S. Francis.

INDEX